Decrypting Justice

Decrypting Power and Coloniality

Philosophical Perspectives from and through the Global South

Series Editors: Ricardo Sanín-Restrepo, Marinella Machado-Araujo, Angus McDonald, and James Martel

The theory of encryption of power (TEP) proposes a fresh understanding of how the use of language monopolizes and hides power, preventing access to it through the denial and neutralization of differences based on class, race, and gender. It argues that coloniality exists because it encrypts power; hence the theory develops insights alongside and in parallel to decolonial theory and critical and subaltern studies. The central claim exposes how, in the name of the people, the people are made vulnerable to dispossession and exclusion, and how in the name of democracy, democracy is undermined and potentially destroyed. Theorizing encryption challenges the linkages between liberalism and colonialism, capitalism and sovereignty, constitution and economy, and their claims of necessity. The insights produced can be brought to bear on such phenomena as information circuits of disinformation on social media platforms, artificial intelligence, weapons, technologies of surveillance, and data mining

Titles in the Series

Decrypting Justice: From Epistemic Violence to Immanent Democracy, edited by Ricardo Sanín-Restrepo, Marinella Machado-Araujo, and Sabelo J. Ndlovu-Gatsheni

Decrypting Justice

From Epistemic Violence to Immanent Democracy

Edited by Ricardo Sanín-Restrepo,
Marinella Machado-Araujo, and
Sabelo J. Ndlovu-Gatsheni

LEXINGTON BOOKS
Lanham • Boulder • New York • London

Lexington Books
Bloomsbury Publishing Inc, 1385 Broadway, New York, NY 10018, USA
Bloomsbury Publishing Plc, 50 Bedford Square, London, WC1B 3DP, UK
Bloomsbury Publishing Ireland, 29 Earlsfort Terrace, Dublin 2, D02 AY28, Ireland
www.rowman.com

British Library Cataloguing in Publication Information Available

Library of Congress Cataloging-in-Publication Data

Names: Sanín-Restrepo, Ricardo, editor. | Machado-Araujo, Marinella, editor. | Ndlovu-Gatsheni, Sabelo J., editor.
Title: Decrypting justice: from epistemic violence to immanent democracy / edited by Ricardo Sanín-Restrepo, Marinella Machado-Araujo, Sabelo J. Ndlovu-Gatsheni.
Description: Lanham, Maryland: Lexington Books, 2025. | Series: Decrypting power and coloniality : philosophical perspectives from and through the global south | Includes bibliographical references and index.
Identifiers: LCCN 2024049775 (print) | LCCN 2024049776 (ebook) | ISBN 9781666961157 (cloth) | ISBN 9781666961164 (epub)
Subjects: LCSH: Justice. | Hegemony. | Postcolonialism.
Classification: LCC JC578 .D44 2025 (print) | LCC JC578 (ebook) | DDC 327.101—dc23/eng/20250106
LC record available at https://lccn.loc.gov/2024049775
LC ebook record available at https://lccn.loc.gov/2024049776

For product safety related questions contact productsafety@bloomsbury.com.

Contents

Prologue

A Conceptual Framework of the Theory of Encryption of Power

Ricardo Sanín-Restrepo

Common to all the chapters in this book is a profound need to take part in shaping another world, as this one has gone awry; it has become a contradiction and a violent simulacrum of itself. Rationality has failed, or rather, it has shown its true grim colors; its supposed universality was never more than an excuse to dominate. Perpetual peace is the pact among the rich to expropriate without limits through perpetual war, and the "adults in the room" are in an unending binge of destruction. Consensuses are simulated or imposed at gunpoint, so everything can be expropriated and commoditized. Commoditize cells, biomes, and planets; blood, children, and death; and cover it all up with the poisoned blanket of transcendent models in the forms of trickle-down economics, national sovereignty, or the rule of law.

Consequently, questions hit us like thunder: How can we even begin to discuss justice when the presuppositions (legal, dialogical) to discuss it are utterly unjust? Is there still something deeply rooted in the concept of justice that can offer us hope amid all the pain? The pain of a world shutting down in violence can easily lead us to despair. The pain of a world that denies its horrors in every possible institutional way can easily lead to rage and denial. Maybe the answer is not deeply rooted in the concept of justice; perhaps it walks on its surface; it colors its atmosphere. Maybe there are living experiences, sprouting all over, people in resistance, people creating through collective imagination and invisible threads of solidarity that can offer a way out. Invisible threads? Yes, that is the point. When we look for them with the registering tools of hegemonic institutions (law, constitutions, science, money, the state), we cannot see and feel but noise and turmoil, and so despair and rage set in. But, when we partake in those experiences, immanently, from what those experiences manifest, our registers are cleansed and transformed immediately, the world opens up anew and shows us how abundant it really is, and maybe we can begin to talk about justice.

The theory of encryption of power acts as a pliable but centered bonding force for the multiplicity of ideas offered in this collection. The theory grounds them, and they coalesce around it, not as a pregiven necessity but as an opportunity to organize and strengthen each other, to produce novel forms of understanding justice, and to illuminate different and unsuspected paths of justice and toward justice.

Given the novelty of the theory, let us draw up a blueprint of the book. To do so, we have methodologically simplified the association. First, in the present prologue, I will be exploring and describing the main concepts that, until the rendering of this book, have been the vortex of the theory—its theoretical framework of sorts. I will concentrate on the concepts that the diverse chapters of this volume use, develop, polish, and especially award new meanings and uses through various case studies and conceptual speculations. This book is packed with refined case studies from the Global South. The latter stems and reveals colonial struggles that compound updated communal practices, novel forms of rendering justice, and political associations that are far removed from the epistemic grammar and accounting methods of the hegemonic West.

Consequently, in a second methodological maneuver, my coeditors and I will schematically introduce the chapters in this book. In a third and final editorial operation, we will put together a brief conclusion (at the end of the book) that describes how each and every chapter has changed, shifted, adjusted, and improved the central concepts of the theory described in this introduction. Instantly, the idea is that the reader will witness the diverse ways in which the conceptual apparatus of the theory of encryption of power is mobilized and deployed, attaining new forms of significations and values while transforming the apparatus itself, improving it, actualizing it, and bringing its sometimes-abstract ideas down to earth. To be sure, this is just one particular reading of the book and by no way an authoritative or canonical one, simply a compass or a practical map that can guide the reader to better comprehend and participate in the thrust and range of the book.

THE CONCEPTUAL APPARATUS OF THE THEORY OF ENCRYPTION OF POWER (TEP)

Chapter 1 serves as a more complete and livelier conceptual framework of the book. Nonetheless, it is an elastic framework that also has a deep speculative drive. Hence, the concepts are not laid down in an encyclopedic manner but are rather permanently interacting and overarching each other, which may result in some difficulty when the need is to extract a systematic conceptual listing of the theory. This puts us at crossroads. There is a certain aridness, a tepidness, in simply describing a theory as if it were a dead anatomy, some loose parts with no connection among them. Hence, the reader must understand that this framework goes under a more descriptive sway, to lay down the conceptual bones of the theory, and it comes with a warning: This "motionless" list only comes alive and truly communicates meaning throughout the workings, struggles, and imaginations of the diverse chapters of the book.

LANGUAGE, POWER, AND ENCRYPTION

"Where there is language, there is encryption." This is a truism that we have dealt with thoroughly before.[1] As we have emphasized, "encryption as an intentional way of hiding the meanings of a symbolic system is an inherent characteristic of any language, it is this that makes all language elastic, mobile, resistant, poetic, imaginative, therefore, this is not disputed by the theory" (Sanín-Restrepo and Machado-Araujo 2020b). However, as we have also made clear, . . . we are faced with a completely different typology when we deal with the encryption "of power." Here, we are facing a primordial prohibition (political, legal, racial) to access the programming and the uses of communication (as the first common of difference) through permanent qualifications and conditions for the exercise of power and, therefore, a rigid stratification for belonging to any possible world (Sanín-Restrepo and Machado-Araujo 2020b).

Here we are left to feel as if power, language, and encryption are so deeply intertwined that they are of the same substance. Hence, it can be argued that the dawn of humanity is marked by a primordial anthropological encryption. As encryption is consubstantial with the emergence of language, the encryption of power essentially creates a prohibition, the origin of all prohibitions, that acts as a boundary of identity and differentiation established by language as law (myth, religion, Freud's Primitive Horde). What is the nature of such encryption? It would seem to allow "the one" or "the few" to freely monopolize, enjoy, and dispose of everything (people, property, power), while limiting it by regulating and neutralizing other people's access through norms (law).[2]

Consequently, the thesis would go, since there is power (as desire and force of the ego), and this power is expressed through language (norms), there is always encryption. Encryption, power, and language coexist as the primordial form of being. The being of what? Of power, language, and encryption. And, although this seems a juicy tautological fruit, we will not bite down on it as the encryption of power we are referring to is a more precise and clean-cut phenomenon that, albeit derived from that triple nature of power, language, and encryption, is not identical to it and signals toward something completely new. The encryption we are referring to implies a new and unsuspected refinement of power as domination that we are certain has never been experienced in history.

ENCRYPTION, COLONIALITY,[3] AND THE CONSTITUTIONAL IDEA

The primordial thesis we are upholding and developing is that the encryption of power is the most sophisticated and seemingly watertight form of power as domination (potestas) ever known, and it has only appeared in late-coloniality. Hence, late-coloniality would not exist without the encryption of power, and the encryption of power is what is proper to late-coloniality.[4] Only in late-coloniality, and through the artifice of modern constitutions, do the people become both the (simulated) sovereign (constituent power) and the index of the state of exception, that is, the excluded (the hidden people). Power in coloniality depends on a sole operation, the creation of a hidden people as the exception, a feat that can only be achieved through the exercise of sovereignty (Sanín-Restrepo 2016, 198). This is a totally new way of deeming the phenomena of power as domination (and resistance) that the theory brings to the table, as it shows a new and more formidable form of power not measured before.[5]

While encryption may have appeared throughout history, it is intrinsic to coloniality, serving as its foundational paradigm. Without encryption, coloniality wouldn't exist.

Through encryption, coloniality[6] has perfected the art of oppression by wielding together sovereignty and the state of exception into a formidable creature: the people. This is its most cunning trick. The combination of coloniality and liberalism forms the most relentless domination machine in history. The encryption of power manifests primarily through constitutions, making the people both the exception (those who can be subjected to violence, displacement, hunger, and death) and the (simulated) sovereign (those in whose name violence, displacement, hunger, and death are carried out). In coloniality, sovereignty and exception merge into one. The order and its exclusions become indistinguishable. As we will develop further in this book, in late-coloniality, with encryption, people are killed in their own name, with no one held legally accountable but themselves. The people become the transcendent model of their own exclusion, of their own destruction.

As we have stated,

> The most sophisticated encryption machine in coloniality is the constitutional idea. Through it, hierarchies (racial, gender, national) are established, the commons are privatized, and democracy is destroyed in its own name, while capitalism is installed as the only global truth. (Sanín-Restrepo and Machado-Araujo 2020b)

POWER AS POTESTAS VS POWER AS POTENTIA

The theory of encryption of power proposes a fresh understanding of how power is concealed and monopolized. Encryption achieves such deed by denying, neutralizing, and/or conditioning differences based on class, race, and gender. The mainstay of encryption is preventing access to power by disassociating power and beingness. Encryption occurs when the mere fact of existing (being and beingness) is conditioned by a transcendent model of power, where "to be" or "beingness" must conform to the conditions of said model. TEP contends that the world fundamentally exists through difference, but oppressive power structures hinder this possibility turning existence (legal, institutional) into a simulacrum.

The concept of power, as explored by TEP (drawing from a rich philosophical lineage including Heraclitus, Aristotle, Spinoza, Buber, Deleuze, Levinas, Fanon, Rancière, and Nancy, among others), emphasizes that existence itself implies power. Hence, "to be" is to possess and exercise power. Power is always the potentiality to become something different; it isn't confined to grand structures like the state, the law, or the economy but resides in the vitality of every entity. Each being exercises power by virtue of its existence. Even seemingly mundane acts—such as water condensing, an algorithm, a kiss, a bomb, a law, the baking of a cake, an information highway, or a poem—express power, shaping possibility, necessity, and contingency.

As shown by diverse fields of study ranging from biology to thermodynamics, from network theories to quantum mechanics, being and power are not separate entities that coincide from time to time. On the contrary, being is power; power is a trademark of beingness, and there is no being that does not produce power. Likewise, being is always within a multiplicity of relations, power is intrinsic to existence, and within relationships, power is both shared and received and thus reality is transformed and fashioned into complexities. Crucially, even the act of determining what matters—what counts—is a fundamental exercise of power, albeit one without a foundational basis. Encrypted human institutions thrive by concentrating, organizing, defining, and monopolizing the meaning and intensities of the exercise of power, ultimately constructing the very structures that shape our reality.

In short, "One thing is power as potentia that belongs and is exercised by every being of difference, with no distinction and finality whatsoever. Another is power as potestas as the operation of absorbing the multiplicity of power, its abundance and horizontal productions into structures of uniformity that solidify it, conditioning and qualifying life as its mainstay" (Sanín-Restrepo 2021).

While power as potestas aims to petrify beingness in final and enclosed structures ordered through necessity (the state, patriotism, racism, etc.), power as potentia means a permanent and incalculable becoming of every being where the finality cannot be predicted or ordered by necessity and is thus always contingent.

SIMULACRA AND TRANSCENDENT MODELS

Encryption "is the imposition of institutional simulations of difference that condition, neutralize or prohibit political agency, reducing difference to static and solid models of identity that pose as the only form of power" (Sanín-Restrepo and Machado-Araujo 2020b). The forms of encryption are the simulacra, which, although based on Deleuze's treatment of Plato's simulacra, are given a sharp twist. For TEP, they are not simply false representations or imitations of reality that conceal the absence or distortion of the original. Rather, the simulacrum is understood as every transcendent model (constitutions, free market, nation) that determines and conditions beingness and imposes a model of identity in its place (where being can only be when it uniforms itself with the conditions of the model). For example, sovereignty, as drawn out in modern constitutions, is a simulacrum that encrypts the power of the people and imposes a transcendent and final authority over them (Ndlovu-Gatsheni 2024). Henceforth, encryption is a process of simulation and concealment that creates illusions of difference and democracy, and thus, political agency can only be exercised by decrypting power, which means exposing and dismantling the simulacra and revealing the hidden structures and forces that shape reality (McDonald 2018).

In understanding the theory, it is paramount to grasp the relations between transcendent models, beingness, and the body politic. As I've put it:

> Since Plato, politics is predefined through extenuating conditions of belonging to the body politic, where "to be" corresponds to an already existing qualification of life, the "idea" as an inner split within forms of identity where some are welcomed into politics, and some are excluded according to qualifications that are detached to beingness but to which beingness must conform to be. Hence, the relationship between power and life is severed, qualified and utterly

> standardized to favour particular models of identity. The hidden origin is the malleable metaphysical center of Western discourse. (Sanín-Restrepo 2018)

Transcendent models are fixed, final, solid, and static structures that simulate power; they act as the metaphysical pinnacle of the world and prohibit or condition being while collapsing political agency into constituted power.

THE HIDDEN PEOPLE

This concept is thoroughly explained in chapter 1 and beautifully developed in chapters 3 to 8. Nevertheless, allow me to announce its main features.

The fundamental political and juridical totality of modernity is both a subject and an agency, "the people." However, it is a totality that is divided in its intrinsic mechanism. "In modernity the key to encryption is the conversion of the concept of the people into a synecdoche. Accordingly, a false totality (the people of human rights and constitutions, the included) become to symbolize and falsely represent an impossible infinity (the excluded, the hidden people)" (Sanín-Restrepo and Machado-Araujo 2020b). Consequently, the people as a totality is a *pars pro toto* synecdoche, where an absolutely arbitrary part (white people within a nation-state) defines an unattainable infinity (the marginalized people, the forced migrant). The people as a synecdoche joins a part that is an excrement of the (simulated) totality and what the totality lacks in order to become a true totality. As the unrepresentable excess of liberal democracies, the hidden people escape all forms of representation and symbolize what exists beyond the representable (Sanín-Restrepo and Machado-Araujo 2020b).

The hidden people have to be falsely included into modern juridical orders to give consistency to the fantasy of totality. The crucial point is that the people as a whole can only exist and exercise power if, and only if, it keeps that other zone of the people "hidden" (Sanín-Restrepo 2016, 44). The constitutive ambivalence is as follows: On one side, there's the strict realm of codified law and reality, represented by concepts like "We the People," as constituent power, or the universal model of human rights that binds reality together; they give substance to the life we live. On the other side, there's the necessary excess that allows this totality to function, the "all but one," or "all minus one," which is the precise formula of liberalism: the totality minus what it must exclude to remain pure (Sanín-Restrepo 2016, 35). The hidden people are those who are excluded, marginalized, or oppressed by the simulations, such as democracy, law, sovereignty, identity, representation, human rights, and capitalism, that encrypt power (Meagher 2022). However, the hidden people are not only passive victims of the encryption of power.

They are also potential agents of resistance and transformation (McDonald 2018) as they are those who have the primordial capacity to decrypt power by exposing and challenging the simulations that conceal it.

SOVEREIGNTY

As we recently explained, "Independently of geopolitical shifts, sovereignty continues to define the shape of the world from the definition of the exceptional. Power in coloniality depends on one thing alone, the creation of a hidden people as the exception, a feat that can only be achieved through the exercise of sovereignty" (Sanín-Restrepo and Machado-Araujo 2020a). The supreme decision on the exception remains the core of the "power machine" as domination. There is a defining transformation in the modern concept of sovereignty that ties together the theory of encryption and the hidden people. The coupling of coloniality and liberalism creates the most sophisticated and impermeable machine of power in history. We can formulate it simply:

> The people must be both the exception and the (simulated) sovereign! Coloniality achieves the most extraordinary exploit: it establishes the people as sovereign as it immediately seizes their sovereignty as absolute power (constituent power). All of this is done while maintaining the simulacrum of popular sovereignty as the political and legal axiom of the people. Therefore, it paradoxically merges the hidden people as sovereign and exception (Sanín-Restrepo and Machado-Araujo 2020b).

I hope that with this conceptual scaffolding, the reader may have gained deeper insights into the theory. I hope one of those insights is that the concepts drawn up here are deeply connected and concatenate to form a systemic theory. Nevertheless, as I also alerted, the theory will only gain momentum when it is moved by the chapters that make up this collection.

NOTES

1. See, for example, Sanín-Restrepo, Ricardo (Ed.). 2018. Decrypting Power. London: Rowman & Littlefield International.
2. As we hold in chapter 1 interpreting Walter Benjamin's idea of violence, "the initial establishment of law is necessarily an act of violence (unfounded decision—constituent power) without legal basis. Once established, the very first heartbeat of the law eliminates any form of violence. However, this exclusion is enforced through additional acts of violence, which serve to maintain the existing power structure."
3. Chapter 1 of this book fully develops the present thesis that is simply described.
4. As stated before,

> We will prove, then, that power in coloniality depends on the neutralization or utter destruction of politics understood as the common of language of the being of difference. Nonetheless, the uniqueness of coloniality as power as domination is not only the stringent qualification it imposes in access to politics, for this would simply be to give a tautological definition of potestas. Potestas as such is the devious art of splitting power apart in order to fix it in a solid state from which it conquers the programming codes of language and then surveils all its points of access. Potestas is thus the capture of the power of language and the imposition of qualifications of its use. The element that above all defines potestas is the construction of schemes of unity and identity through the direct cancelation of any being that produces difference.
>
> Nevertheless, our main target is not potestas per se but to clamp down the uniqueness of potestas in coloniality. Hence, we will discover that the uniqueness of coloniality is that in order for potestas to act expansively and frictionlessly it must simulate democracy and thus necessarily encrypt power. (Sanín-Restrepo 2016)

5. As previously argued: "When the 'theory of encryption of power' is used as a conceptual leverage of political philosophy it unveils something unique. The orders of globalization through the hegemony of capitalism based on coloniality exists as a whole because they produce a specific form of power: the encryption of power! Hence, the encryption of power is not a secondary aspect of the organization of power as domination of our times, it is its defining and central feature. Encryption is a form of power that has only existed within these networks, within this history" (Sanín-Restrepo 2021).

6. "With the Monroe Doctrine as its spearhead and through an exercise of variable speeds and intensities that defy traditional colonialism, the United States manages to create mimetic but aberrant copies throughout America. The processes of independence in Latin America, as a transition, simply marked the continuity of elites housed in another skin. However, in this transition there is a dense paradigm shift, the transition from classical European colonialism to the apparently anonymous coloniality of global capital led by the United States" (Sanín-Restrepo Machado-Araujo 2020a).

BIBLIOGRAPHY

McDonald, Angus. 2018. "The Equivocation That Lies Like Truth." In: *Decrypting Power*. Edited by Sanín-Restrepo. London & New York: Rowman & Littlefield, 27–49.

Meagher, Thomas. 2022. "Decrypting Caliban's Immanence: A Meditation on Ricardo Sanín-Restrepo's Being and Contingency." https://caribbeanphilosophy.org/blog/decrypting-caliban.

Ndlovu-Gatsheni, Sabelo, J. 2024. *Beyond the Coloniality of Internationalism: Reworlding the World from the Global South*. Dakar: Codesria.

Sanín-Restrepo, Ricardo. 2016. *Decolonizing Democracy: Power in a Solid State*. London: Rowman & Littlefield International.

Sanín-Restrepo, Ricardo (Ed.). 2018. *Decrypting Power*. London: Rowman & Littlefield International.

Sanín-Restrepo, Ricardo. 2021. *Being and Contingency: Decrypting Heidegger's Terminology*. London: Rowman & Littlefield International.

Sanín-Restrepo, Ricardo and Marinella Machado-Araujo. 2020a. "Keys to Decrypt the Republic Against Democracy." *Law and Critique* 33(1): 41–62.

Sanín-Restrepo, Ricardo and Marinella Machado-Araujo. 2020b. "The Theory of Encryption of Power: Itinerary of an Idea." *Revista da Faculdade Mineira de Direito* 23(45): 18–33.

Decrypting Justice

From Epistemic Violence to Immanent Democracy: A Brief Presentation of This Book

Ricardo Sanín-Restrepo, Marinella Machado-Araujo, and Sabelo J. Ndlovu-Gatsheni

According to the theory of encryption, there is no world unless the world is composed of all perspectives, of all that is immanently becoming and in an infinity that points toward continual transformation. Therefore, the world we live in, that world of hierarchies and domination, cannot claim to be the world, although, as the theory proves, trying to shush it or wish it away is also a psychotic mistake, as hierarchies and domination shape the way of the world as we experience it. Being true to that dictate, we understand the polysemic, ticklish, and incomplete nature of the word justice. Of how every Western thinker, within dogmatic traditions, has tried to capture, frame, tame, reduce, and shape it to particular visions and prefigured models. Consequently, the book's driving force is to liberate its multiplicity so we may begin to learn from it. Ground zero is justice, but it is a movable, contouring ground zero. We try to penetrate it, explain it, and ride it through decryption as the vehicle to clarify and potentialize it.

The theory of encryption of power is deployed to decrypt justice. This immediately presents us with the splintering action of decryption. Between Justice, written with massive hegemonic capital letters as an overarching institution in the Sacrosanct book of Western ideas, and justice, in its everyday workings within disparate communal forms and its deep spiritual exercise of multiplicity.

As all the chapters from the book prove through different pathways, late-coloniality through the hand of liberalism, as a precondition of its existence, shattered the possibility of a true community—a shared existence. The very essence of being-in-common was fractured and resignified as being in obedience to the model. While chapters 1–3 serve as the speculative backbone of the book, chapters 4 and 5 emancipate the communal through alternate practices that beat as one heart, the practices of "Quilombismo" in Brazil and "Corazonar" of the Tseltal women in Mexico. From the practices of the Tosepan in Mexico, chapter 7 decrypts the hegemonic forms of territory, the fallacious and profit-driven creation of space, and the people and things within it. Chapters 6 and 8 decrypt the many and entangled ways in which modern Western judicial systems encrypt communal practices and disempower the possibility of alternate communities that inhibit straying from the model of "man," through the practices of the migrants of Central America and the critique of the justice system arising from the peace process in Colombia.

Nevertheless, they do not stop at the signaling of the malaise, this is just a first step. All the case studies build precise forms of achieving justice through detailed constructions of communal practices. In doing so, they prove how the alternate and marginal construction of worlds, polities, and justice dwarf Western traditional transcendent models. The studies show, in the raw, the incompleteness and tendentiousness of the latter, as opposed to the amplitude in the aims and goals of the alternate. It is in this alternate where we truly find the universal as a synergy of humans and nature, as discrete and thus elastic forms of knowing and producing unconditioned becomings, proving that the backward, the primitive, and the violent is on the side of the transcendent models that serve as the building blocks of Western thinking and doing.

For the chapters in this book, there is no naiveté in this move to approximate justice from multiplicity. The world in its current shape is not overlooked in a gesture of detachment or immaturity; rather, it is confronted to its roots in a gesture of eyes-wide-open rebellion, of a living struggle for another, better world that must confront and break through the world as it stands. Thus, they approximate justice with theoretical sophistication and a deep compromise to the truth, put to the service of multiplying the voices that can utter and show what the word justice means—what it means in movement, what it can create in action. The book is above all a dialogue of plural disciplinary works that use the theory of encryption of power in varied and novel ways that shape it with plasticity while landing it in living experiences.

In this aspect, every author employs diverse keys of the theory in versatile ways. Sometimes the reader will see these keys combine, conflate, contract, extend, meet, and depart, but they are always alive, alive in the sense of participating in a world that resists and creates difference. Therefore, the codes and lexicons of every specialized area where the authors come from (philosophy, law, anthropology, those big formal disciplines) are not a *tabula rasa* of sorts, a harsh zone of demarcation; they are also decrypted as an open log, a platform where they meet and complement each other with openness and generosity.

What galvanizes the chapters of this book is to share in the peripheral and marginal, in what is occluded below thick crusts of formal language and magnificent institutions. To listen with attention to all that breathes difference and multiplicity amid the mummified air of the conventional, of the supposed superiority of the human creature as we unveil how "humanity" has also been a subterfuge of a minority to extract life and limb from everything that doesn't belong to the model of "man." To look for all that sparkles in the dark surface rising from the deepest layers of time and space.

There is a distinct configuration of the book. While chapters one through three are more speculative in nature, and chapter 4 is a powerful hinge between theory and praxis, the rest of the book is devoted to case studies. Although, as the reader will attest, they are all built on solid theoretical ground and speculative sophistication.

Allow us to make a brief presentation of every chapter that comprises this book.

CHAPTER 1

The first chapter, authored by Ricardo Sanín-Restrepo and Marinella Machado-Araujo, has a double function. First, to set the table for the rest of the book by explicating the keys to the theory of encryption of power. Second, to decrypt justice. Regarding the first function, it is simply that, a setting of a very general framework of the theory—it is not, however, a canonical function, as the theory stands firmly against any type of canon. According to the theory, a true model is just a sample, an object, an idea, or a discourse comparable to others, extending the line of representation infinitely, and thus opening the possibilities to signify anew. This part does not pretend to set a rhythm or even draw lines within which to draw lines but simply expounds on particular ideas. The second function, however, is deeper.

The authors establish that the theory of encryption of power reveals a major paradox that is built into the meaning of justice by Western theoretical and practical constructions. They announce it as: "How can there be justice, better yet, how can we even discuss what justice means when the preconditions to discuss it are utterly unjust? The paradoxical shines even brighter when we announce it not as a question but an affirmation: We cannot discuss justice until there are just conditions to discuss justice."

The paradox is liberated and potentialized in its poetic core and span by two nuclear theses of the theory of encryption of power. The first is that decryption creates a theory of justice immanent to radical democracy. The second is that coloniality, as the archetype of transcendent models, exists because it encrypts. Encryption here means a very particular thing: turning the people (the hidden people) into both the simulated sovereign (We the people) and the exception (excrement), through another transcendent model, the constitution.

The theses underscore the three keys of decryption, and so the chapter moves on to create a symbiosis of the three to solve the paradox, or better yet, to bring out all the power of the paradoxical to bear its fruit upon the encryption of justice.

Nevertheless, it is through the concept of the hidden people that they loosen the tight grip of encryption over justice. Through a composite of how the people are built from transcendent models (the people as a synecdoche) and, more importantly, what the people do when they resist the homogenizing and oppressive rule of the transcendent model, the paradox shows that the contradiction lodged within it was only apparent. This move turns the tables on difference and simulacra. As they say, "as we begin to understand that everything that hides power and neutralizes or denies agency as difference is a simulation, while everything that produces difference is the only possibility of being in and of the world." This point will prove that the theory proposes something altogether different from the deaf new-wavy-post-modern celebration of insubstantial difference.

In a final drive to decrypt justice that engages extensively with AI and studies of posthumanism, the chapter describes and decrypts what it recognizes as the three main pipelines of transcendent models to encrypt justice. They are: "1. They must create a sense of totality (simulated order). 2. They must instill finality (hierarchy). 3. They must function as an extensive calculating machine (immunity-autopoiesis-reverse alignment)."

CHAPTER 2

Secrets and lies. Neoliberalism tightening its grasp on everything that lives and breathes. Technology turned into a bludgeon of hyper-surveillance against the rest of the world, spreading the virus of neoliberalism as ideology, as scarcity, as destruction. It becomes difficult to tell the difference between secrets and lies. "Only lies," responds the author, Oscar Guardiola-Rivera, and continues:

> We know that the masters of today's financial universe produce nothing. They weave nothing, like the weavers in Hans Christian Andersen's tale of the emperor's new clothes. They seem to make something out of nothing, for the new wealth they accumulate seems to come from something that is an appearance,

> the derivative-form, rather than from the production and exchange of concrete commodities. Everyone knows this, but nobody would say it.
>
> If they were to reveal this secret, it would mean that the very structure that determines a great deal of their ordinary lives, the current economy, cannot be grounded in material reality or devalues the latter and has nothing else to go on. . . . Because people feel anxious about not having something to hold, they will turn an appearance—like the supposed magical qualities of the emperor's appearance or the temporal patterns appearing to them in the shape of data and prices—into a mode of being.

Not having something to hold, not having someone to tell them what to do, and especially to signal out their enemy amongst a mass of noise and dazzling darkness. Where do they hide when everything can disappear with a whisper? When invisible monsters can devour you in the blink of an eye. Encryption is pretending that life is otherwise, that it is worth it, that we are happy in the middle of perpetual debt, and that it is then a private affair that must be defended tooth and nail against the brutes at the gates. But the gates are vaporous, and they won't protect against intelligent bombs or financial bombs exploding in the cloud, tearing through your body, gnawing away at your soul, and taking it all, leaving only bones to be commoditized, again.

And still, we participate in it, as the author says, we wanted it all mapped out, framed, and coded.

What should we do when injustice is the rule? Decrypt. Through poetics, communal imagination, magic, and dancing, test the limits of the possible, or rather, what encryption shows us as possible. Through magic, a language that had been reduced to count, discipline, and number can be unleashed from within to create truths that are beyond the reach of formulas of totality.

The author raises a fundamental question about encryption. As he states it, "sure, x is constructed or encrypted and, thus, it can be deconstructed or decrypted. But what do we do with this revelation? . . . If life, or at least the life of power, is constructed and encrypted, how come it appears so immutable? How come everybody sees and knows it and yet they carry on acting as if they did not know?"

The author picks up a penetrating aspect of the theory, one directed to unravel and clarify not only what is behind the confusion of meaning, but how it got to be that way, within the "key of our twenty-first century discourses of cybersecurity." With great sophistication and allure, the author uses encryption as a tool for unveiling that today's form of encryption of power corresponds to a derivation of "older martial knowledges (such as siege architectures, poliarcetics, castrametation, surveyance, and forensics) as encryption converts the initial representation of the information or a cruder representation of real conditions, known as 'plaintext', into an alternative form known as 'cyphertext.'"

In the same vein, the author finds the tip of the iceberg in this dark ocean, in the drive of encrypted power to install the idea of "harmony" as the central organizing principle of power as domination. Harmony imposes an aesthetic that installs the image of continuity and order. A straight arrow of time of Western epistemology and its institutions, not only accounting for everything that has happened, but imposing that what has happened, must have happened.

The author shows us the salting of nature by reason; nothing will ever grow but by its hand, and it will be a simulacrum of growth; it will be impotent harmony.

Before this monumental hurdle, he proposes a lateral approach to the encryption of power. What does it accomplish? It rids the confusion; it separates the thick membranes that unified the idea of the "original" and "primitive," so the world and all its makings could be read through Western privileged registers and methods. It removes the presupposition of necessity, showing the contingent nature of the registers and methods, and opening up new avenues of possibilities.

CHAPTER 3

In this chapter, Sabelo J. Ndlovu-Gatsheni advocates for a "decolonial paradigm of justice," challenging traditional Eurocentric theories of justice that are rooted in the overarching transcendent model known as coloniality. The author shows that these conventional theories are inherently flawed due to a very precise form of violence: epistemic violence. Violence is incorporated at their core and programs their operation entirely. Epistemic violence creates what should be deemed a contradictory creature. On one side, these models of justice are built on narrow, even parochial, epistemological foundations. On the other, they become universal, and their traction irresistible, due to their systematic universalization through violent enforcement. And here is the absurdity unveiled: this violent enforcement not only assures their universalization but encrypts their operation in such a manner that hides and fortifies (in jurisprudence, for example) the obvious sleight of hand between narrowness, violence, and universality.

Epistemic violence involves the imposition of a particular worldview and set of values that are branded, pushed, and enforced onto diverse cultures with the aim of neutralizing and edging them into a model that is nonexistent beyond permanent violent decisions by the encryptors. We must ask ourselves, is there a worse form of violence than having theories of justice, which are supposed to prevent violence and ensure fairness, which have themselves been built, spread, and maintained through the rule of violent domination?

The theoretical compound is a varied concatenation of movements and strategies of decryption. On one side, the chapter pinpoints with millimetric precision the shortcomings of traditional theories of justice (Rawls, etc.), analyzing their figureheads and claims that, when seen under this light, begin to melt into the insubstantial stuff that they are made of. On the other hand, it proves that a decolonial approach to justice relies on thoroughly examining the supposed origins and histories of the systems, structures, and institutions (transcendent models) that perpetuate injustice.

CHAPTER 4

In chapter 4, Bethania Assy and Rafael Rolo pose fundamental questions for the theory of encryption of power: "Is it possible to present encryption differently than as a technique to ascertain a potestas? Is it possible to think of decryption not only as an emancipatory tendency?" To which a firm proposal follows: "Instead of a binary contraposition, we present a more nuanced picture, in which encryption and decryption are not judged simply for what they might abstractly mean, but for how they actually function."

It is decryption in action, as a praxis of liberation instantiated through the actualization of the ancient Afro-Brazilian practice of quilombismo.

Henceforth, the authors create a huge magnetic field for decryption through the release of the multiplicity of power inherent to the political actions of quilombismo and aquilombar-se. They are simultaneously movements to create a community (to exist) and to resist. A symbiosis the authors identify as (R)existence. Quilombismo is used as a slick decrypting tool, as a new form of imagination of the political and a garnering of a common language and praxis of resistance. It also serves as a common platform for any form of resistance. Given the inherent decryptive nature of quilombismo, it is not reserved for certain types of struggles and for a given set of people, but it is rather an articulation point of an array of struggles and beings in the world.

The authors contribute to pinning down the nature of encryption with what they name "bastard power." They understand it as the encrypting ploy that intends to sow the origins of power in an immaculate moment of creation in the land of plenty of the mighty state. Taking power away from the popular, twisting the lines of belonging between the people and their constituent power.

This leads the authors to another powerful insight. Encryption creates a rigid and stale regime of time that occludes the temporality of the becoming of difference. When it imposes a mystic origin of origins, the encryption of power acts as a lock that shutters all forms of becoming, while turning the transformative power of history into a blind accumulation of events folded within a narrow scope of time. Encryption collapses time, history, and events into one single point, a monolith called the state. The state, as a point zero of time, history, and becoming, overturns the potentiality of the popular, of everything that produces difference to create difference, and as such, it limits our very perception of time and space, and finally our possibility to move and transform ourselves and the world through them.

One of the mainstays of the chapter is that it demonstrates that the theory of encryption does not repeat the trite gesture of some postmodern theories that simply affirm that "everything is a social construction" as its starting point. On the contrary, the chapter recognizes that this is precisely another form of encryption that the theory identifies and supersedes. As the authors demonstrate, for the theory, there is no final and absolute "x," a given of the social that is constructed. As they put it, "absolute encryption would be a paradox in its own terms, for it would actually constitute a mere form of murmuring, or a senseless soliloquy." Here, the authors show us a way forward through Quilombismo.

Through decryption, they demonstrate that the Quilombo represents more than a physical space; it is a symbol of resistance, an axis for the production of cultural multiplicity, and the permanent creation of new realms of reality.

The term extends to various forms of Afro-Brazilian communal life—from religious houses of worship (Umbanda and Candomblé) to samba schools and social clubs. Each one embodies the spirit of quilombismo, a spirit that is not a mere reflection of Hegel's master–slave dialectic that creates a mirror image, a form of mimesis tending toward the reproduction of a faithful copy, instead asserting its own identity and agency as immanent and autonomous difference. As the authors follow Charles Mills' "racial contract" and Sueli Carneiro's "racial device," to ascertain that while the racial model of the state begets a reproduction of its own image as a line of demarcation and exclusion, Quilombo and quilombismo beget difference and multiplicity in an immanent way through resistance.

CHAPTER 5

The chapter is about *Corazonar*, another action of resistance and existence of and through the community, and as such, it stands in an intimate connection to chapter 4; they both weave a vibrant political map for decryption.

There is a vitality in this chapter, written by Laura Edith Saavedra-Hernández, that invites us to share in the action permanently; it is the vitality that emerges from the site of enunciation of the author. In her own words, "my analysis will be crossed by my experience, my militancy, my gender, my mestizo identity and my class, which will surely give or take away epistemic privileges over certain discussions." As we have learned from critical theory, there is nothing more partial and limited than pretending to speak about acute human dramas from supposedly neutral and objectively built places. The author offers us a work of refined and rigorous translation of the multiplicity and tenacity of the cosmovisions of the "Tseltal Women's Experiences in the Pursuit of Self-justice." That refinement and rigor are attested by the fact that the author learned the Tseltal language. What the reader will find is a true gift of shared intellect and spiritual kinship.

The primary aim of the study is to examine the disparities and conflicts between the dominant definitions of Western theory and the diverse, often overlooked, and subaltern, lived experiences concerning violence, justice, and human rights of marginal groups. The concept of epistemological hegemony is understood here as a transcendent model. It inherently possesses and exercises forms of dominance that encompass coercion and the unchallenged acceptance of particular views that are elevated fraudulently to universal laws. Nevertheless, they are also the place that incites both resistance and subordinate forms of power. The author highlights the importance of recognizing the insights and philosophies of the Tseltal and Tsotsil women from Chiapas's highlands in Mexico as they open veins in a time and space that seem shuttered by traditional models of justice.

In stark contrast, the chapter shows how encryption is a powerful and destructive alloy, concocted from an epistemology that established an encrypted world (language, rules, laws, but specifically a hegemonic language) and the injustice that then follows from its application by the judicial branch. In said application, ironically but logically, all the tenets of the transcendent model, such as rule of law, due process, and so on, stand in integrity while destroying worlds at whim.

Is there another way to compose a world from where we could accomplish another kind of justice? The author is certain that we can. The call is to use decryption to erode the traditional models of justice while creating a space of resistance where the visions and languages that have been banished by the model may flourish again.

In a very well-grooved proposal, the chapter discovers an alternative in the Tstsal forms of justice(s): Corazonar, which means: (1) There is no individual kind of justice, or of reparations; (2) Injustice is committed not against an individual but against the sense of community. Henceforth, it wounds the social as well as the spiritual fabric. They are not things to be repaired by servicers or welders; they are meanings and senses appertaining to the community that need to be healed by the community, and decryption is the meeting point that invigorates the possibility of us seeing that possibility.

CHAPTER 6

War, displacement, concentration of wealth, inequality, but also plebeian imagination and resistance melt into a pot that makes Colombia a symbiosis of the troubles of the colonial world while also announcing the possibility of its liberation.

The authors, Michael Monclou-Chaparro, Julián Trujillo-Guerrero, and María Daniela Delgado-Álvarez, boldly tackle the Colombian recent peace process and the transitional justice system that it installed, which the authors call "liberal transitional justice" (LTJ). They are not content to highlight certain technical shortcomings of the system that could be adjusted or improved upon; more importantly, they prove with great precision that the system constitutes a primordial encryption of power. Its veiled purpose is to maintain capitalism, as a transcendent model, intact. Furthermore, they prove that the system is invariably used as a cog in the machine of neoliberalism, where post-war means ample profits for traditional elites from the reconstruction of torn societies, in a macabre cycle of destroy-profit-reconstruct-profit.

As they undertake the crudest manifestation of human conflict, war, they do so with great tact and theoretical elegance to show how encryption can be tucked away in the most refined and apparently benevolent liberal institutions.

As the authors state, they use "encryption and decryption of power as a useful tool for understanding how liberalism functions in societies at war and, above all, how it constructs forms of justice that are a simulacrum of democracy." LTJ is therefore not designed to bring a dialogue between included and excluded about the nature of the split, or regarding immemorial injustices, nor the cause of fractured societies and structural inequalities, but to maintain the functioning framework of the status quo. It represents a waning down of hostilities, a smothering of certain forms of violence, but it does not confront the fundamental questions of the conflict, of what originated the armed conflict in the first place. Hence, everything is negotiable, except for the transcendent model that left the victims in shambles.

Here, their thesis is crystal clear: "Based on the encryption/decryption of power, our study on LTJ argues that it is a theory and practice of justice that assumes the capitalist development model as a formula for peace and, in doing so, risks promoting and deepening economic injustices. It establishes a limited and transcendent notion of justice rooted in mechanisms that construct a particular narrative about the past, a definition of victims, an inventory of what rights they can expect, and an idea about the future of society."

Accordingly, another fundamental aspect comes mightily to the fore, as the authors wager the possibility, through decryption, of liberating transitional justice by deliberalizing it. Insofar as for liberals, LTJ is a form of re-telling history, of constituting shuttered totalities, of determining what can and cannot be said, and who can say it. It all derives from who or what can be and what can't be, which is ultimately frizzing the limit of the possible and the impossible.

Through this sharp contrast, the authors achieve a major form of decryption as they tie up their keys (hidden people, simulacra, transcendent models) in one powerful pack, offering us a clear way out of an apparent conundrum.

CHAPTER 7

In yet another chapter deploying the theory of encryption of power as a living experience, the authors, María Elena Rojas and Jaime Ortega, develop the paradigm of the Social Solidarity Economy (SSE), as a particular manifestation of territoriality as opposed to the Western construction of territory.

What is vital in their work is the knowledge that the fact of following social movements stepping away from traditional Western forms of communities and social links requires a profound shift of vision, theoretical structure, and methodology. Only then can they attain a clear understanding of the intensity and breadth of such transformations. As soon as they lay their groundwork, the authors make it clear that their critique not only puts hegemonic Western institutions and theories of the liberal strand between their pincers, but all hegemonic forms. In a bold move, the authors denounce and prove the incapacity of traditional European socialism (so stiff and linear, so dependent on transcendent models) to deal with, understand, and most importantly, help to create a new reality for these social movements that are deeply embedded in Indigenous practices of justice.

As they understand it, "in this case, a portion of Mexican territory, which is the focus of our attention, shows the concrete way of decrypting the power of the conventional economy." The theory helps them unravel how hegemonic economic power networks, money dynamics, and market structures act and pervade societies. Additionally, all of this is accomplished under the auspices of traditional disciplines and legal practices, but specifically, the preponderant role the state plays to create the situation. It is germane to these apparatuses to create a perpetual crisis, which has led societies to seek alternatives for social organization and reproduction. The existing order, driven by mercantile forms and capital expansion, generates havoc and squalor. It breaks the bonds among societies, and one of its main targets is to disenfranchise the people. On the other hand, social solidarity economies emerge as their antithesis, advocating for different ways of organizing "life in the present" and repairing the deep wounds inflicted on these societies by colonialism and coloniality.

The chapter expands on the Tosepan cooperative, deeply rooted in Mexican history, as a paradigmatic example of an alternative economic model. Collective action, symbolic elements, and politicization processes play a crucial role in this alternative economy. Nevertheless, the key point to it all is that this new alternative model emphasizes constructing an economy based on an utterly new notion of space.

In another fundamental move, the chapter shows how one of the most pervasive powers of transcendent models is to create, hedge, control, and define space, "the territory." Insofar, the power of the modern state manipulates space to manipulate the peoples and things in it. The state manipulates space, slimming it down, deflating it, privatizing it and its resources, prohibiting access, or opening the door to exploitation, all under the iron rule of the law. The authors here follow in the steps of the work of Polanyi and Ostrom, but basically of Brazilian geographer Porto-Goncalves, who has "set guidelines to think about the multiple dimensions called on behalf of the territory."

CHAPTER 8

Chapter 8 meticulously tackles the complex problem of forced displacement, asylum, and its administrative and judicial treatment as a paradigmatic case of the encryption of power.

The author, Luisa Gabriela Morales-Vega, understands that forced migration has painfully shaped our world and is a sharp and brutal result of the conflicts of our time (for land, ecological, food security, drug wars, etc.). As such, it possesses a myriad of components with a high intensity of encryption of power: division among peoples that underscores the manipulation of soft and hard types of sovereignty under the cover of "national security." Revolving doors moving at high speeds between the judicial and the executive branches are truly unearthed from opportunistic political decisions. The capacity of established power to hide its horrors within the armor of the law, reducing the problems to administrative matters, and then making processes difficult and muddled.

In this chapter, she gifts us with the results of her rigorous research on the Mexican case. With chirurgical precision, she breaks down the painstaking process refugees must submit to as they suffer being drowned in a legal and political maze of rulings.

In this taxonomy of encrypted power, we can see clearly how the concept of the "hidden people," incarnated by the refugee, is a permanent challenge to the notion of the people as a sovereign subject, that is, as a totality. Through this challenge, and in the way the author decrypts it, we can also see with clarity how concepts such as national security take a legal hierarchical upper hand encrypting law.

Chapter 1

A Prolific Paradox of Justice and Two Theses on the Encryption of the Hidden People

Ricardo Sanín-Restrepo and Marinella Machado-Araujo

A PARADOX AND TWO THESES

Let us announce a paradox,[1] simply to carry it with us as it will come alive gradually: How can there be justice, better yet, how can we even discuss what justice means when the preconditions to discuss it are utterly unjust? The paradox shines even brighter when we announce as an affirmation: We cannot discuss justice until there are just conditions to discuss justice.

Now, let us announce two theses emerging from the theory of encryption of power (TEP) that working together will liberate all the power of the paradox, opening a new dimension of understanding the complexity of justice and injustice. Let us go even further and anticipate that the liberation of the paradox[2] lies in a new reading of what the people are (hidden people as a *pars pro toto synecdoche*), and what the hidden people do, the permanent exercise of resistance.

The first thesis was put forward as soon as the theory began to take shape, and it reads: The theory of the encryption of power, "far from being a 'new method' or another analytical theory of language, is substantially the theory of justice immanent to radical democracy" (Sanín-Restrepo 2016, 8). This is the moment to develop this premise, but above all, to prove it.

The second thesis takes a bit more time to unload: What sets late-coloniality[3] apart from every other regime of power? It is that it encrypts power. Even if we can find examples of encryption hither and tither in history, it is proper only to coloniality—as the paradigm of a transcendent model.[4] There would not be coloniality without the encryption of power that fundaments it.

Coloniality, through encryption, has refined power as oppression into perfection. The interplay between coloniality and liberalism creates the most implacable machine of domination in history. Attention to the detail of how the encryption of power materializes: primarily (but not exclusively) through constitutions, the people become at the same time *both* the exception (the excluded) and the (simulated) sovereign! Sovereign and exception become one. What the *order is* and *what the order excludes*—in order to be—becomes one and the same thing. An authentic *Coup de grâce*. "We the people" is the most splendid and horrifying fusion of power and sheer violence under an impermeable armor of legitimacy. The people become the transcendent and mystic model of their own exclusion, of the war to subdue and expropriate them. Injustice is naturalized as justice. The outside becomes the inside, as the exception becomes the (simulated) sovereign. An anthropophagic, narcissistic, and at the same time nihilistic political and legal design,[5] that, nonetheless, is the open slit within the structure of power as domination through which resistance and transformation are possible.

We are before a fundamental concept of the theory of encryption of power: "the hidden people."

As we will develop, hand in hand with Roberto Esposito's concept of *immunitas*, Posthumanism—especially in Rosi Braidotti's view and Franco Berardi's concept of "reverse alignment"—is that transcendent models[6] (described below) are also a massive mechanism of creating, controlling, anticipating-programming, and simulating conflict. Therefore, three mechanisms are fundamental for a transcendent model to work as encryption: (1) They must create a sense of totality (simulated order); (2) they must instill finality (hierarchy); and (3) they must function as an extensive calculating machine (immunity-autopoiesis-reverse alignment).

Bear with us, as the paradox will initially appear as an insurmountable contradiction. Let us unpack it through a first approximation to the theory of encryption of power. Encryption of power is the constitutive institutional exclusion, neutralizing, or lessening of beings through stringent qualifications or conditions to belong to the world, crafted through a transcendent and unaccountable cluster of models (race, nation, nature, law, the market, the constitution). Therefore, being, any kind of being, in order to be and to act, must conform to an invisible model that dictates the totality of reality, where *to be* is to obey the model. Transcendent models constitute the very fabric of the logic of inclusion-exclusion. They are used to create and maintain a hierarchy and a boundary between those who belong and those who do not share the privileges of the body politic, based on arbitrary and artificial criteria that have nothing to do with beingness.

Decrypted power would have to prove that power is not exclusively produced by said models, but that it is immanent to every single unqualified being (*Energeia*[7]). Ultimately, the world can only exist through the intense production of power-as-difference of every single being, and, as such, the world is always a potential of being other than itself, of being infinite. For decryption, the world does not come first, as a collection (an arithmetical totality) of differences, an accountable sum of them, stretched out in a straight line of time. Rather, the world is difference in permanent becoming (*potentia*) or better yet, the infinite and immanent becoming of difference.

The ontological condition of the political (of what counts, of how things communicate) lies in the absence of conditions or qualifications beyond difference to belong to the body politic. If the latter is true, politics can only exist in democracy (Rancière 2001)—a non-place where meaning is potentiality, being is unqualified, and everything is yet to be decided.[8]

The creative power of difference is hidden, better yet simulated, by institutional structures that impose fixed and static models of identity and difference, such as the state, the law, or the constitution. These structures are transcendent models, and their primordial role is to create simulacra (of difference, of people, of life), and they act as forms of encryption that prevent or condition the expression of political agency.

Very well, then the paradox follows. If the aforementioned is true, then it would seem that we can only discuss the meaning of justice when every being that produces difference is part of the world, that is, when power is decrypted. An encrypted world means that there is a constitutive lack, a constitutive exclusion of beings that turn the actual world we live in into a simulacrum of the world. Therefore, any discussion on the meaning of justice is tainted as it would be done by beings that were arbitrarily included in a political association, as they correspond to the model at hand, and the political association is so because it has excluded others. Accordingly, the paradox seems here as a circularity: We cannot discuss justice as there is a lack at the heart of the composition of the community, but the very composition of the community is unjust as it is *a given* that excludes a part of it in order to conform itself.

This throws us into an abyss. Justice remains unnameable, untouchable, in one word, encrypted, as long as there is no possibility of there being a world where difference is not at the base and the people are decrypted. Justice, or any discussion of it, whether it is a system of distribution of rights and obligations, if it is relational, and so on, is a moot question, a simulacrum. The outcome is already decided from the outset, from the very outline of what it means to be, to have power, and to count, but also to be able to feel and understand. It may seem obvious, but that is just the point; we take for granted that we may reach consensuses (ideal, virtual, comparative, distributive) without everyone and everything having the power to intervene in the discussion.

Here is the catch and the intensification of the paradox: Can we discuss under circumstances of inequality? It would appear we must. A logical reading of the thesis and the paradox would seem to force our hand to decide that the first discussion has to achieve the forms in which the excluded may intervene. Until then, justice is but a projection, and thus determining that it can be achieved without the excluded is an exercise of injustice. The paradox deepens when we realize that groups that have been not only neglected but on whose oppression the system was built cannot speak of justice. Language is missing, as the language to prefigure even a claim is precisely the one designed to keep them in a state of oppression, and oppression is the lifeline of the system. Consequently, is any discussion of justice truly a mere discussion of the correct association?

Let us land it. The paradox seems like a contradiction because this view is still unilateral; it is still hegemonic. We are still caught up in the strings of the model, and it certainly looks like some kind of Jacobinism *where we, the included,* will clear the way for the true people. Consequently, the paradox becomes a prophecy shouted from the balcony of hierarchies. How do we retain the power of the paradox? We must come down from the balcony and look and partake in the forms and acts of the hidden people, what they mean immanently and what they do transcendently.

The paradox shows us all its poetic splendor when we interrogate the place and function of the hidden people as standing in resistance. Let us explore, first, the anatomy of the hidden people as a synecdoche and, second, and more importantly, how people's resistance (agency) is the permanent exercise of difference and the dispelling of transcendent models.

First, What the People Are

As Schmitt (2006) and Agamben (1998) verify, the sovereign's decision—whether defining normality, abnormality, order, or chaos—becomes logically possible only when operating outside the established norm . . . but not totally outside of it. It is only in a state of exception that the sovereign can declare both the norm and its suspension (if the sovereign was inside, it would be logically bound by the norm of normality, and if it was outside, it would be utterly disconnected from the norm). As Žižek reminds us: "However (and this is the core of Schmitt's argument) the decision that crosses the gap does not impose a *concrete order*, but primarily the *formal principle of order* as such" (Žižek 2001, 153. Italics are ours). Henceforth, the hidden people are constructed through a dual act: exclusion from normality and inclusion as the reverse of the law.

> We stand before the constitutive paradox of the legitimacy of liberal constitutionalism. On the one hand, we discover the rigid zone of codified law, of

> codified reality, that manifests itself in archetypal concepts such as the totality of the people as constituent power (We the People), or the totality of the human rights model (everyone) that announces an abrasive universality that holds together the fruit of reality. On the other hand, we have the excess that is compulsory in order to make such totality work as such, the-all-but-one, the all minus one, as the exact mathematical formula of liberalism, the totality minus what it needs to exclude to keep itself immaculate. (Sanín-Restrepo 2016, 35)

In the context of coloniality, crystallized in modern constitutions, the concept of the people becomes the axiological and overdetermining[9] parameter of power, of every form of power. The people are legalized as an impossible totality where they are both subject and agency, zenith and bottom, chosen and disposable. However, this totality is necessarily split at its core. The key lies in how constitutions transformed the concept of "the people" into a *pars pro toto synecdoche*. Here, an arbitrary part—such as the white population within a nation-state, the debtor, the citizen—defines an unattainable infinity, the people. Nevertheless, it nominally needs to incorporate the marginalized, including forced migrants, the homeless, racialized people. The interplay is not accidental or merely operative; it is constitutive. The hidden people are not just an excess or a surplus of the concept of the people as a synecdoche; on the contrary, they are the foundational sustenance of the totality of the people. Without the hidden people, the concept of the people would not exist or function. Nevertheless, at the same time, they are what is missing in the totality, for it to declare itself a true totality. It is thus a crack, an opening that seals the system and at the same time makes it function through an absence.

The people, as a synecdoche, bridge a gap within the (simulated) totality. They connect a part that is essentially a residue of the totality to the totality itself. This residue fills the void necessary for the totality to pretend to be authentic. Yet, there's a twist. The hidden people, as an unrepresentable excess within liberal democracies, defy all forms of representation. They symbolize what lies beyond the realm of the representable, and here is where the second part breaks through the paradox, resistance.

Second. What the People Do

What breaks through the interstices of sovereignty and its flawed creation of totality is the power of the people to create anew from sheer contingency. Being inside and out, in the crack of beingness and its impossibility means that the paradox of power is the hidden people themselves.

Consequently, if the transcendent model creates itself through the exclusion of difference and is ontologically founded in the necessary uniformity of being, then it follows that the hidden people logically define politics as the truth of *the being of difference* in permanent resistance.

While transcendent models tame and neutralize the people through unanimity, so they can uniform and pack them into homogeneous and obedient niches, the hidden people are, by definition all that resists. The wretched and their struggle, the dissent and its dances, the unbound creature. Resistance is then not something occasional; it is the permanent exercise of power to counterattack the form. It is what prevents the law of identity and unity of coloniality from shuttering upon itself, appearing as the spotless creation of reason and human industry—such as our constitutionalists would want to sell us their master's creation.

Difference as resistance is not the frictionless or unbounded exercise of difference where *everything goes*. Rather, resistance is always exercised within a plane of consistency in a dialectical struggle against a model of oppression that needs to shutter difference in order to survive. In this sense, the resistance of the hidden people is not co-relative to any mind; it does not need *the included* to bring it to fruition by law, philosophical theses, or any other institution. It needs not to be thought about, in the sense that Quentin Meillassoux (2008) proved radical contingency, and with it, buried every form of co-relationism from Kant to Heidegger.

The core rejection of politics lies in its refusal to accept any finality dictated by invisible and untouchable models, orchestrated by elites, as these models operate under the guise of a simulated totality (people as a simulated totality, as a synecdoche). This is the meaning of decryption.

Democracy is a force that resists historical hierarchies and is synonymous with the unyielding and irrevocable exercise of difference. It matters not if we speak of operative or inoperative communities (Nancy 2000), or the community to come (Derrida 2004); the hidden people are both, and they are none. We will dare to paraphrase here, "Don't tell the people what to do." Democracy is not an elusive Promised Land perpetually deferred. Instead, it is a consistent reality, a quotidian experience that stands in opposition to the domination of the transcendent model. Democracy is, first of all, difference, as the unbounded origin of the world, but simultaneously it is also resistance as a result of the exercise of its potentia. Finally, it is a permanent vocation for the actualization (actuality) of a new legality that distributes difference in the world as an absolute law of the production of truth.

Even if it is true that the hidden people are created as the negativity of sovereignty and its law, their permanent exercise of power is not a utopian or idealistic fantasy, but a realistic and pragmatic truth that emerges from the concrete struggles and movements of social transformation. More than a pragmatic possibility, they are twofold: they are the people in permanent resistance to traditional forms of domination, but within this struggle, they announce what is to come, the world that must be, as the exercise of difference.[10]

The traumatic confrontation between the deceptive totality and the excluded (those who represent the missing part of the whole) gives rise to an intimate mechanism of resistance. This dialectical[11] mechanism embodies a sense of shared existence that opposes the illusory eclipse of all conceivable origins, the simulacrum of all forms of being and becoming.

At this critical juncture, the boundary between inside and outside dissolves, and the people, as a constitutive element, take form. The hidden people—unnamable and inherently excluded from the impossible totality—serve as the base for the emergence of a new truth, one that arises from what is fundamentally absent.[12] When we view the hidden people as the realm of absolute differentiation, opposed to the univocity of the model, we understand that the paradox is truly a looking glass.

THE THREE MECHANISMS OF ENCRYPTION (TOTALITY, FINALITY, *IMMUNITAS*)

Three mechanisms are fundamental for the transcendent model to fully realize encryption: (1) They must create a sense of totality (simulated order); (2) they must instill finality (hierarchy); and (3) they must function as an extensive calculating machine (immunity-autopoiesis-reverse alignment).

If we say that the building block of democracy is that constituent power belongs exclusively to the people, what happens when someone or something that is not the people determines "these are the totality of the people," and adds "the people are the people, *if and only if,* they conform to this ideal or finality?" Are we still talking about democracy? Constituent power? The people? If only one of those questions is negative, doesn't the whole construction logically crumble?

People, relations, and things of the world, or in other words, beingness, prefigured as a totality, logically supposes that there is an external architect to being, a master who counts, labels, categorizes, and defines those things and relations unilaterally and arbitrarily. An external and superior force hedges and limits any possible relation or change that is not anticipated in the total sum of things. This can only mean the utter impossibility of immanence, difference, and infinity that, as we proved, are the index of beingness and therefore of the world.

A political community as a finality logically supposes that there is an external architect, a master who imposes, from a hidden exterior, what that community must strive for in order to be (Plato's *areté,* Aristotle's *Eudaimonia* as virtue, but on a grimmer side, it can also be race or money as models, etc.). This logically means that a community (a people) cannot set or become their own finality but must instead obey the finality set forth in an external constituent moment by some power other than themselves. Even worse, in order to belong to the body politic, an admission test must be passed; the candidate must prove that it complies with the requirements of membership, and as a consequence, democracy is impossible.

Insofar as is becoming evident, totality and finality, as constitutive features of a community, negate democracy.

The fundamental insight is that for those rigid boundaries of totality and finality to work, transcendent models must also be, to some extent, elastic and resilient. Every boundary is a liquid structure that contours, changes, and accommodates variations; furthermore, it must be able to quickly respond to any variation with precision. Transcendent models are a complex machine that calculates outcomes through a fixed code (in the case of sovereignty, its code is: falsely include the abnormality, the hidden people, so they can be excluded). By shifting our perspectives, we may even discover that they are not a programming entity as much as an instance of self-fulfilling prophecy (Merton 1948), where the chain, *law-conflict-code of immunity-resolution* are one and the same, simply displayed as different points in time.

Plastic Totality

The "encryptor" (those who hold the keys of the transcendent model) defines reality by controlling the communication (language, images, data) used to discuss it. To achieve this control, the image of an absolute totality is created. This totality could be a nation-state or a constitution. It acts as a predefined framework that governs all interactions and discussions within its domain.

A transcendent model must impose the things of the world as a final and done totality, an arithmetic formula that counts beings, but most importantly, that calculates and programs every possible interaction. For encryption,

> . . . it is fundamental to create the idea of a totality (the nation state, the constitution) that is previous and superior to any interaction that may emerge. Totality holds within it the design of parts that are integral to it, creating simultaneously the mechanism to calculate every emergence of possible relations. A regime of encryption anticipates the emergence of difference and tries to paralyze the formation of truths trough difference. Within a totality, the possibility of meaning is already distributed among centers of significance. Encryption is thus the negation of democracy (the order of difference) from the impossibility of politics through the alienation of language that makes the world possible. In the end, the impenetrability of language becomes the impenetrability of the political. (Sanín-Restrepo 2018, xix)

Totality refers to a state of being complete, final, and closed. It also implies finality, as it announces perfection (nothing else can be added). It implies that every relationship depends on an external guiding force that defines the boundaries of all possible forms. When we inquire about the world, the answer is already predetermined.

Totality operates like a mythical recipe. It brings disparate elements together, announcing an unattainable ideal, while always preserving the impossible model intact and out of reach of difference.

The kind of totality that encryption creates with the interplay of the ideas of the people as totality, and the hidden people, is an *orientable surface* that simulates a Moebius strip: for the transcendent model, it ideally symbolizes infinity, but it is a closed totality to the extent that interiority and exteriority are mutually suspended and permanently denote each other. But, for the hidden people in resistance, it is truly a Moebius strip, a *non-orientable* potentiality as there cannot be a shuttered definition of a singular space and direction.

Totality opposes infinity, and infinity is the sign of contingency. Infinity means that the potential relations among beings are incalculable and immanent to the relations themselves.

Imagine the color palette, with all the sophistication that it implies. Beginning with the definition of what color is, how it is perceived, what it means in the dark, how it refracts with light, the meanings and functions of absorption, change, emission, hue, luminance, and irradiance. Think also about its tonalities, and even the human capacity to divide light and shades, tinctures, and turn color itself into moral and aesthetic symbols. Now imagine that a transcendent model determines that these things called colors can only be used in a certain way to form only certain totalities in predefined and fixed interactions or patterns. Now we can see the role of transcendent models arbitrarily turning infinity into totality.

> Being cannot be attributed to a model, a model within language can only be deemed as a sample. The sample (model) is a means of representation of singulars and passages to composites (either in creation or destruction). The only difference, logically speaking, between the sample of green in a haberdashery, the sample of macadamia nut brittle ice-cream and the sample of humanity in a declaration of rights is that in the latter case something inexistent is elevated to serve as the only possibility of existence of what potestas (power as oppression) may decide to apply to it and to every other sample, including the green fabric or the macadamia nut brittle ice-cream. (Sanín-Restrepo 2021)

Let us reflect, again, emanating from these new findings, on the interactions between the hidden people and the people as a totality. "The concept of the people becomes a synecdoche, where a false totality (the people of human rights and constitutions, the included) incarnates (symbolizes and falsely represent) an impossible infinity (the excluded, the hidden people)" (Sanín-Restrepo 2021, 13).

The encryption of power determines who counts within the totality of a political society. While decisions are ostensibly made for the entire population, and beyond it, for an infinity of beings, the programming of values remains accessible only to a privileged minority. The hidden people—the marginalized and excluded—are constitutively absent from this definition of politics and democracy.

On the other hand, contingency, a primordial concept for decryption (see Sanín-Restrepo 2021), within a totality suggests that the possibility of this completeness is perpetually held in check by an absent element, in our case, the hidden people. This missing component disrupts the harmony between the existing state of affairs and the overarching totality. However, if the latter is true, then if totality could exist differently (contingently),[13] it logically implies that reality is not fixed and final, but rather open and boundless. In essence, totality and contingency are incompatible concepts.

> While contingency is the unleashing of immanence, generation, transitions, and creativity; necessity is the sovereign grip of every definition of time and space from a predefined point zero. While in necessity, the contingency of the future is captured in what is presently actual; contingency is the edge where possible and impossible are to be decided. Contingency is always the unbound multiplicity of becoming. Hence, there is no expression of difference that is not contingent as there is no negation of difference that does not always fall back into necessity. Contingency and necessity are then the gridlocks of power, that is, of what is possible and impossible. (Sanín-Restrepo 2018, xi)

Justice, in this framework, is not a universal constant but a dynamic concept shaped by singular interactions, differences, and the ever-changing landscape of contingency.

Theories of justice that embrace totality, either as an ideal community (Rawls 2001), its conditions of dialogue (Habermas 1998), the improvement of conditions that take the totality of the system for granted (Amartya Sen 2009), and what and how goods and services are divided by a deciding group (distributive), are pregiven as natural, necessary, total, and are thus encrypted.

Plastic-Finality

Decrypting power means rejecting finality established by invisible models as the condition of belonging to a body politic.

Virtue (as doing well),[14] as a personal finality or aim to attain, could be a transcendent and beautiful voyage for the soul. The problems are not solely of a logical nature: who can define virtue? And, by what means can it be established? Or beauty, or even race for that matter, which is in itself walking on a heck of a slippery slope. However, why should anything other than the possibility to belong to a body politic define the body politic? And, furthermore, how can we define a condition to belong to the body politic before the possibility of the appearance of the body politic? To the last questions[15] you may be inclined to answer that it is almost germane to groups to demand conditions of admission, but then you are talking about private clubs, reading groups, aristocracies, but certainly not democracies. Because, if virtue (or anything else other than difference) takes the place of the condition of a body politic, then virtue (or better, they who establish its need) is the true constituent power of said body. When we impose virtue (as Aristotle and Plato do) or any other value as the very condition for belonging to a community, a monumental fracture immediately opens up at the base of politics.[16]

> Politics is defined by *a doing well*, but the very confines of the description of doing well can only be posited by those who are already inside politics! Politics is thus reduced to the level of a techné: if to play the harp is to play it to perfection, then to live means to live to perfection according to a logos. But the logos cannot define an abstract, a priori, and universal property of perfection, and thus the power to define perfection is deferred to those already belonging to the political body (as myth) . . . Only those who live in virtue, who have dominated the techné of life, are allowed to be called into the political. This is the primordial encryption of politics. (Sanín-Restrepo 2016)

"We the people" is turned to "We (some of us who are virtuous,—or white, or Christian) are the people as long as we conform to the mystical and mythical dictates of a transcendent model whose mysteries are not completely clear to us."

This simple exploration of finality reveals the crux of the matter. The encryption of democracy is something much deeper and all abrasive: it is the encryption of the possible.

Decrypting power is, then, the fundamental rejection of politics as any finality established by invisible and untouchable models. What *finality* denies is the very possibility of a relation of power stemming from difference, immanence, and infinity.

Let us see these problematics of the encryption of the people through finality and totality via artificial intelligence and what it can mean for our world. After the said exploration, we will land in the decryption of what we have termed "the calculating machine" and immunity.

AI and the Post-Anthropocene

Artificial Intelligence[17] puts in check what humans have sternly built as the dividing line between their uniqueness and superiority and every other form of matter considered as minor beings (animals, inanimate objects, microorganisms, tools). The line is drawn somewhere along a given superior activity of the ego, be it creativity, imagination, free will, intentionality, rationality, and, above all, the creation of orders and institutions determined by and generating forms of power as organization.

> . . . AI constantly probes the boundaries of and taken for granted assumptions about qualities supposed to be quintessentially human. One of such qualities was supposed to be creativity: the result of allegedly exclusively human consciousness, emotionality, and drive, impossible for other beings, let alone digital entities, to replicate. Nevertheless, recent developments in AI and related fields have enabled a flourishing of what is often called computer-generated art—essentially, artificial creativity. (Kalpokas and Kalpokiene 2023)

Although we cannot delve into detail here, suffice it to state that the monument of human superiority was already cracked at its seams before AI. Colonialism and coloniality made clear that the only worthy subjectivity around which science, morals, aesthetics, and ontology were constructed was the white European male. Freud broke the ego, as a supposed core of uniform and integral subjectivity bestowed with a linear and clear-cut intentionality. Scientific revolutions, such as Darwin's theory of evolution, quantum mechanics, and thermodynamics, shattered the idea of the sterilized separation between humans and nature and the utter control over the latter through the absolute objectivity and neutrality of a "scientific method" created by humans to award meaning onto it. The Industrial Revolution, with advances in apprehending reality, such as the camera, obliterated human art's stronghold on their claim that objective perspective belonged exclusively to human creativity given to them by a central perspective of things and that this was consequently the only legitimate way to see. The idea of agency as strictly human and consciously driven was revoked, or at least put into question, by Peirce's thirdness and Foucault's BioPolitics, to mention just a couple of spokes in the wheels of subjectivity and rationality that led to what we now call studies of posthumanism.

As Rosi Braidotti explains, ". . . across the spectrum of cognitive capitalism, of posthumanism on the one hand and post-anthropocentrism on the other. The former focuses on the critique of the humanist ideal of 'Man' as the allegedly universal measure of all things, while the latter criticizes species hierarchy and human exceptionalism" (Braidotti 2019).

The jaw-dropping advances in AI simply evinces what studies of post-humanism have been signaling for some time now; the concept of man is fractured, and its claim of symbolic, aesthetic, moral, ontological, and epistemological superiority[18] rests in tatters. The idea of "humanity" as encompassing a universality of beings is nothing but a ruse, yet another synecdoche, where "man" and "human" always referred to a (racial, gendered, proprietorial) minority who have held on to the strings of power and have used the concept of "humanity" to dominate and expropriate whatever is not them. As Braidotti hits the nail on the head, "(human) . . . never was a universal or a neutral term to begin with. It is rather a normative category that indexes access to privileges and entitlements. Appeals to the 'human' are always discriminatory: they create structural distinctions and inequalities among different categories of humans, let alone between humans and non-humans" (Braidotti, 2019).

Henceforth, power as potestas rests in a model we can safely say operates as a "model of all models": Man. The transcendent model that programs, limits, and determines all other transcendent models such as "the market," "freedom," "the nation," and so on. The model is not a generic and open-ended prototype, elastic enough to fit changes and transformations, but rather a shuttered system of identity and power.[19] Certainly, the idea of the superiority of man is illusory, limited, and destructive. The illusion of a creature disconnected from its environment, acting on it without being acted upon. The limited shallowness of imposing a model of a finalized shape on everything that is becoming in time and space, the shallowness of necessity over contingency that dictates that we must swallow the bitter pills of "we live in the best of possible worlds" (thus nothing must change) along with genocides perpetrated in the name of democracy and sovereignty. The destructive hubris of believing that this creature can consume and destroy at whim without limit and consequence.

However, no other event like the coming into being of AI is pushing the anthropocentric fable to its bursting limit, showing that everything that "man" held dear as their uniqueness was but a chimera.

What exactly is transformed by AI regarding the Anthropos? How dense is its power of encryption/decryption regarding the creature's illusions, limits, and destruction?

Let us center on a small set of questions.

First: Does AI simply replicate the hierarchies and inequalities of its programming? Or, said in another way, does it replicate human biases and is it therefore implicitly encrypting power?

Second: How far can programming really go? That is, how much of the active process can it control when machine learning supposes the autonomy of the learning and acting of the machine? We are referring to the unleashing of forces that cannot be contained by the very logic that created them. In a sense, the question leads to another, deeper one: what will happen when and if AI gains "singularity?"

Third: To what extent is subjectivity fragmented by "cognitive capitalism" and its unregulated surveillance and algorithmic dictatorship? How much has the compact and monumental "I," that supposedly acted as a rational free being, become multiple and scattered little "Me's" floating aimlessly in the amniotic fluid of the web, creating profiles of consumerism and becoming fixed only as a being in perpetual debt?

Fourth: Connecting all the aforementioned questions, has AI created other realms of reality, of nature, of actuality, of imagination? And what does this mean for the "other" or "second" natures that humans had created beforehand? We are referring to the "economy" or the "state's sovereignty" as autonomous human "natures" that were constructed under the claim that they functioned with the predictability and rationality of the "first" nature.

Allow us to tackle all the questions as one.

For now, the answer to whether AI replicates established human hierarchies and exacerbates existing inequalities is yes. Only a handful of Gargantuan corporations, operating in an entirely unregulated and unrestricted environment, control the programming of AI inputs and outputs, driven solely by an insatiable quest for profit. As Kalpokas and Kalpokiene have put it, ". . . a paradigmatic case of AI pushing the boundaries of otherwise taken-for-granted anthropocentric assumptions. Particularly, resistance to acknowledging algorithmic creativity is located in a hierarchical and discriminatory view of the world, characteristic of the anthropocentric thinking of Western modernity" (Kalpokas and Kalpokiene 2023).

Here, we must separate AI and other machines. In cybernetics, a non-trivial machine represents a system where the output is not directly predictable from its input. This type of machine exhibits characteristics of agency and autonomy. In contrast, a trivial machine operates in a repetitive and predictable manner (except for printers, but we all knew that), as its functions remain unaffected by previous operations. The behavior of a non-trivial machine is inherently reactive, unpredictable, and dynamic, as its current input–output relationship is influenced by its past outputs. This makes non-trivial machines complex and adaptive, capable of evolving over time in response to their operational history (Heßler 2023; Fischer and Cretu 2023).

Consequently, we have the main elements for a plausible answer. These handful of profit-driven corporations feed AI a reproduction of the world they want to preserve and intensify, a world of racial hierarchies, profound social divisions, and the unlimited exploitation and destruction of society and nature. This would seem to point to the idea that there is no autonomy as such in AI, as it is created and driven under human aesthetic and ethical mannerisms and truisms; it is still programmed through a human language, desires, and absences. Nevertheless, the previously quoted authors point toward something more convoluted. "Algorithmic creativity" and the extensive and intensive method by which AI machines learn (they are all connected horizontally; this process is unlimited; when one machine learns something, it is not individual learning, but it is immediately shared with all other machines). Hence, machine learning is not only the capacity to think and create by itself, but the very possibility of the creation of a new dominium of unpredictable signs, meanings, and objects, not only blurring the dominance of the Anthropos but signaling toward a brutal separation from it.

Franco Berardi calls "reverse alignment":

> What will happen in terms of alignment will be the opposite of what is promised by the builders of the automaton: it is not the machine that aligns itself with human values but humans who must align themselves with the automatic values of the intelligent artifact, whether it is a question of assimilating the indispensable procedures for interacting with the financial system, or learning the procedures necessary to use military systems. (Berardi 2023)

We are thus looking toward unpredictability and the split, a point where programming becomes diffuse because machine learning is lateral and integral, the line blurs, and we cannot predicate that the outcomes are the direct result of programming. "Moreover, widely available and easy to use AI tools that do not necessitate independent training or extensive parameter tinkering" (Kalpokas and Kalpokiene 2023).

The point raises the question that if AI is initially programmed as x, it will not remain on the same straightforward path, in another whip of posthuman humbling. Nevertheless, this may not be a novelty. Think of how capitalism has taken its own chaotic and destructive path, a runaway train with no one at the controls, or rather, a gigantic Ponzi scheme, where everyone, including the great capitalists, does nothing else but obey its blind designs (see Harvey 2011). Maybe no other event than this, of turning things and setting them loose, should have taught us so much about our discreet place in the universe, and nevertheless has made our narcissism more acute. Maybe because this was the grain of its core all along?

Adam Smith's idea of the economy as natural, as simply another mightier nature imposed on human relations, a second skin, shares the floor with Hobbes' idea of sovereignty as the true nature of political society. They have wedged and sculpted our world. Regarding the second nature and the unleashing of uncontrollable forces, "the point here is not so much that our domination of nature has led to our downfall, but that those hubristic claims of domination are exposed as hollow now that we have unleashed processes and events that we may be unable to control or reverse" (Choat 2018).

And we may be arriving at a crucial stage. Cognitive capitalism is the force that drives and encrypts our relationships, that builds our sensitivities and our vision of the world. Braidotti tells us:

> . . . these developments do not take place in a void, but rather within the axiomatic and profit-driven system (Toscano 2005) of "cognitive capitalism" (Moulier Boutang 2012). This system rests on advanced technologies, the financialization of the economy and the overwhelming power of the media and cultural sectors. The practice of labour in such a system is simultaneously highly sophisticated, as it requires cultural and algorithmic fluency, and also highly unregulated and hence open to exploitation. (Braidotti2019)

The rise of cognitive capitalism creates a new logic in bio-power and bio-politics. Bentham's macabre conception of the Panopticon, instrumentalized by Michel Foucault, may need to give way to new metaphors, as the level of pervasiveness and perversity of bio-politics has garnered newfangled planes of sophistication.

Frank Pasquale invites us to symbolize it as a one-way mirror, where the state and powerful corporations have absolute visibility into our lives, while their actions are utterly opaque and even mystical to us, or in a word, encrypted. "But while powerful businesses, financial institutions, and government agencies hide their actions behind nondisclosure agreements, 'proprietary methods,' and gag rules, our own lives are increasingly open books. Everything we do online is recorded" (Pasquale 2015). This new panopticon is not a zero point of visibility but a sophisticated field of elastic vision, there seems to be nothing else but the visual apparatus itself. It moves and penetrates, it hides in plain sight, we are imbued in it, and we are it. But most importantly, we are the ones that seek to fatten it. Aldous Huxley already warned us that the secret police would not be invading our homes clandestinely to hide cameras and such; no, we will happily desire, buy, enjoy, and gloat about the apparatuses that keep us in a state of total surveillance. As Pasquale continues: "Surveillance cameras, data brokers, sensor networks, and 'supercookies' record how fast we drive, what pills we take, what books we read, what websites we visit. The law, so aggressively protective of secrecy in the world of commerce, is increasingly silent when it comes to the privacy of personal affairs" (Pasquale 2015).

Nevertheless, the one-way mirror seeks not only a kind of knowing or stripping us down to the bones of desire, but it is substantially a way of shaping us, of awarding us with multiple and pliable personalities, of kneading desire, converting the complexity of what is human to a single gooey form, the debtor, the inexorable form of subjectivity of cognitive capitalism. "Connecting the dots of past behavior to predict the future. Are you a fierce comparison shopper, or the relaxed kind who's OK spending a few extra dollars for a plane ticket or a movie if it saves some trouble? Firms want to know, and they can find out quite easily. Every business wants a data advantage that will let it target its ideal customer" (Pasquale 2015, 20).

The effect on subjectivity, or rather on agency, is deeply seeded. The conceited idea of a supreme "I," bathing in the waters of free will and liberty, is upended and taken to the other extreme. Multiple "Me's," quartered, atomized, profiled, into a perpetual debtor (debtor of financial systems, but also debtor of image). "Commodities never fully appease or release but keep us coming back for more. Addictive and toxic, capitalism is an entropic and self-destructive system that 'eats up' the future and endangers the very sources of its wealth and power (Holland 2011)" (Braidotti 2022). Here we must add Mark Coeckelbergh's insights "AI, especially machine learning, has made significant progress. This has enabled algorithms to take over many of our activities, including planning, speech, face recognition, and decision making." Coeckelbergh M (2020). We are left looking, without fully knowing, through a double barrel of a gun. On one side, political speeches and ads installed in the cortex of our sensations and responses, all fabricated by the dictatorship of algorithms, shout at our ego that we are chosen, powerful, and free. On the other barrel, multiple and inane "Me's" are being created and fattened by desire to produce the docile perpetual debtor.

Immunity, the Calculating Machine, and the Hierarchization of Lexicons

However, isn't a transcendent model the paradigm of a technology of power? Who else but Plato (2005) uses *techné* as the precondition of the origin of political philosophy as specialized knowledge that begets the social division of labor? *Techné* is at the heart of the modeling of power and of the dyad power/knowledge. Heidegger, following Plato, tells us how *techné* "means neither art nor technology but a kind of knowledge, the knowing disposal over the free planning and arranging and controlling of arrangements" (Heidegger 2000, 49). Of course, it is Foucault (1978, 1985, 1990) who drives this understanding the furthest, establishing a clean-cut map of how knowledge, technology, and discipline intertwine to create concrete and magnificent models of power.[20]

Transcendent models are enmeshed in the latter form of power as *techné,* and as such, they remain a mystical form of creating obedience. They possess and project that double nature of omnipotent power and adoration. *The model* holds the mystery of the word—flesh made spirit; we are in perpetual lack, spiritless flesh. There is this mystical aura shrouding transcendent models; it is how they are able to function as the very lifeline of ideology. The imbedded belief that they represent a kind of mysterious perfection. A *Deus Absconditus,* where there is a secret mechanism tirelessly ticking inside them that allows them to absorb any amount of external information, to ward themselves off against any kind of menace, and return all that noise and chaos to the world as a clean and coherent reality. As redemption for our ignorance, doubt, and impiety.

Developing his concept of "Coloniality of internationalism," Sabelo J. Ndlovu-Gatsheni reminds us that the transcendent model need not be an institution or a single system of beliefs, but a cluster of disciplines, institutions, and hegemonical forms of producing knowledge that work as a cluster, bleeding into mighty power structures and discourses:

> The DNA of imperial/colonial/liberal hegemonic internationalism is coloniality. The leitmotif of coloniality is encryption of power. Coloniality of internationalism is a *sine qua non* of transcendental model of power. It is conceived and driven by leading figures (philosophers and statesmen) and countries (empires and nation-states) at particular moments in human history aimed at impositions of particular orders favourable to the powerful. The most enduring and longest internationalism is one that emerged in the fifteenth century predicated on what James Blaut (1993) termed the "colonizer's model of the world." This long-standing imperial/colonial/liberal internationalism was characterized by Carl Schmitt (1996) as the "second nomos of the earth." What hangs it together, animates it, galvanizes, and sustains it is what the Latin American decolonial theorists termed "modernity/coloniality" (power structure) consisting of "colonial matrices of power." (Ndlovu-Gatsheni 2024, 12)

Let us now weave in between *Autopoiesis* (Maturana and Varela 1972, Varela 2017, Luhmann 2012), *Immunitas* (Esposito 2005) with some preliminary insights of artificial intelligence, to understand how transcendent models function as the machine of encryption through the creation of reality and ideology. We must be very attentive, because there is a permanent interchange between autopoiesis and immunitas, where sometimes one, both, or their mutual interplay are simply simulated, that is, they function *as if.* For example, how the state simulates its full capacity to absorb and solve every conflict that erupts on its surface.

Insofar, transcendent models are not only artificial edifices that possess (or pretend to possess) the capacity to self-organize and perpetually propagate and enhance their existence through the iterative execution of their own processes (Keenan 2022). What we need to grasp is that the process is all-encompassing, as the chain law-conflict-code of immunity-resolution are one and the same thing simply displayed as different points in time. Yes, in brief, there is a trick of sorts, a game of mirrors, where the machinic spirit splashes out law-conflict-code of immunity-resolution as differential points and processes in time and space, while there is truly a simulacrum of such things, and they are all tied up as one substance into a perfect programming bundle inside the model. The key takeaway is that the component of *conflict* within the chain law-*conflict*-code of immunity-resolution is simulated; true conflict subsists in reality within the interstice inside/outside (racism, expropriation, poverty, etc.) but is absorbed, transported,[21] and transformed into a simulacrum of a conflict that is then interiorized as the only truth of the situation. The conflict is turned into an anemic semantic and legal scheme, now centering around words like property, quotas, and so on, where the stakes that are simulated are principles of the system such as rights, due process, and the rule of law, which replace racism, expropriation, poverty, and so on.

> . . . a logic where liberalism, through a colossal deployment of institutions, simulates conflict and difference to naturalize and legitimize the horrors of capital. The court, the screen of a smart phone, the law, the false sense of expression and the fantasy of dissent create a monumental stage for the spectacle of difference that enervates the capacity of power as domination to thrive on its own. (Sanín-Restrepo 2016, 42)

What is more relevant to our discussion regarding politics, democracy, and the people, is that the simulation of difference and conflict creates a lexical encryption. With it, hierarchies are established among beings and objects in the world, while engagement (the execution of the control of the machine) is reserved for those who hold the codes of usage (encryptors). The bitter aim of all this contraption is to allow the machine of appropriation through violence to efficiently devour in deafening silence.

The simulation of difference and conflict is then the cornerstone of the autopoietic machine. In doing so, they behave very close to what we now know as artificial intelligence, where the supposedly contingent outcome is already determined and schemed out bit by bit from the outset within the interplay of input and output. The secret to all, where we dispel its mystical aura, is that the input –what conflict is—and output—how conflict is solved—are entirely simulated, leaving a bloody trail of the real conflict that was simulated.

Following Esposito (2005) and Benjamin (2010), we understand that the law does not see the community as a unity but as a disparity of forces that can always destroy it. How does the law respond? It imposes the ideal of union of forces, which involves coercing transcendent models as the anima of the community, as an essence that each individual must pursue as their highest destiny: country, race, and so on, all in the name of the people. The main interest of the law, or rather its implicit structure (its determinism or machinicism), is to protect itself.

The theory of encryption of power, ruminating on Roberto Esposito's concept of *Immunitas,* finds that the integrating parts of the totality of a transcendent model are not only designed to maintain the status quo, but to calculate every emergence of possible relations, reinforcing existing hierarchies. Immunity, as a part of encryption, perpetuates hierarchies, chokes difference, and controls the narrative of reality to its most vascular detail.

Let us pursue Esposito's work on immunitas:[22]

> According to this approach, one should not miss the view of the circumstance that immunity, as a private category, does not acquire relevance more than as a negative modality of the community. This negative dialectic acquires particular relevance in the sphere of legal language or, to be more precise, of the law as an immune device of the entire social system. (Esposito 2005, 18)

Immunitas is not only the waiver of an obligation or the exemption of a tribute but something that interrupts the social circuit of reciprocal donation; this is what the original meaning refers to (Esposito 2005, 16). We then have a situation where everyone is linked in terms of equality to an obligation, and then the reality, where privileges and exceptions are granted arbitrarily, interrupting the social circuit. Consequently, every community is really immunity to the extent that the group or system is internally designed and, at the same time, armed from what it needs to avoid (either excluding or including falsely, that is, encrypting).

Immunitas can be an exception to the rule on multiple levels. On one side, privilege for some who do not have to fulfill the rule; on the other, an exception in the sense that only some must satisfy the rule; and even, third, those who fall outside the rule of privilege (migrants, prisoners—the hidden people). At its core, law already possesses a code to establish what the relevant conflicts are, what can or cannot be discussed, negotiated, claimed, and, more importantly, changed. Notwithstanding, what is fundamental to grasp is that there is a systematic articulator within the rule, a distributor, which is installed deep in the hardware of the institution and already provides forms of exclusion when defending itself. A basic component of encryption is that it is elastic. The structural programming of the law prevents the threat with a rigorous codified reaction. When this operation fails or is not enough to suppress or neutralize the conflict, the decision centers become fluid, and the solution will be deferred to a qualified interpreter (constitutional courts, the Fed, etc.), who, following the code, will decide under the canopy of some kind of supposed discretion of the law.

Immunity is an anti-community, a system of rules, institutions, and speeches as machines that anticipate results of encryption.

Esposito follows Simone Weil's powerful insights into the inherently private and exclusive character of all rights, including those that are defined as public. Law, in its historically constituted form, is always for someone, never for everyone, and a privilege cannot be, by logical definition, universal (Esposito 2005, 20). Joining this explosive insight with *immunitas*, Esposito produces a refined conclusion: the main objective of the law is to shield the community, which inherently gives it a negative connotation. Due to the contrasting interdependence of the two concepts, the goal is to safeguard not against an outside threat, but against an element that is intrinsically part of the community and, indeed, defines its very essence (Esposito 2005, 36).

The logic is then very simple. A community is built on top of particular privileges that pass as rights of the whole community. And this is when it becomes uncanny; in order to sustain said privileges, the law defends them against those who would constitute a true community if the privilege was lifted. There are various forms of immunity, and this last one is the liberal breed; it is based on the simulation of rights and of the people, that if realized, would destroy itself. What truly would constitute a community is held at bay to protect the immunity of *some*, in the name of the community that cannot exist as long as it remains as such. The proof of the simulacrum is then that the hidden people would realize the false simulacrum (people as a totality), closing the gap of the primordial exclusion.

As Esposito clearly puts it

> . . . the risk from which the law aims to protect life in common is represented by the same relationship that it constitutes it as such. This relationship breaks the limits of identity of individuals and exposes them to alteration, and therefore, to a potential conflict—on the part of the others. Since the relationship and the alteration are not a pathological possibility, but the original form of the community, this means that the law, by immunizing it, inverts it, making it its opposite. (Esposito 2005, 36)

Law does not immunize from exterior threats but against interior forms of relationality, of links that would constitute the community (the hidden people). To protect and keep the community alive, the law empties the community's core and tears it away from its most intense meaning (Esposito 2005, 37).

We are forced to a further conclusion: the bridge between the sovereignty of the people and appropriation of the people is the law.

Following in Walter Benjamin's steps, we understand that violence is not limited to preceding the law; rather, violence constitutes the law (Benjamin

2010). Law is both the scheme of visibility of the community and its denial; they become one in the same stroke. This is why violence and law, for Benjamin, are not two separate parts of a concerted movement but are one and the same thing. The function of the law is to reduce all power to its monopoly, co-opt every being to its belonging, and shutter the gap between it and any kind of difference that would defy it.

The intermingling of Esposito and Benjamin shows us that the initial establishment of law is necessarily an act of violence (unfounded decision—constituent power) without legal basis. Once established, the very first heartbeat of the law eliminates any form of violence. However, this exclusion is enforced through additional acts of violence, which serve to maintain the existing power structure. Essentially, it's a cycle of violence used to regulate violence itself, used to perpetuate itself perpetually. As Esposito asks, "what is exclusion of something external but its inclusion?" (2005, 47). The law does not want to eliminate violence, but to regulate it and convert it to its interior. What threatens the law is not violence but its duplicity inside/outside. Its most refined form is evident when we grasp that the outside that has to be included is its own inside, the hidden people. With it, the great leap is taken, and it is the total closure of the crack of the exception between sovereign and excluded/included. Here, "violence derives its legitimacy not from its content but its location" (Esposito 2005, 47). With the hidden people, the gap is closed, and the inside and the outside are made to coincide. Communities and immunity become one.

Subsequently, we begin to fully understand that myth, and not politics, is the simulacrum of Western powers. As Glissant put it masterfully, "the Plantation is not the product of a politics, but the emanation of a fantasy" (Glissant 1997, 93).

What becomes fundamental is the idea of point of contact (friction, encounter), or rather the utter lack of it (its simulacrum). The model creates an interface; it is contact without sensitivity, without immanent communication. Information is transferred or conducted without altering the beings that are supposedly in contact, without truly depending on their power. Another thing altogether is transported; maybe it could be the simulation of being together, maybe obedience in its crudest form, but neither being nor their power, which remain static. The final product is not known in the factory; we are only cogs in a machine.

Today's artificial intelligence was not built in a vacuum; it adopts the codes of production, the programming, and defensive systems of historical forms of artificial intelligence: the state, the law, and so on. The state is a great example of this artificial intelligence deployed over the control of time and space, a complex program that anticipates every form of conflict or, at least, sets out the rules to do so.

In that same line:

> What the encryptor accomplishes, through very sophisticated uses of Artificial Intelligence and downright monopolization of information, (for example through the military-industrial-virtual-technology complex) is to create a funnel where all human intelligence is distilled, bottled, branded, and destined. All this process is conducted from within five or six corporations and an alliance of a handful of nation-states. "Resource" which is Heidegger's funny little corporate name for the way in which objects will come to appear and be experienced are inverted by this type of encryption. In our times of unleashed neoliberalism human flesh is the dire fuel of the machine. (Sanín-Restrepo 2021, 63–64)

Maybe the problem of AI, and by extension, of what we are learning of classic transcendent models, is not that it (AI) will mirror the ethics of destruction of capitalism through highly elitized and centralized programming. The problem is that every human individual (most of us) that interacts with the machine (feeds it information, teaches it how to mimic purpose and desire) is in itself encrypted, as a highly elitized and centralized program. The big techs need not worry about encrypting their chat boxes (hiding in them and directing them toward racism, misogyny, and elitism), we do it for them in every single contact we have with the machines. We are the encrypted machine of language that has fed and fattened transcendent models for centuries. It is a fine time to partake in the difference production machine, the insurrectional machine, the hidden people.

NOTES

1. The poetic (paradox, parody, satire, etc.) creates novelty without a preexistent model. It breaks the siege of any regime of predictability anchored in the utter control of time, space, and beings. Eroding necessity and its rule of brutality, it allows us to see, feel, and partake in the world again. "(I)f philosophy is the extraordinary questioning of what ordinarily seems reality, poetics is the answer of and through the extraordinary" (Sanín-Restrepo 2018, xxii).
2. Liberation or solution, not as if a paradox was a riddle to solve or a contradiction to be overcome, but as a means to intensify its poetic power.
3. As will become apparent, the definition of "late-coloniality" is tied to the emergence in history of constitutional phenomena (Sanín-Restrepo and Machado-Araujo 2020).
4. "The perseverance of models of identity means two interconnected things: first, politics has served as a harsh demarcation line of life, and second, that to belong to a body politic, any agent (before becoming a subject, before exercising difference) must conform to the qualifications of identity set forth by an invisible (transcendent) model" (Sanín-Restrepo 2018, xiii).

5. We have yet to explore the aesthetic and psychoanalytic consequences of this new form of power, although the table is set:

> Renouncing God, transcendence, and veiling its own principles modernity has set forth a paradoxically divine force: its own nihilism. From within the carcass of divinity, a flood of power-thirsty deities struggles to subdue the production of time and space and to harness every kind of creation of life as its own creation. The dogmatic slumber becomes the linguistic (nihilist) psychotic awakening. Their enemy: any living form that produces difference as the trait of its own existence, because such a thing defies both the deities' control of the creation of life and their claim to dominate space and time through transcendence. The antidote to difference: to solidify power in ever greater and more sophisticated machines that simulate politics in law and culture and trace origins to aberrant communities. The finality of this machine: to grind bodies into automated units and to scorch the earth clean of difference. Its psychedelic architectural model: to create a center of light as positivity and then ignite the centrifugal fuse at its core, creating peripheries of negativity where the perverted infra-human must dwell under the cloud of error while transfusing every ounce of energy to replenish the center. Coloniality is the name of the form of power we are describing. (Sanín-Restrepo 2016, 19)

6. In an upcoming volume of this series, we will explore the convergences between James Martel's concept of "Archism" and the theory of encryption of power. For a definition of archism (Martel 2021), Martel has defined how "Archism . . . seeks to go nameless insofar as it claims to be ubiquitous and just 'how politics is', is that violent and hierarchical form of power that dominates the world today."

7. For a complete study, see the fourth chapter of Sanín-Restrepo 2016.

8. This serves, so far, to unpack the paradox, but it is not yet a complete definition of decrypting or encrypting power.

9. In Althusser's sense (2016).

10. While reading a draft of this chapter, James R. Martel was reminded of a powerful passage of Nietzsche's *Thus Spoke Zarathustra:*

> Then a roaring wind tore its wings apart; whistling, shrilling and whipping
> it threw down a black coffin before me:
> And amidst the roaring and whistling and shrilling the coffin burst
> open and spewed forth thousandfold laughter.
> And it laughed and mocked and roared against me from a thousand
> grimaces of children, angels, owls, fools and butterflies the size of children.

11. See Sanín-Restrepo 2016.

12. "In other words, democracy can only produce itself through a dialectical approach that recognizes the *constitutive* contradiction between the totality and its hidden counterpart. As we will ascertain, the democratic synthesis does not involve the reconciliation of opposites, but first the total alienation of the false opposition (Adorno 2004, 18) and second the structuring of a true ontology of difference" (Sanín-Restrepo 2016, 44).

13. And here we refer to contingency as absolute contingency in the terms of French philosopher Quentin Meillassoux (2008).

14. As defined by Aristotle and Plato, for example.

15. Even if you can somehow circumvent the logical impossibility.

16. For a thorough study, see Sanín-Restrepo 2016.

17. This section is part of a larger study that is under way; we will focus here on a comparative description largely on Esposito's work.

18. "This dominant anthropocentric paradigm is rooted in an overstretch that encompasses ontology (humans as privileged entities), epistemology (humans as exclusive sources of knowledge), and ethics (humans as bearers of supreme moral value)" (Kalpokas and Kalpokiene 2023).

19. "Hence, Grear's (2015: 231–32) critique of the anthropos benchmark for law as 'a thoroughly gendered, raced construction' whose 'marginalised, colonialised 'others' were rendered susceptible to acts and forms of domination legitimated by assumptions concerning (white) masculine superiority and mastery' is particularly powerful. It also shows posthumanism to be not anti-human but radically egalitarian" (Kalpokas and Kalpokiene 2023).

20. However: "A scathing relation power-knowledge was uncovered by Foucault, nevertheless, what he missed is that philosophy too (not his discrete sciences alone) is executed to give ground to the predominant forms of power. Is there a philosophical theory that is not compromised or that is not the product of a specific form of power? It is high time to begin understanding philosophy from power so we may begin to understand power from philosophy" (Sanín-Restrepo 2021, 126).

21. In the sense proposed by Deleuze and Guattari (1987).

22. Free translation from a text in Spanish.

BIBLIOGRAPHY

Agamben, Giorgio. 1998. *Homo Sacer: Sovereign Power and Bare Life*. Stanford, CA: Stanford University Press.

Althusser, Louis, et al. 2016. *Reading Capital: The Complete Edition*. London: Verso Books.

Aristotle. 2015. *Nicomachean Ethics*. Perseus Digital Library. http://www.perseus.tufts.edu/hopper/. Retrieved December 2015.

Benjamin, Walter. 2010. *Para una Crítica de la Violencia*. Madrid: Biblioteca Nueva.

Berardi, Franco. 2023. "The Completion." Journal #137. E-flux.com. https://www.e-flux.com/journal/137/544269/the-completion/. Retrieved December 2023.

Braidotti, Rosi. 2019. "A Theoretical Framework for the Critical Posthumanities." *Theory, Culture & Society* 36(6): 31–61. doi: 10.1177/0263276418771486.

Braidotti, Rosi. 2022. "The Virtual as Affirmative Praxis: A Neo-Materialist Approach," *Humanities* 11(3): 62. doi: 10.3390/h11030062.

Choat, Simon. 2018. "Science, Agency and Ontology: A Historical-Materialist Response to New Materialism." *Political Studies* 66(4): 1027–42. doi: 10.1177/0032321717731926.

Coeckelbergh, Mark. 2020. *AI Ethics*. Cambridge, MA: The MIT Press.

Deleuze, Gilles and Felix Guattari. 1987. *A Thousand Plateaus: Capitalism and Schizophrenia*. Minneapolis, MN: University of Minnesota Press.

Derrida, Jacques. 2004. *Dissemination*. London: Continuum.

Esposito, Roberto. 2005. *Immunitas: Protección y Negación de la Vida*. Buenos Aires: Amorrortu.

Fischer, Thomas and Andrei Cretu. 2023. "The Ashby Box: A Contextualization and Speculative Remake." In: *Frictions: Inquiries into Cybernetic Thinking and Its Attempts towards Mate[real]ization*. Edited by Diego Gómez-Venegas. Lüneburg: Leuphana University of Lüneburg, 163–93.

Foucault, Michel. 1978. *The History of Sexuality Volume I: An Introduction*. New York: Pantheon Books.

Foucault, Michel. 1980. "The Confession of the Flesh." In: *Power/Knowledge: Selected Interviews and Other Writings*. Edited by Colin Gordon. New York: Pantheon Books, 194–229.

Foucault, Michel. 1995. *Discipline and Punish: The Birth of the Prison*. Translated by Alan Sheridan. New York: Vintage Books.

Glissant, Edouard. 1997. *Poetics of Relation*. Ann Arbor, MI: University of Michigan Press

Habermas, Jürgen. 1998. *Between Facts and Norms, Contributions to a Discourse, Theory of Law and Democracy*. Cambridge, MA: MIT Press.

Harvey, David. 2011. *The Enigma of Capital and the Crisis of Capitalism*. London: Profile Books.

Heßler, Martina. 2023. "Artificial Intelligence. Traditional Expectations and a New Category of Machines." In: *Actor & Avatar a Scientific and Artistic Catalog*. Edited by Dieter Mersch et al. Bielefeld: Transcript Verlag, 259–64.

Huxley, Aldous. 2004. *Brave New World and Brave New World Revisited*. New York: Harper.

Kalpokas, Ignas and Julija Kalpokiene. 2023. "Creative Encounters of a Posthuman Kind – Anthropocentric Law, Artificial Intelligence, and Art." *Technology and Society* 72: 102197.

Keenan, Bernard. 2022. "Niklas Luhmann: What is Autopoiesis?" https://criticallegalthinking.com/2022/01/10/niklas-luhmann-what-is-autopoiesis/. Retrieved March 2024.

Levinas, Emmanuel. 1979. *Totality and Infinity: An Essay on Exteriority*. The Hague: Martinus Nijhoff Publishers and Duquesne University Press.

Luhmann, Niklas. 2012. *Introduction to Systems Theory*. Cambridge: Polity Press.

Martel, James R. 2021. *Anarchist Prophets: Disappointing Vision and the Power of Collective Sight*. Durham, NC: Duke University Press.

Maturana, Humberto R. and Francisco J. Varela. 1972. *Autopoiesis and Cognition: The Realization of the Living*. Dordrecht: Reidel.

Meillassoux, Quentin. 2008. *After Finitude. An Essay on the Necessity of Contingency*. Translated by Ray Brassier. London: Bloomsbury Academic.

Méndez-Hincapíe, Gabriel. 2017. "From the Cybernetic World War towards a Cybernetic Civil War." https://criticallegalthinking.com/2017/08/16/cybernetic-world-war-towards-cybernetic-civil-war/. Retrieved March 2024.

Merton, Robert K. 1948. "The Self-Fulfilling Prophecy." *The Antioch Review* 8(2): 193–210.

Nancy, Jean-Luc. 2000. *Being Singular Plural.* Stanford, CA: Stanford University Press.
Ndlovu-Gatsheni, Sabelo, J. 2024. *Beyond the Coloniality of Internationalism: Reworlding the World from the Global South.* Dakar: Codesria.
Nietzsche, Friedrich. 1999. *Thus Spoke Zarathustra.* London: Penguin Classics.
Pasquale, Frank. 2015. *The Black Box Society, The Secret Algorithms That Control Money and Information.* Cambridge, MA; London: Harvard University Press.
Plato. 2005. *Phaedrus.* London: Penguin Classics.
Rancière, Jacques. 2001. *Ten Theses on Politics.* Baltimore, MD: Johns Hopkins University Press.
Rawls, John. 2001. *Justice as Fairness: A Restatement.* Cambridge, MA: Harvard University Press.
Sanín-Restrepo, Ricardo. 2016. *Decolonizing Democracy: Power in a Solid State.* London: Rowman & Littlefield International.
Sanín-Restrepo, Ricardo (Ed.). 2018. *Decrypting Power.* London: Rowman & Littlefield International.
Sanín-Restrepo, Ricardo. 2021. *Being and Contingency: Decrypting Heidegger's Terminology.* London: Rowman & Littlefield International.
Sanín-Restrepo, Ricardo. 2021. "Many Worlds Interpretation, Critical Theory and the (Immanent) Paradox of Power." https://criticallegalthinking.com/2021/11/22/many-worlds-interpretation-critical-theory-and-the-immanent-paradox-of-power/.
Sanín-Restrepo, Ricardo and Marinella Machado-Araujo. 2020. "The Theory of Encryption of Power: Itinerary of an Idea." *Revista da Faculdade Mineira de Direito* 23(45): 18–33.
Schmitt, Carl. 2006. *The Nomos of the Earth in the International Law of the Jus Publicum Europaeum.* Translated and annotated by G. L. Ulmen. New York: Telos Press Publishing.
Sen, Amartya. 2009. *The Idea of Justice.* Cambridge, MA: Belknap Press of Harvard University Press.
Varela, Francisco, et al. 2017. *The Embodied Mind: Cognitive Science and Human Experience.* Boston, MA: MIT Press.
Žižek, Slavoj. 2001. *El Sujeto Espinoso.* Buenos Aires: Editorial Paidós.

Chapter 2

Let's Dance (On Fantastic Critique)

Oscar Guardiola-Rivera

What is offered by way of hope in the twenty-first century years of meltdown and plague? Models, plans, blueprints, wiring diagrams, numerical keys to secure the message and guarantee its arrival at a pre-set destination. Cybernetic prospects of ever more intrusive communications systems linking virus to virus everywhere. Secrets and lies. Or no secrets, only lies.

Public secrets. Lies that everyone knows are lies. However, even though everyone knows about them, everybody acts as if they didn't know. A public secret is truthful, not just a part of the imagination but a connection with reality, yet it's kept hidden in plain sight. Its reality may be undervalued or disavowed, placed or displaced beyond the horizon line of visuality. Encrypted, to use Ricardo Sanín-Restrepo's parlance. Or a structure of ignorance, to borrow from Linda Martín-Alcoff's reading of Charles W. Mill's epistemology of ignorance.[1]

For example, we know that the masters of today's financial universe produce nothing. They weave nothing, like the weavers in Hans Christian Andersen's tale of the Emperor's New Clothes. They seem to make something out of nothing, for the new wealth they accumulate seems to come from something that is an appearance, the derivative form, rather than from the production and exchange of concrete commodities. Everyone knows this, but nobody would say it, just as in Andersen's story.[2]

If they were to reveal this secret, it would mean that the very structure that determines a great deal of their ordinary lives, the current economy, cannot be grounded in material reality or devalues the latter and has nothing else to go on. This is idealism. Because people feel anxious about not having something to hold, they will turn an appearance—like the supposed magical qualities of the emperor's appearance or the temporal patterns appearing to them in the shape of data and prices—into a mode of being.

To seize hold of it. Also, to justify on those grounds and make invisible the aggression that lies beneath the desire to seize hold of something, to accumulate. In this respect, they behave in the same way in which schools of thought and declarations of enmity have been used for centuries to devour one another.

"Little closed orbiting test-tubes full of viruses, put up by the L Society in perfect obedience to our compulsion to . . . 'build the future';—to be Zeus, to have power over what happens," to predict, pre-empt, and control or exterminate, tells us the science fiction writer Ursula K. Le Guin in a text that so influences my efforts to think out this piece that I would love for it to be just a collection of her quotes and footnotes. But in what follows, I promise to exercise refrain. "Knowledge is power, and we want to know what comes next, we want it all mapped out," she says in this respect.[3]

She means to tell us that in history, not only in fiction, slogans like "build the future" often turn out to mean "exterminate all the brutes." So, on the one hand, structures of disavowal or ignorance. And on the other hand, "we want it all mapped out," framed and coded.

These are but the two sides of the same coin, as our friend Ricardo Sanín-Restrepo contends when he says this same unity is a characteristic of language and discourses: "Encryption, as the intentional way of hiding or confounding the meanings of a symbolic system is a characteristic proper to any language, that is what allows every language to be elastic, creative and resilient," he observes. "Nevertheless, we are before a whole different kind of creature when we deal with the 'encryption of power.' Here we are before a primordial prohibition (political, legal, racial) controlling access to the programming and uses of language (as the first common difference)," he argues, "through permanent qualifications and conditions for the exercise of power and therefore a rigid stratification for the belonging-to of any possible world."[4]

Thus understood, for Sanín-Restrepo there is no dispute about this being a problem of an epistemological kind: the confounding of the meanings of a sign/symbolic system. He explains that in the case of power, there is a "primordial prohibition" controlling access to the framing and uses of such systems and language. This is Sanín's "decrypting turn."[5]

Let us say two things about it. First, this move is to be welcomed as both a reflexive and profoundly relativizing turn: what seemed absolute or self-evident, for example, the elasticity and resilience of language, is compromised by being exposed in a forensic, juristic manner. And what is exposed is, precisely, a secret: the law-like "primordial prohibition" that lies behind or before it. But, second, why primordial? Here, the eureka moment of his theory of encryption and turn, different though it may seem from other mainstream critical approaches and turns, shares with them the basic manner of anthropological thinking that at once invokes the *originary* quality of prehistoric dualisms or liminal prohibitions and the *contemporaneity* of relativizing deconstruction.

I fear this basic attitude of the a-ha moment of intellectual relativization may lead to relativism—the confusion of what were mere preambles to an investigation, such as "x is a primordial social construction" with conclusive statements about essentialized attributes such as "belonging to any possible world." What is most problematic about such a confusion between the norms of operation of knowledge, of the sign and symbolic system of language transmission set by master-experts, and the hierarchy of beings and objects in the world is that, in being exposed as mere construction these can be made into straw men enemies.

"Our rules concerning access to original information, which frame our hierarchies of belonging in any possible world, are but a social construction," the academic critic tells his students. But is the shock value of its revelation, burning the husk of the problem, still valuable because it is shocking? Or is the brilliance of this pronouncement blinding?

For me, the problem may be altogether different: sure, x is constructed or encrypted and, thus, it can be deconstructed or decrypted. But what do we do with this revelation? Thus formulated, the problem appears to be something else entirely, like a film that has gone through a chemical bath: If life, or at least the life of power, is constructed and encrypted, how come it appears so immutable? How come everybody sees and knows it, and yet they carry on acting as if they did not know? To say the problem is encryption and, by implication, that our negative deconstructive critique suffices, may be akin to shooting an arrow straight at the heart of a straw man.

HOW TO GROUND ETHICS, LAW, AND POLITICS WITHOUT FALLING BACK ON METAPHYSICS OF IGNORANCE

In contrast, my proposal in this chapter is to take up the key insight of this theory of the confusion of meaning, Sanín-Restrepo's encryption theory, rendered in the key of our twenty-first century discourses of cybersecurity, and run with it!

In other words, let's transit from the epistemological, the linguistic, and the focus on socially constructed relations to the outer limits of such extensional logics. In the process, we shall make full virtue of their capacity to stop judgment—to suspend the pedantic reasoning of forensic exposure procedures and decisionism on its tracks. Thereby placing a bomb under what appears reasonable just because it's familiar, within our given horizon of visuality. To explode what's known now and judged or decided once and for all. In favor of what we may not see or imagine yet. "He has no clothes!" says the child in Hans Christian Andersen's story.[6] In doing so, we hope to save some lives and hope itself as a different kind of principle.

I aim for a different kind of critique, which I call "fantastic critique." This proposal emerges out of the recent interest that the topics of visuality and visibility have acquired not only in aesthetics but also in postmetaphysical theories of ethics, politics, and normativity. Both visuality and visibility constitute an increasingly pertinent theme in forms of cultural critique that highlight the lack of attention to the social and political impact of structures of ignorance and encryption in our public imagination and media of communication.[7]

This is also borne out by recent neuroscientific investigations that observe how a system that does not appear to itself cannot suffer, but once it does, it becomes something else: a subject of ethical concern. Ethical flesh, suffering in concrete and perhaps different circumstances depending on what the relevant material environments offer or not. The keyword here is affordances. "The affordances of the environment are what it offers the animal, what it provides or furnishes," as James J. Gibson put it in his pathbreaking 1979 book *The Ecological Approach to Visual Perception.* This talk of affordances brings together our call for further attention to imagining capacities, visibility, environmental aspects of perception and action, and the study of some basic elements of cultural cognition and imaginative normative orientation.

Chief among them, the interplay between the displayed and the hidden (occluded, deleted, or encrypted) can be associated with and illuminated by evidence concerning the so-called "discovery of the occluding edge" in the study of environmental perceptual affordances. This phenomenon occurs when texture is gradually revealed (accretion) or occluded (deletion) over time at the edge of another surface. Occluding edges are typically revealed with movements of the perceiver and relative movements of environmental features. The implication is not only that this is a relational property of environment–organism processes but also that (the occluding edge of a closer surface) is visible only *over time.* This is to say that in the absence of motion and transition this aspect of phenomenal modeling is not present. Further, perceiving an occluding edge entails awareness of a now-hidden surface and a yet-to-be-revealed surface of a farther object. Meaning that perceiving and percepts have both retrospectivity (moving backward) and prospectivity (looking forward). Simply put, it is a past-oriented and future-oriented process.

These signs carry natural information, as states of affairs are non-accidentally correlated or in mimetic correspondence to other states of affairs. They may be indexes of change, and as such, as indexicals, the sign component is not opposed or external to, but part of the signified, articulated into components and, thus, can be composed and re-composed (or "figured"). The strength of a sign in a context can measure how likely it is that, within that context, a sign with that surface form (moving backward, looking forward) signifies a certain state of affairs. Put simply, a sign is what can serve or be used as a sign, that which provides and shows, or affords, an orientation. A sign carries natural information relative to an animal or sentient entity that can interpret it, not because that entity possesses exclusive, unique expertise or mastery but because the environment affords it.

In other words, the properties identified in this kind of process—environmental affordances—are neither purely subjective nor purely objective. Just as the capacity for image-making begins neither in pure thought nor in the external world of art or ornament. As contemporary archaeologists suggest, based on the evidence they have unearthed while doing fieldwork around the world, image-making and visibility have to do with "the sympathetic meeting of human minds with specific materials in their vicinity."[8] Furthermore, this capacity seems to be tied "to what we now see as an evolved capacity for mental time travel," or chronoesthesia.[9] Meaning "the ability to project oneself, consciously, into the past or the future" connected to the non-mastery arts of memory, self-modeling, and orientation.[10]

To insist, the properties identified in environmental affordances are neither purely subjective nor purely objective. Instead, they pertain to complementarities between the animal and the environment, to an idea of nature as the "inorganic" body of humans and other living sentient beings, and to the corporeality of the ethical agent. Which is to say, to being-alive and being-with-others (including being-in-public or appearing to others) as the very condition of possibility of ethical and cultural agency.

This means not only that we must think of ethical/cultural agency as ethical flesh riveted to history (in the sense of moving backward/looking forward) or as motion and transformation. It also means that, environmentally and historically speaking, the old positions, furnishings, limitations, and liminal prohibitions are going through a process of destruction while new ones are in formation. This process can be seen and projected in a similar way to how a now-hidden surface gives place to a not-yet-revealed or becoming-present surface *over time*. This ontological dimension of past-future and the not yet in environmental affordances of visibility is as crucial to our investigations of the conditions of ethical and historical agency as a supporting surface is for animals to move.

It can be said that where such surfaces exist, the surfaces support locomotion by the appropriate animals. Similarly, it can be said that when corporeality riveted to history and the environment exists, environmental affordances support motion, transformation, and transposition (the formation of new positions in lieu of older ones) by the appropriate agents. "Supportability" exists by virtue of both the material nature and arrangement of environmental surfaces and history as well as the capability of specific sentient creatures. Likewise, "graspability" and "ready-to-handness," as well as "appearability" or "visibility" exist because there are bodily entities that can grasp, appear in, or see environmental surfaces of a size, shape, rigidity, and mobility that allow grasping or seeing.

The crucial point here is that these entities point both ways: to the "objective" environment and to the "subject" animal or other tracing, imaging entity. They are real, rather than spooky or spiritual in some subjective metaphysical sense. "Real" means here, precisely, pointing both ways: "objective" and "subjective" in relational terms; "descriptive" (describing what is the case, what the world provides or furnishes) and "directive" (representing or directing what is to be done with such furnishings, making clear possible uses) in terms of the functions of percepts, representation, and action in the sense proposed by people like Ruth Garrett Millikan; neither "purely internal" in a spiritual sense nor "purely external," purely ornamental or inert material when it comes to art and self-projection; and, finally, "backward" and "forward" in the sense of retrospective and prospective dimensions of tracking, orientation, and disclosure or revelation of processes happening in/over time.[11]

This includes the changing nature of processes and of the "ready to hand" environs and objects, works, and the imaging and orientation agencies and work that such critical concepts as "decryption," "aesthetic trespassing," "transposition," "worlding" figuration, or envisioning across and beyond thresholds, try to disclose and clarify. This is the kind of naturalist realism espoused by and associated in this book with the living work of activating presence and survivance, with hope and plebeian courage as ethical-political virtues.[12]

FANTASTIC CRITIQUE

In the previous sections, we have learned to see our ethical investigations as also aesthetic, cultural, and political, even a matter of natural history. Discovering these layers of a material process invites us to continue to explore its unfolding. Let's call this an archaeology of ethopoetic cores. That is, "the ethical creativity of those who challenge the ruling" morality and frameworks of visuality via the invention of techniques of liberation and appearance to themselves and to others.[13]

This kind of approach may also help us to understand why ethics must always be prefaced by global histories of moral/ethical frameworks and hopeful ways of seeing (which may be assisted by and in dialogue with archaeology and anthropology, among other humanities) as well as scientific approaches that investigate how and when pain signals, states of emotional distress, negative thoughts, devaluation, injury, and suffering can be integrated into a transparent self-model and appear to someone (oneself and others)—and when they do not or cannot. Here's where a fruitful dialogue can take place between our renewed sense of critique, certain tenets of neuroscientific research, theories of visibility, and encryption.

Here we may also find a new and enticing entry point into the dimension that critical theorists call the labor of the negative. In this respect, let's clarify that this proposal doesn't conceive its task in terms of exhaustive explanation, final judgment, or definition starting from incontrovertible premises, or a decisive meeting between opposing parties. Such a head-on confrontation would not suit its subject matter.

Let's speak, rather, of figuration and/or characterization as the approaches best suited for our critical archaeology of ethopoetic systems—our fantastic critique. Like the characters and figurations that appear in children's stories like Andersen's "The Emperor's New Clothes" or the Indigenous tales our parents told us.[14] And since characterization cannot confront its matter head-on, let us then settle for sideways and backward moves. As in dance, which happens in the interzone of aesthetic trespassing, or in poetics, storytelling, filming with a camera and seeing aspects.

SEEING OTHERWISE, SAVING HOPE

We aim to see things otherwise, to envision another kind of critique—fantastic critique—in dialogue with encryption theory and other such post-metaphysical approaches to ground a hopeful ethics, and to save hope from becoming fully privatized, either subsumed under the cold stream of economic reductionism in its consumer-friendly form or encoded in the frame of cybersecurity and pre-emption in its financial investor and user-friendly derivative forms. We have learned that the key encodes, hides, and may provide an illusion of control over the process of transmission of information in space and time. To encode is, basically, to set the frame and a system of rules to convert information (perception, sensing, and sense or sense-making), such as letters, words, gestures, or images and simulacra, into another form, sometimes shortened and other times secret, via a communication channel figured as a flat extension or through storage in a storage medium.

This process, also known in cryptography and other derivations of older martial knowledges (such as siege architectures, poliarcetics, castrametation, surveyance, and forensics) as encryption, converts the initial representation of the information or a cruder representation of real conditions, known as "plaintext," into an alternative form known as "cyphertext." The latter may be more or less refined, more or less invisible, more or less magical and fascinating, like the clothes of the emperor's tale, but must doubtlessly amount to something real. And like the magical qualities of the clothes in the old tale, the process makes the kingly figure of authorization and those authorized by such figurations half human and half superhuman. At least in the sense that, although encryption does not itself prevent interference or disruption from below, it can deny the intelligible content to a would-be interceptor or hacker, thereby setting or re-setting the very framing conditions of spatial perception in terms of extensional binaries. For example, below/above, outside/inside, exclusion/inclusion, and so on.

This is so because, in principle, only authorized parties are supposed to be in a position to see or decipher a ciphertext back to plaintext and, therefore, gain unimpeded access to the initial, original, "primitive" or cruder representation of the truer or real information about the conditions of the situation.

Here comes the twist. Historically speaking, encryption techniques seem to have arisen out of the necessities of military messaging but, as it is the case with almost all military and security or securitized forms, they emerge out of the self-differentiation of time and space that is often imagined and essentialized as a sort of pre-cosmos or primordial, "mythical" time. This is important both because it suggests the reason why we can use old folktales like that of the Emperor's New Clothes to approach phenomena of public secrecy from a lateral angle, a different movement like a new dance move, and because it helps us to steer clear of the customary notions of the familiar normative and anthropological idea according to which origin myths and tales posit an "original state of undifferentiation," or the mode of being that political and legal philosophies refer to in modernity as a "state of nature." The time of primitive accumulation.

To imagine the original state of information in communications or political philosophical and information security approaches as "primitive" and then, in turn (or is it a re-turn?), to imagine the Amerindian or Indigenous pre-cosmos as such a state of indistinction and originality tends to weigh the scales of those approaches on the side of cosmo-legal numerical harmony and spiritual continuity at the expense of the embodied consciousness and discontinuities that a lateral perspective, a sideways move or approach such as the one attempted in this article, would like to run with. Or dance.

The tendency toward harmony through calculation and spiritual, natural continuity is as old as it is problematic.

Another starting point for the investigation undertaken in this piece is the argument that the apparent progress from "mystical" or religious forces driving us through progress in the direction of harmony to "dialectics," or the re-cognitive model of speech/communication and harmonious circulation, is not an accident of history. For a very long time, the search for ultimate points of reference and something to hold on to, a framework, and a system of rules which would determine the world's order, regulate its motion, and the motion of everything within it has combined notions of laws and ciphers or numbers. Either through metaphysical mathematics and physics in the case of the order of nature, or through (no less metaphysical) accounts of law and the economy in the case of the social order. Something similar has occurred in the case of religious orderings in which submission or allegiance to divine law and the mystical vision of absolute, unchanging premises are recognized as the two sides of one and the same knowledge providing exclusive access to the timeless to a lucky few.[15]

This is to emphasize that neither the encryption of power nor the governance of numbers may be a completely new turning point in the history of political power, and as such, it may not entail the disappearance of law. Rather, it entails the subordination of politics and the law's content to a calculus of utility, framing them within and putting them to the service of the utopian view of "economic harmonies" that would supposedly regulate, once and for all, the functioning of human societies.

In the case of European Law, for example, this harmonization, representing both the dialectical union of opposites and the final resolution of differences and conflict, is put forward as "the juridical realization of the economic liberties guaranteed by the treaty and, also, as the spontaneous progress that would result from the [utilitarian] uses of such liberties." Thus, in the terms of Article 151 of the Treaty on the Functioning of the European Union (TFEU), the "harmonization of social systems" must be the result of "the functioning of its internal market." Which means to say "the field [of the market] emancipated to [be bound by the repressive force of] the calculus of interests of the economic actors". This framing determines the nature of public regulation and the legislative approach as purely subsidiary (and, hence, the privatization of hope). At the same time, this framing perspective hides from (public) view the interdependence between the emancipated forces of the internal market and the aggressive unleashing of those same forces upon external markets or spaces.[16]

In that respect, at least, the arrangement of the spaces of the world external or "peripheral" to EU internal space is not so different from the Westphalian arrangement that saw peace within the European space defined by the treaty and its signatories at the expense of war everywhere else (the colonial scramble between European kingly and sovereign powers organized under the imperative to "exterminate all the brutes"). Further, such an arrangement is not that different from that in which the visible world is arranged for the spectator as the universe was once thought to be arranged for God. This is the same viewpoint and conventional perspective through which missionary eyes saw Amerindian society as "brutish."

This drive toward harmony through calculation and the naturalized view of spiritual continuity is problematic. Not least because it tends to render the differences between the characters in the scene (which can be scaled as actors in the world, in global history, or as species in an ontological account) logically as well as chronologically derivative. Which is to say "lower," or inferior in the same sense in which we tend to predicate the "lower resolution" of a copy inferior in respect of its original. This would be tantamount to a logically discontinuous or extensional passage and vision, so to speak, covering the totality from the continuous to the discontinuous.

Here, we reach the limits of both the resources of extensional logic—its linear perspective and encoding vocabulary—and the very notion of binary opposition leading to harmonious destiny and unity for coping with the multidimensional capacities or relations of actors and actants in history and in the stories in which they are protagonists. Such relations perfuse and constitute a mythic matter, as shown in this chapter via the tale of the Emperor's New Clothes.

In this respect, Brazilian anthropologist Eduardo Viveiros de Castro explains how "the actants of origin myths are defined by their intrinsic capacity to be something else," in a way that traces a lateral move from (symbolic) epistemology to (political) ontology. "In this sense, each mythic being differs infinitely from itself, given that it is posited by mythic discourse only to be substituted, that is, transformed. It is this self-difference which defines a 'spirit,' and which makes all mythic beings into 'spirits' too." Spirits capable of demonic alliances in this world.[17]

SPIRITS IN A MATERIAL WORLD

To take the insight of encryption and public secrecy further, and to put this part of the imagination in contact with real relations, let us add that secrecy, encryption, and the (extensional, perspectival) logic of pre-emption that they use to frame space and time not only provide us with an illusion of control or "legitimacy." But it also allows for the delusion of calculation and control of spacetime. It does this by computing a mathematical, continuous, and homogeneous spacetime that it declares to be natural and reality. As Sanín-Restrepo says, "for the encryption of language it is fundamental to create the idea of a totality that is previous . . . to any interaction that may emerge" within it.[18]

He seems to be describing a framework or a plane of representation. But if so, this is no longer simply a matter of signs, symbols, and linguistic construction but the entire paradigm that has long dominated our sensing and sense-making capacities: linear perspective. Only that its stable horizon and single point of view is being supplemented nowadays by cybernetic keys, doors, and overlapping windows. Still, this means that our capacities for "painting pictures" in the mind and projecting them onto the world, which establish visuality and foresight as well as pre-emptive abilities, are dependent on a framework that "holds within it the design of parts that are integral to it, creating simultaneously the mechanism to calculate every emergence of possible relations," to predict or pre-empt such emergence.[19]

Put simply, the illusion of a quasi-natural view to the outside is created by the artificial computation of a mathematical, homogeneous, flattened spacetime. The spacetime thus artfully defined, yet normatively declared natural, becomes calculable, navigable, and predictable. It allows the calculation of future risk, which can be pre-empted or anticipated and, therefore, managed. If the first meaning of *perspectiva* is to see through and onto a space out there (or "nature" as an exterior extension opposed to an interior space), then the second meaning of perspective is temporal: a view onto a calculable and homogeneous space, empty and thus ready to hand. Out there for the taking.

Furthermore, the kind of perspective that allows temporal computation as the condition of possibility of encryption and public secrecy also guarantees profit to the secret (of the kingly figure of "sovereignty"). It does so by allowing wealth historically obtained by means of "primitive accumulation" to accumulate and accrue in value unimpeded.

Notice that "primitive accumulation" is a metaphor, an image, or a trope. As such, it condenses both the image of a pile-up, as in the display of a pile of earth one shovels when extracting something from somewhere, but also the removal of that action behind the veil of a supposedly "primordial" time which obscures the contemporaneity of the extraction. Putting the extracted something somewhere else, the imagined figuration of a homogeneous time flattens and stretches it, subjecting that real dimension to an imaginary extensional logic or spatializing it to justify the pile-up, the accruement of value. It is this accumulation of wealth that allows historical injustices to propagate and expand spatially as well as temporally.

In contrast with the hegemony of this calculating perspective, explained by means of a metaphor that does justice to the secret (the "accumulation" metaphor), we follow in the footsteps of poets and anthropologists. It shall be argued that the myths, stories, and tales we tell our children, whether these are the children's tales collected by Hans Christian Andersen or the collection of Amerindian myths by Jaime de Angulo, or the fieldwork collections by Latin Americanist ethnographers such as Michael Taussig or Claude Lévi-Strauss, abidingly emphasize the continuity of differentiation against the flattening of such differentiation by perspectival ontologies like the political philosophies of "brutishness" and encryption. The latter are critically defined here as ontologies of the continuity of continuity.[20]

Amerindian myths, but also folktales like Andersen's story and ethnological fieldwork notebooks reflect on the ontological conditions of possibility of the differences between characters or species that are the actors of post-original worlds and fields of information in which mimetic capacities operate. They are reflective of the fact that the differences between these species or characters are, in any case continuous with each other or can be synthesized in the mathematical sense that they are all differences of perspective.

Our sideways move to recover and reinvent plebeian perspectives of hope and courageous feelings, inspired by the poetics of myths and folktales, is to insist on the insight that differences of perspective amount to something real. But this is not a mode of being. Instead, it is a mode of appearing, of being-in-public. In turn, the latter must be situated in the context of enthusiastic yet highly precise and critical reception and selection of totalizing perspectives and encrypting discourses, and the refusal to follow such perspectives to the end with the understanding that they always involve and depend upon the interplay between the displayed and the hidden.

This highly precise attention to interplay, to interzones, and the observation of events of transition is a crucial lesson, which arises from the archaeological and anthropological record that suggests an intimation of the synthetic relationship between thought, image, and the making of social worlds. A lesson that is also increasingly borne out by the findings of modern neuroscience, "as well as being richly exemplified in ethnographic studies . . . and in the first-hand testimonies of Indigenous experts and artists."[21]

The challenge for us is to notice how the task of image-making begins neither in pure thought nor the imaginary faculty nor in the great outdoors of naturalistic, naïve "art" or "ornament." But rather, "in the sympathetic meeting of minds with specific materials in their vicinity; and moreover, that the capacity to make images is ineluctably tied to what we would now see as an evolved capacity for mental time travel." This ability to project oneself into the past or future, to move backward looking forward can perhaps be extended to the ability of materials to image themselves, which investigative counter-forensic approaches deploy in an effective manner when, for example, dealing with cases of human rights violations. And, thus, to the arts of memory and navigation as well as to the political arts of projecting hopeful visions that are not linear models of what is to come while gathering the courage to live and enact them.[22]

Our move is itself transitional, mobile, and transformative.

HIS-STORY

Consider again the main characters in the Emperor's New Clothes story, retold by Hans Christian Andersen. On the one hand, the kingly emperor. It is his-story. His story revolves around getting new clothes for his procession. Vanity? Is that the point of the story? Perhaps, but if we settle for that reading, we may miss what matters most. Are the clothes only for showing off? If they were, pretty ones would suffice. Why, then, magical cloth? A procession is part of a ritual marking the transformation of this kingly body into something else. We may assume the king has become a king by inheritance the minute the former king or queen died. If so, why the need for a coronation or a procession marking passage or transformation?

The answer is that the body of the king is not just any body, but both a particular body and one supposed to encode the totality of passage, transformation, and time itself. Rites such as the coronation or the procession in the story of the emperor's clothes do not just mark time. Instead, time, the forces of creation and destruction are incarnated in that body. Remember that, as it is the case for gods and other supernatural characters, there is no need for the king to situate himself in relation to others. He is himself the situation.

Which means there would be no time and no continuity without the continuity of kingly bodies. The point of rituals like a coronation or procession is to allow for this to happen—apotheosis or transcendence. Thereafter, the king becomes something else: the key for the continuity of continuity. That's part of the magic of the state. For rulers and kingly figures to become half god and half man, half alien and half local—a widespread phenomenon according to the archaeological and anthropological record.

On the other hand, there's the child. He bears an intimate relation to a spirit, like the spirits of the forest or the underground and other primordial forces sustaining everything that exists. As such, the child of Andersen's folktale resonates with the spirit of love given definition in the voice of the woman mystic Diotima by Plato, as one "who conveys the messages to the gods from men and to men from the gods, prayers and sacrifices to the one, commands and rewards to the other."[23]

Messenger, medium, and message. These are old motifs that resonate very strongly with our contemporary concerns about communication, mimetic excess, information overload, and hyperesthesia leading to the fascination of abomination and the misery of desire in our global era. Diotima goes on to say that "being of an intermediate nature, a spirit bridges the gap between them [gods and men] and prevents the universe from falling into two separate halves."[24] There it is, continuity, in the sense that everything that is spirit or incarnates fundamental forces—underground beings, forest sprites, earth-beings, talking animals, tricksters, hobgoblins, and kings, perhaps also cybernetic avatars and AI—is half god and half man.

Through this class of characters, what is represented is the seemingly supernatural skill of kingly or priestly figures in sacrificial rituals. That is, sovereignty as such. Their supposed exceptionality is incarnated in their public/private bodies.[25] Consider, for example, the coronation of King Charles III in twenty-first-century Britain, featuring a scene of cleansing when the soon-to-be-king is undressed and clothed once again in the regalia that is supposed to make him reappear in all its majesty, exceptionality, and sovereignty. Following Graeber and Sahlins, we might say that what takes place in that ritual is the privatization of sacred goods like sovereignty, projective vision, and so on, and thus also what Sanín-Restrepo calls the encryption of a people. Can we say that something similar happens in the case of the quasi-divination powers of derivatives' investors and other financial masters of the universe? What about wannabe-kings like the Trumps and Bolsonaros of our televisual universe?

What about hi-tech tycoons and artificial intelligence? Isn't the clunky reality of their hi-tech tools and garb what makes them reappear, magically so to speak, as masters? Perhaps. But if there is continuity with the child/eros character of stories, there is also discontinuity and differentiation. The child of Andersen's story or Plato's Eros is different from the "exceptional master." Instead, he looks more like a non-master. Consider in this respect Socrates' very first question to Diotima, which indicates that a spirit is inherently rebellious and childish: "Who are his parents?" he asks her of Eros. He's a strange character, for when he wins, he loses; when he walks, he gets lost or makes people lose themselves (falling in love, for instance). Or to fall without anything to fall to, like in some kind of interstice, interzone, or sunken place. He is neither wise nor ignorant, neither good nor bad, but both. Definitely, he's not temperate. Double. Devilish.[26]

He's like the trickster in Amerindian stories. In such stories, trickster makes the world. Imagine that. The kind of world that can come out of double entendres, misunderstandings, and negations. Imagine Eros coming out of the sunken place. That would be a force to be reckoned with. But would anyone recognize that world as utopia? I think not. It won't look the way utopia ought to. It may look more like some kind of place Coyote or Donkey made "after having a conversation with his own dung." [27]

All this is to say that the child in the emperor's story, like the symbol which trickster embodies, is never a static one. Rather, it contains within itself the seed of differentiation, the kernel of men and women within the shell of a god. This also means that the best way to explore, experiment, and investigate god-like figures is child-like. To say of kings and all other seemingly exceptional beings, "But he doesn't have anything on!"

In this respect, the force of negation that underpins hope can be understood as a kind of atheism. To get to the kernel of humanity (which is labor, work, creation, and figuration, but also hesitation and pulling the handbrake; even failure) by dissolving the shell of a god. Hence the proximity between the thought of the power of negative, determinate all-too-human judgment and the motif of the death of God.

Hope has more to do with a philosophy of decoding the magical and divine, a thought of death and rebirth, thoroughly transformative and human, than with any thought or fantasy of transcendence and deification. The latter is both forensic and pedantic (fascination with misery, desire, and abomination). Pedantic, discriminatory judgment. The former we call fantastic critique and judgment in the sense that it does not discriminate but brings into being something new and different.

Isn't that also what wizards, shamans, and alchemists do? Instead of cracking a nut by using a hammer, which might provide access to its interior but at the risk of pulverizing its contents or rendering any internal differences meaningless, they immerse the problem in a more general field within which it can be won over with much subtler elegance and nuance. This softens the hard shell of the nut, allowing the appearance of its kernel.

THIS IS THE WAY (GET OUT)

Let's not call it a method (it is emphatically non Cartesian, it is not ocular-centric). Rather, a practical approach. A way to make things public. Perhaps you may want to call it a different aesthetic. Consider the fact that the way of immersion to dissolve the shell would lose neither precision nor direction, nor would it render insignificant the local differences. Instead, it dissolves irregularities, habits, and conventions that have been naturalized and taken for granted, or thought of as unchangeable, as if they had a magical quality or timelessness. Our way is, in this sense, apotropaic: magic against magic, or *limpieza* (in the older sense of making visible the sources of terror, clarifying truth, and stopping the repeated occupation of your home by spiritual attack) as opposed to cleansing (the forced displacement or killing off of innocents). This aesthetic of visibility, synthesis, and active presence makes present (all too human) contradictions and possibilities in a living, changing, wider or more encompassing and transformative figuration.[28]

Call this practical approach to dissolve the shell, the habits, or the conventional framework and its irregularities the labor of the negative, which is always task-oriented because it does not seek to control time but acknowledges its reality—passage, thorough transformation—and therefore also death, without which there is no rebirth. But consider also, as someone said somewhere, that to uphold the work of death is a task which demands the greatest courage. Impotent harmony hates this acknowledgment, which is why it tends toward timelessness or stasis. The latter is the true enemy of hope, and a most destructive drive.

Put simply, the life of the spirit that the child or Eros and trickster represent is not the life that is frightened of death or seeks to cover in secrecy the sacrificial violence unleashed in reality to maintain the continuity of continuity and the fantasy of harmony by calculation that sovereignty and capital represent. On the contrary, the life of the spirit confronts phenomena of violence without stripping it of its political character, accepts the possibility of failure, the inconsequence of its actions, demands, and protests, as well as of death and lives with it. Spirit achieves truth and the power of truth only to the extent that it looks at the negative in the eye and dwells with it.

Like Chris does in one of the initial scenes of Peele's movie *Get Out*.[29] Having hit a deer on the way to his girlfriend's house, where unknown to him the sunken place awaits, he gets out of the car and contemplates the dying deer in the eye. The scene prefigures the rest of the movie and explains its title. But it will also take the love of a friend (who is a bit of a sideways detective) for the task of the negative to be completed in the film. Ditto, eros, childhood friendship and sideways and backward trickster moves are the way out of a sunken place, also the way to solve a case of disappearance. In that respect, also the detective-like investigator, who may be a mathematician finding the solution to a problem synthetically, or a counter-forensic investigator of human rights violations and historical injustices decoding the magic behind *desapariciones* and displacements, also represent the life of the spirit.

To foreshadow our conclusion, if what becomes present after a counter-forensic investigation on the making and unmaking of god-like kingly figures is that they are, after all, all too human, a continuity, then it also becomes clearer that when everything is human—plants, animals, kings, spirits, those seen as inferior because or class or gender or race, and intelligent machines—then the human is an entirely different thing. This is the way of the child in the folktale retold by Hans Christian Andersen. He wants the secret out. He wants out.

His father may see that desire as immaturity or innocence, which is another way of saying stupidity or silliness and to disavow it. Instead, let us see this as the mastery of those who have not achieved mastery: the mastery of knowing what not to know, of secrecy, encoding, encryption, and pre-emption. The child, eros, the way of sideways savage detectives (i.e., determinate negation), they're all for anti-mastery. This is the way of hope.

The child pulls the handbrake in the continuity of continuity. He (or is it she?) determinately refuses the mastery of smoke and mirrors' publicity, the trickery of the displayed and the hidden, or the single frame of visuality and encryption. Perhaps that is because children are true experts in the art of hiding. Hide and seek. Hide behind places. There they discover interstices and interzones between different sets of the visible. They can see between two frames.

In conclusion, the child can be seen as truth incarnate. But not in the sense that makes truth too close to innocence and impotent beauty or madness, which are often bywords for stupidity. On the contrary, the child unleashes a different kind of energetic violence: that of seeing between frames and seeing through, backward, from behind, or in retro projection—the negativity of making visible and of understanding—versus the purity of impotent beauty of the fantasy of continuity and the dream of harmony by calculus. Which is impotent because, being a pure dream, it cannot act or create anything. Just like the weavers of beautiful cloth in the story, whose impotence is reflected in that of the king.

Hope is not a pure dream. It is active, which puts it on the side of the abyssal aspect and a tough down-to-earth aspect—falling, contemplating the negative and death in the eye. This means hope is to be found where opposed figures like the child and the emperor or the people in general confront each other in their differentiation and diverse possibilities and assemble in this task. They assemble in alliance rather than pure allegiance, going to the kernel and the root of the problem. This requires such figures to move where roots are usually found, back in the countryside or under a rock crevice. Hope is, therefore, radical. It is about work, task orientations, and class struggle. It is anti-racist, and it is not masculinist because it is the practice of those who have been introduced into History backward and from below or behind. It can be violent. It is not innocent.

END OF INNOCENCE

Let's rid ourselves of the myth of the origins of the innocent child and the *bon sauvage*. A quite different way of seeing the child's act is as anything but innocent. This means that his position is radical and advantageous, even violent, in the sense that he takes full advantage of the father's positioning of the child as innocent or ethically immature to see between visual orders of encryption, to untwist or decrypt the public secret to get to the root of the problem.

Namely, that the emperor has no clothes is a revelation that will inevitably be seen as violent. The child is a critic, even a criminal in the sense that to be declared a criminal by the state and the market means your position does justice to the secret that sustains the supposed magical qualities of the state and the market: he knows that magical clothes, like most of the fictions we live by, are, as they say nowadays, socially constructed. He's woke.

But there's more. When it is enthusiastically pointed out within the memory of our present Academy that political power, kingly power, and public power are, like race, gender, or the nation and the crimes of the nation, so many social constructions, the risk is that what is merely a preamble to our investigations may be, or indeed has been, by and large, converted into a conclusion: "Sex, or gender, is a social construction." "Race and the nation are an invention." "The crimes of the state are history," and so on and so forth. So, it is said by establishment liberals and revisionists of fascistic history alike: "Oh, let's indeed celebrate difference. We are all fluid, neither this nor that, and therefore I will choose to be this or that, I will choose this or that element of the narrative of history, or none, or all, and balance the narrative just like we balance the books. It's all the same to me."

The problem is that if it is all the same, then there is no real difference, and everything can be reduced to some common denominator. Like, say, money or the obligation to return like for like in an exchange of gifts or commerce. As in that hell of neoliberalism which is the luxury real estate project Lana in the Beit Hanina quadrant of Jerusalem, offering Palestinians an elegant lifestyle with a view of the separation wall. Or as in the illusion that because all information and prices can be expressed as numbers, these belong to a temporal pattern that can be subject to, reduced to, the power of probabilistic reasoning and encryption, prediction, or pre-emption. What follows is the pedantic application of the rules of pre-emption and derivation to everything in society and in history.

In such a world, which is our world, according to such an ontology, which is our base ontology, not only is it all the same to some observer posited outside of the visual scene that has been arranged for him the same way the universe was once thought to be organized for God. It is also the case that in such a world, according to such an ontology, time itself is no longer. Because the entire universe is being projected onto the one eye of some spectator posited out of time, which explains it. But to explain time-bound phenomena by appealing to some timeless realm no one has ever had access to (or to postulate that mathematics is such a realm) is at best dubious. It is to explain nothing at all.

The king of the story would better fit the position of the one for whom the visual world has been organized the same way it was once thought the universe was arranged for God. To become emperor, half human or more human than human and half god, he must go through the coronation and ritual procession. It involves a kind of magic, the assertion by the swindlers who mimic weaving and dressing him up that a stupid person, inconstant in politics, cannot see the especial cloth. Also, secrecy, the information that designers created nothing, that everyone can see it, but nobody will say it. The information is, therefore, encoded. And only those authorized with the right lingo and code are supposed to access the original information, to see through and hold on to the correct perspective.

Consider, also, the spreading of rumor and revelation through the media and the whole population. The rumor that the entire rite is fictive or, as postmodern critics would say nowadays, socially constructed. However, the key here is that such rumor and revelation do not do justice to the secret, as it is proven by the fact that, after shivering, "for he was certain that they were right," the king internalizes the revelation ("I must bear it until the procession is over") and then, "he walked ever more proudly." This is the moment when he becomes emperor. Deification. The apotheosis of market and war.[30]

But if so, his being more than human, which makes him or his perspective see the world the same way God would have supposedly seen it, is thoroughly dependent on all-too-human means—smoke and mirrors, rumor, social media, pretense, and disavowal—that it would be impossible to continue to assert his essential difference. Put simply, superhuman or kingly sovereignty dissolves into the medium of popular sovereignty, and the latter is nothing more than the displacement of kingly sovereignty onto a substance or essence called "the people." Here, again, everything changes so that nothing changes. It's all the same to you and me. Everything converges onto your eye or mine as to the vanishing point of infinity. The problem has not been solved: the visible world is still arranged for the spectator just as the universe was once thought to be arranged for God.

Remember that according to the convention of perspective, there is no reciprocity. There is no need for God to situate himself in relation to others because he is himself the situation, the framework, and the system of rules. The ultimate frame and common denominator. But of course, we're modern, so, no need to call him God. Call it money, or the market's perspective, or that of the masters of the universe. Or AI. It's all the same to me. No looking forward. Just the continuity of continuity. The same story. History.

HISTORY, REPEAT

"I am not real, I am just like you," says jazz musician Sun Ra upon entering a black community center in full childish disguise, flanked by mythical figures wearing masks in the key scene of the film *Space Is the Place*. "You don't exist in this society. If you did, your people wouldn't be seeking equal rights. You're not real. If you were, you would have some status among the nations of the world. So, we're both myths. I do not come to you as a reality. I come to you as the myth," he says to the kids in the center. As for history, he says: "History is his-story. But you haven't heard my story. Not yet." [31]

NOT A CONCLUSION: THE GIFT

Things are different with the child. He knows well what not to know, but what makes him and his position so strange and fantastic is that he cannot pretend and carry on. He can't help but blurt it out: "But he doesn't have anything on!"[32]

He refuses the unspoken contract, the natural contract, and the social contract presupposed by the obligation to give back a gift of the same kind in exchanges—not something too precious, not in full view but in secrecy. It is the middle play between the displayed and the hidden, and no ceremonial but only commercial relations that involve no visual or social reciprocity.

In the middle plane between the displayed and the hidden—which is the plane of contractual commercial relations—the parties involved, the individuals, have themselves been elevated to the status of the sovereign and are the situation. There's no time here to take time to pause, to pause to think, to relate to the relation not only as the object of our investigations but also as the means of investigation, let alone to give the gift of time. No time at all.

It is not that the child refuses the gift, the secret, the art of knowing what not to know. Perhaps he accepts it, but instead of reciprocating in kind he gives it away, spends it, or commits it to sacrifice like the cannibals of lore. Indeed, like them. Like the Indians encountered by Christian Europeans for whom the inhabitants of the Americas appeared as inconstant. If so, the sacrifice offered by the child is not like the sort of sacrifice envisaged in Plato's dream of revealed truth, which is the kind of hammering of truth that destroys it in the very act of revealing it. Instead, as our anthropologist friends suggest, the child's act would be a truly cannibalistic act of profitless loss.[33]

His is indicative of a different communication and a truly different economy, one that is perhaps best thought together with Georges Bataille's sociology of expenditure in which sacrifice consecrates that which it destroys. Or with Giorgio Agamben's history of law emerging from states of emergency in the shape of the consecrated man. Notice, however, as pointed out to us by Miguel Taussig, in these cases the same emphasis as that placed by the anthropologist Evans-Pritchard in his 1936 study of Nuer religion in central Africa on the fact that the point of sacrificing cattle is not really the gift of flesh; not even the feast of meat after the pageantry has ended (which also applies to the case in which the coronation of a king is followed by a feast, or a holiday, and a concert).

Instead, it is the gift of time.

This is also borne out in the gift paradigm advocated by the Anti-utilitarian Movement in the Social Sciences. Based on Polanyi, Marshall Sahlins's *Stone Age Economics* and Marcel Mauss's *The Gift*, put together, they have sought to fight the seemingly complete hegemony of price economics and its constructivism in academia and over the world. Or, at least, the reduction of economics and society to the one-dimensionality and linear representational bias of a pre-emptive, speculative, rentier market economy hell-bent on encoding (that is, financializing) every and all aspects of social life. From nature to culture to the metaverse. To the fragmentation of the life of the spirit, which is "the fragmentation of our minds" as put to us by Ahed Tamimi in his house in Nabi Saleh, under order of demolition by the state of Israel acting as sovereign on illegally occupied land. This is an economy that often maintains links with mafia-like, dark web, international criminal or nearly criminal and not-so-tangible links with financial networks in opaque tax havens whose existence is indebted to, predicated on, and legitimized by sovereign, imperial, kingly power.[34]

In this context, that of the gift paradigm, the gift of pause, hesitance, and negation of the child in the story indicates a way of perceiving, figuring, sensing, and making sense of the history and becoming of the social bond, as what Sun Ra called "his-story." It is a plebeian way of decrypting power. But it is also indicative of the turbulence created in history by the active presence or survivance of those who, like the child of the story, give and give freely. These "childish" societies are the protagonists of Mauss's ethnography.

But there is nothing childish or stupid in the initial idea that the decision to give one's adversaries goods, good words, precious people, or names and positions makes it possible to turn from war to peace, to bring about a discontinuity in time, and transform enemies into allies. The end idea is that what matters is not the direction of change or exchange, the destiny of the message and information, as is the case in contractual obligations and encryption seen through the frame of utilitarian relations.

What matters is, instead, its volatility or turbulence.

Turbulence and volatility are different terms for the continuity of time's self-differentiation. This perspective is the one we would like to emphasize as other than the one which dominates the present, what just is. It is also a way not to confuse what just is with justice. A way to avoid turning what was an invitation to begin the project of analysis and cultural reconstruction—the revelation that power, politics, communication, race, and nation or national and international history were so many constructions—into a conclusion. Rather, our aim in focusing on turbulence and volatility as we end this piece has been to ask, like children, are we there yet? If not, what's the next step? Or, how come if things are constructed, they appear so deep-seated and immutable? And is this the end of the story?

We know Sun Ra's answer to that question. But to the question "what comes in the place of construction and its apparent opposite? More invention or no invention at all?" Let us reply that from the standpoint of gift-giving societies and the child of the story, what matters is not the direction of change in (contractual) exchanges but its volatility. Let us also say that this insight is the key to unlocking the secret of today's financial engineering, which seems to most of us as some kind of magic, able to make money out of nowhere and take power everywhere.

To conclude by not concluding, this is an invitation to reflect on an aspect of our really existing financial practice and discourse that is reflexively about its ability to create new investment technologies or vehicles of transmission, whose changing values, represented in prices, yield new information, different information, deriving from changes in underlying indexes. That is why I have been insisting on the fact that we must see the actions of the king, the child, and the town's people as indicators or indexes of change.

The crucial insight is that such indexes have no common denominator. From the standpoint of today's financial engineer, which in principle seems to be a million light years away from that of gift societies, there's no need to flatten space and time in order to place within such a plane of representation two points in time and relate them extensionally by reduction to a common plane, a common frame, or a common denominator. That is not how contemporary finance works in our contemporary market society.

How does this relate to gift societies that are clearly non-market in that sense? Well, one only needs to envision an insurgent and perhaps even subversive perspective of financial design that is not necessarily reductionist in the sense of committing itself to treating what is not a market as a market. Instead, one can envision marketable tokens or remedies (which means this vision is applicable to a jurisdiction of historical wrongs, such as, for example, the Special Peace Jurisdiction created in Colombia after the 2016 Peace Accords) of the market's coexistence with its non-market others without needing to regard them as therefore similar or homogeneous.

This kind of envisioning is an exemplary instance of what Roman Jakobson called a poetics. That is, a self-consciously trans-discursive practice able to connect heterogeneous practices and modes of appearing, or thought-images, by registering the changing rates of change among them. This is also what surrealist poets often do, as well as the trickster figures of Amerindian songs and stories. Additionally, this is also the reflexive aspect of contemporary financial discourse and practice, about its ability to yield different information derived from changes in underlying indexes with no common denominator. In turn, this resonates with the argument being developed by activist thinkers like dancer Ray Martin and human rights theorist Bob Meister, that the ability to gain or lose from heightened volatility is also the primary site of struggle in contemporary capitalist society.

What if this is the point of convergence between progressive movements active during the protests of the last three to five years, like Black Lives Matter or the Primera Línea of young protesters during the 2021 General Strike in

Colombia, and the historical trajectory of gift-giving societies? Perhaps this is what we witnessed when, during Colombia's General Strike, the gift-like performance of *la minga* by Indigenous and native peasant peoples joined the youth that had revolted against the crude conditions of hunger and psychological misery left in the wake of war and plague in that country.

Theirs would be an example of continuity of discontinuity. And, thus, also of a way to avoid the devouring force coming at us from the other direction, the one which, playing on our Platonic yearning for the true real, demands that we choose between cruel pessimism and naïve optimism, encoded as political realism or the familiarity of "what just is." The example of the kids in struggle and the native peasants of Colombia has given me and many of us pause and time to think.

It invites us to take time to garner courage. To take and give time. In other words, the virtue to bring into being, out of that capacity for differentiation, different concepts (such as mimesis, movement, derivation, and transposition) that can be translated into parts of the imagination but are also points of contact with real relations, as well as the means of investigation, experimentation, and negotiation on the making of different things public.

Put simply, we aim to provide time and space, public spaces or imaginary domains, for other publics and diverse economies. Again, our inspiring example is the act of the child. Not only the child in the story but also the kids in struggle of the last five years. And the example of all spirit-beings like them, who, in their commitment and investment of the gift to profitless sacrifice, not only exercise the gift of negation but also add something positive and constructive to their critique: volatility, ensuing turbulence, and other kinds of value.

In the end, we will all dance better.

NOTES

1. See, Ricardo Sanín-Restrepo, *Being and Contingency: Decrypting Heidegger's Terminology* (Lanham, New York and London: Rowman & Littlefield International, 2020); and Linda Martín-Alcoff, "Epistemologies of Ignorance: Three Types," in *Race and Epistemologies of Ignorance*, ed. by Shannon Sullivan & Nancy Tuana (New York: State University of New York Press, 2007), 39–57.

2. Hans Christian Andersen, "The Emperor's New Clothes" at https://andersen.sdu.dk/vaerk/hersholt/TheEmperorsNewClothes.html.

3. Ursula K. Le Guin, "A Non-Euclidean View of California as a Cold Place to Be." In Thomas More's Utopia (London: Verso, 2016), 191.

4. Ricardo Sanín-Restrepo, "The Meaning of the Encryption of Power as the Razor's Edge of Politics." In *Decrypting Power*. Ed. by Sanín-Restrepo, R. (New

York & London: Rowman & Littlefield Publ. 2018), xii. Also, *Being and Contingency: Decrypting Heidegger's Terminology.*

5. Ibid.

6. Hans Christian Andersen, "The Emperor's New Clothes" at https://andersen.sdu.dk/vaerk/hersholt/TheEmperorsNewClothes.html.

7. See, Ricardo Sanín-Restrepo, *Being and Contingency: Decrypting Heidegger's Terminology* (Lanham, New York and London: Rowman & Littlefield International, 2020); and Linda Martín-Alcoff, "Epistemologies of Ignorance: Three Types," in *Race and Epistemologies of Ignorance*, ed. by Shannon Sullivan & Nancy Tuana (New York: State University of New York Press, 2007), 39–57.

8. David Wengrow, "On Image Systems in Human History," in *Image, Thought, and the Making of Social Worlds*, ed. by D. Wengrow (Heidelberg: Propylaeum, 2022), 3–18 at 4, citing Tulving, E. "Episodic and Semantic Memory," in *Organization of Memory*, ed. by E. Tulving & W. Donaldson (New York, 1972), 381–402.

9. David Wengrow, "On Images in Human History," 4–5. See also, Michael Taussig, *Mastery and the Art of Non-Mastery in the Age of Meltdown* (Chicago: The University of Chicago Press, 2021), 5–12.

10. Ibid.

11. Ruth Garret Millikan, "Pushmi-Pullyu Representations," in *Mind and Morals. Essays on Ethics and Cognitive Science*, ed. by L. May, A. Clark & M. Friedman (Cambridge, Mass.: The MIT Press, 1996). Chapter 8, also available at https://philosophy.uconn.edu/wp-content/uploads/sites/365/2014/02/Pushmi-Pullyu-Representations.pdf. Also, *Beyond Concepts: Unicepts, Language, and Natural Information* (Oxford: Oxford University Press, 2017).

12. Ricardo Sanín-Restrepo, *Being and Contingency: Decrypting Heidegger's Terminology*, 51: "The ready to hand is thus forever changing in its own nature while its use is also made out of emergent properties and a wide range of orders that bombard language from every flank." Also, Mariana Ortega, "The Difference that Art Makes," in *Contemporary Aesthetics (Journal Archive)*, vol 14, Article 20 (2016) at https://digitalcommons.risd.edu/liberalarts_contempaesthetics/vol14/iss1/20/ and "Exiled Space, in-between space: Existential Spatiality in Ana Mendieta's *Siluetas* Series," *Philosophy & Geography, 7:1* (2004) 25–41, DOI: 10.1080/1090377042000196001.

13. Amy Allen & Eduardo Mendieta, "Introduction," in *Decolonizing Ethics. The Critical Theory of Enrique Dussel*, ed. by Amy Allen and Eduardo Mendieta (University Park: The Pennsylvania State University Press, 2021) 1–21 at 12–3: "This is why ethics must always be prefaced by a global history of ethical systems—the memory of the vanquished and victims in and of history. It could be argued, then, that the ethics [developed by Dussel from the late 1990s onward] is an ethics of liberation of the community of life." This is also, for us, the point of contact between such ethics, the question of techniques of liberation, and theories of encryption or structures of ignorance. See also, Oscar Guardiola-Rivera (ed.), Special Edition: *Photoelectric Technologies of Liberation*, in *Discourse. Journal for Theoretical Studies in Media and Culture 39.2* (Detroit: Wayne University Press, Spring 2017); Ricardo Sanín-Restrepo, *Being and Contingency: Decrypting Heidegger's Terminology;* Linda

Martín-Alcoff, "Epistemologies of Ignorance: Three Types," in *Race and Epistemologies of Ignorance*, 39–57.

14. Hans Christian Andersen, "The Emperor's New Clothes" at https://andersen.sdu.dk/vaerk/hersholt/TheEmperorsNewClothes.html. Also, Jaime de Angulo, *Indian Tales* (North Point Press, 1997) and *Popol Vuh. The Definitive Edition of the Maya Book of the Dawn of Life*, ed. by D. Tedlock (Austin: Touchstone, 1996).

15. See Alain Supiot, *La Gouvernance par les nombres. Cours au Collège de France, 2012-2014* (Paris : Fayard, 2015).

16. Treaty on the Functioning of the European Union—Consolidated Version in Official Journal of the European Union C 326/47 ff. October 26, 2012, art. 151: "The Union and the Member States, having in mind fundamental social rights . . . shall have as their objectives the promotion of employment, improved living and working conditions, so as to make possible their harmonization. . . . They believe that such a development will ensue not only from the functioning of the internal market, which will favor the harmonization of social systems, but also from the procedures provided for in the Treaties and from the approximation of provisions laid down by law, regulation or administrative action." Available at https://eur-lex.europa.eu/LexUriServ/LexUriServ.do?uri=CELEX:12012E/TXT:en:PDF.

17. Viveiros de Castro, Eduardo. "The Crystal Forest: Notes on the Ontology of Amazonian Spirits." *Inter Asia 9*, 2 (2007): 153–72 and "Intensive Filiation and Demonic Alliance." *Deleuzian Intersections in Science, Technology and Anthropology*, ed. by CB Jensen and K Rodje (Oxford: Berghahn Books, 2009).

18. Ricardo Sanín-Restrepo, "The X-Game of Language: Decrypting Heidegger's Ready to Hand." *Critical Legal Thinking* blog, posted October 20, 2018 at https://criticallegalthinking.com/2018/10/20/the-x-game-of-language-decrypting-heideggers-ready-to-hand/.

19. Ibid.

20. Hans Christian Andersen, "The Emperor's New Clothes" at https://andersen.sdu.dk/vaerk/hersholt/TheEmperorsNewClothes.html. Also, Jaime de Angulo, *Indian Tales* (North Point Press, 1997). Also, Michael Taussig, *Mimesis and Alterity. A Particular Theory of the Senses* (New York & London: Routledge, 1993) and Claude Lévi-Strauss, *Mythologiques* (Paris: Plon, 1964).

21. David Wengrow, "On Image Systems in Human History," in *Image, Thought, and the Making of Social Worlds*, 4.

22. Ibid.

23. Plato, *Symposium*, trans. by W. Hamilton (London: Penguin, 1951), 81.

24. Ibid.

25. See on this, Marshal Sahlins and David Graeber. *On Kings* (Boston: Hau Books, 2017).

26. Plato, *Symposium*, 81.

27. Ursula K. Le Guin, "A Non-Euclidean View of California as a Cold Place to Be," 179.

28. See on this, from the standpoint of mathematics and philosophy, Fernando Zalamea, *Synthetic Philosophy of Contemporary Mathematics*, trans. by Zachery Luke Frase (Cambridge, Massachusetts: MIT/Urbanomic, 2012). Also, Eyal Weizman and

Matthew Fuller, *Investigative Aesthetics. Conflicts and Commons in the Politics of Truth* (London: Verso, 2021).

29. *Get Out*, dir. By Jordan Peele, 2017.

30. Michael Taussig, "The Adult's Imagination of the Child's Imagination." In Aesthetic Subjects, ed. by Pamela R. Matthews and David McWhirter (Minneapolis: University of Minnesota Press, 2003) Chapter 19. Also, Hans Christian Andersen, "The Emperor's New Clothes" at https://andersen.sdu.dk/vaerk/hersholt/TheEmperorsNewClothes.html.

31. *Space Is the Place*, Dir. By John Coney, 1974. See also, *Sun Ra: Brother from Another Planet,* Dir. By Don Letts, 2005.

32. Michael Taussig, "The Adult's Imagination of the Child's Imagination." In Aesthetic Subjects, ed. by Pamela R. Matthews and David McWhirter (Minneapolis: University of Minnesota Press, 2003) Chapter 19. Also, Hans Christian Andersen, "The Emperor's New Clothes" at https://andersen.sdu.dk/vaerk/hersholt/TheEmperorsNewClothes.html.

33. Michael Taussig, "The Adult's Imagination of the Child's Imagination." In Aesthetic Subjects, Chapter 19 for quote and the source of some of the ideas expressed in this and previous paragraphs. Our gratitude to Michael for his generosity and guidance all these years.

34. Callé, Alain. 2020. *The Gift Paradigm. A Short Introduction to the Anti-Utilitarian Movement in the Social Sciences.* Chicago: Prickly Paradigm Press, i–viii. Also, Kojo Koram. 2022. *Uncommon Wealth. Britain and the Aftermath of Empire.* London: John Murray Publishers.

BIBLIOGRAPHY

Allen, Amy and Eduardo Mendieta. 2021. *Decolonizing Ethics. The Critical Theory of Enrique Dussel.* University Park, PA: The Pennsylvania State University Press.

Adorno, Theodor W. 2005. *Critical Models: Interventions and Catchwords*, trans. by H. Pickford. New York: Columbia University Press.

Andersen, Hans-Christian. 1837. "The Emperor's New Clothes." https://andersen.sdu.dk/vaerk/hersholt/TheEmperorsNewClothes.html.

Axelos, Kostas. 2024. *Alienation, Praxis, and Techne in the Thought of Karl Marx*, translated by R. Bruzina. Austin, TX: University of Texas, 1976.

Callé, Alain. 2020. *The Gift Paradigm. A Short Introduction to the Anti-Utilitarian Movement in the Social Sciences.* Chicago, IL: Prickly Paradigm Press.

De Angulo, Jaime. 1997. *Indian Tales*. New York: North Point Press, 1997.

Dussel, Enrique. 2016. *14 tesis de ética*. Madrid: Trotta editorial.

Garreth Millikan, Ruth. 1996. "Pushmi-Pullyu Representations." In: *Mind and Morals. Essays on Ethics and Cognitive Science*. Edited by L. May, A. Clark, and M. Friedman. Cambridge, MA: The MIT Press, 145–62.

Garreth Millikan, Ruth. 2017. *Beyond Concepts: Unicepts, Language, and Natural Information*. Oxford: Oxford University Press.

Guardiola-Rivera, Oscar (Ed.). Spring 2017. "Special Edition: Photoelectric Technologies of Liberation." *Discourse. Journal for Theoretical Studies in Media and Culture* 39(2): 153–94.

Kluge, Alexander. 2019. *Difference and Orientation*, ed. by R. Langston. Ithaca, NY: Cornell University Press.

Kluge, Alexander and Oskar Negt. 2001. "Geschichte und Eigensinn." In: *Der unterschatzte Mensch: Gemeine Philosophie in zwei Banden*. Oskar Negt / Alexander Kluge Vol. 2. Frankfurt am Main: Zweitausendeins, 475.

Koram, Kojo. 2022. *Uncommon Wealth. Britain and the Aftermath of Empire*. London: John Murray Publishers.

Langston, Richard. 2020. *Dark Matter: A Guide to Alexander Kluge & Oskar Negt*. London & New York: Verso Books.

Le Guin, Ursula K. 2016. "A Non-Euclidean View of California as a Cold Place to Be." In: Thomas More's *Utopia*. London: Verso Books, 163–94.

Martín-Alcoff, Linda. 2007. "Epistemologies of Ignorance: Three Types." In: *Race and Epistemologies of Ignorance*. Edited by Shannon Sullivan and Nancy Tuana. New York: State University of New York Press, 39–58.

Martin, Randy. 2012. "A Precarious Dance, A Derivative Sociality." *TDR: The Drama Review* 56(4): 216–91.

Mendieta, Eduardo. 2024. *The Philosophical Animal. On Zoopoetics and Interspecies Cosmopolitanism*. Albany, NY: State University of New York Press.

Ortega, Mariana. 2016. "The Difference that Art Makes." *Contemporary Aesthetics (Journal Archive)* 14: 20. https://digitalcommons.risd.edu/liberalarts_contempaesthetics/vol14/iss1/20/.

Plato. 1951. *Symposium*, trans. by W. Hamilton. London: Penguin Books.

Sahlins, Marshal and David Graeber. 2017. *On Kings*. Boston, MA: Hau Books.

Sanín-Restrepo, Ricardo. 2018. "The Meaning of the Encryption of Power as the Razor's Edge of Politics." In: *Decrypting Power*. Edited by Ricardo Sanín-Restrepo. New York & London: Rowman & Littlefield International IX–XXX.

Sanín-Restrepo, Ricardo. 2018a. "The X-Game of Language: Decrypting Heidegger's Ready to Hand." *CriticalLegalThinking*, 20 October. https://criticallegalthinking.com/2018/10/20/the-x-game-of-language-decrypting-heideggers-ready-to-hand/.

Sanín-Restrepo, Ricardo. 2021. *Being and Contingency: Decrypting Heidegger's Terminology*. London: Rowman & Littlefield International.

Supiot, Alain. 2015. *La Gouvernance par les nombres. Cours au Collège de France, 2012-2014*. Paris: Fayard.

Taussig, Michael. 2003. "The Adult's Imagination of the Child's Imagination." In: *Aesthetic Subjects*. Edited by Pamela R. Matthews and David McWhirter. Minneapolis, MN: University of Minnesota Press, 449–68.

Taussig, Michael. 2021. *Mastery and the Art of Non-Mastery in the Age of Meltdown*. Chicago, IL: The University of Chicago Press.

Tulving, E. 1972. "Episodic and Semantic Memory." In: *Organization of Memory*. Edited by E. Tulving and W. Donaldson. New York: Academic Press, 381–402.

Viveiros de Castro, Eduardo. 2007. "The Crystal Forest: Notes on the Ontology of Amazonian Spirits." *Inter Asia* 9(2): 153–72.

Viveiros de Castro, Eduardo. 2009. "Intensive Filiation and Demonic Alliance." In: *Deleuzian Intersections in Science, Technology and Anthropology.* Edited by C. B. Jensen and K. Rodje. Oxford: Bergahn Books, 219–54.

Viveiros de Castro, Eduardo. 2010. "Claude Lévi-Strauss: Fundador del postestructuralismo." In: *Lévi-Strauss: Un siglo de reflexión.* Edited by C. Bonfliglioli and S. Millán. Mexico: Juan Pablos Editor, 17–42.

Viveiros de Castro, Eduardo. 2012. *Radical Dualism: A Meta-Fantasy on the Square Root of Dual organizations, or a Savage Homage to Lévi-Strauss.* Kassel & Ostfildern: Hatje Cantz Verlag/Documenta.

Weizman, Eyal and Matthew Fuller. 2012. *Investigative Aesthetics. Conflicts and Commons in the Politics of Truth.* London: Verso Books.

Wengrow, David. 2022. "On Image Systems in Human History." In: *Image, Thought, and the Making of Social Worlds.* Edited by David Wengrow. Heidelberg: Propylaeum, 3–18.

Zalamea, Fernando. 2000. *Ariel y Arisbe. Evolución y evaluación del concepto de América Latina en el siglo XX: Una vision crítica desde la lógica contemporánea y la arquitectónica pragmática de C. S. Pierce.* Bogotá: Convenio Andrés Bello/ Tercer Mundo editores.

Zalamea, Fernando. 2009. *Filosofiá sintética de las matemáticas contemporáneas.* Bogotá: Editorial Universidad Nacional de Colombia.

Zalamea, Fernando. 2009. *América - Una trama integral. Transversalidad, bordes y abismos en la cultura America de los siglos XIX y XX.* Bogotá: Editorial Universidad Nacional de Colombia.

Zalamea, Fernando. 2010. *Razón de la frontera y fronteras de la razón. Pensamiento de los límites en Peirce, Florenski, Mareay, y limitantes de la expression en Lispector, Vieira da Silva, Tarkovski.* Bogotá: Editorial Universidad Nacional de Colombia.

Zalamea, Fernando. 2012. *Synthetic Philosophy of Contemporary Mathematics*, trans. by Zachery Luke Frase. Cambridge, MA: MIT/Urbanomic.

LEGAL SOURCES

Treaty on the Functioning of the European Union – Consolidated Version in *Official Journal of the European Union* C 326/47 ff. 26 October 2012.

FILMOGRAPHY

Space Is the Place, Dir. By John Coney, 1974.

Sun Ra: Brother from Another Planet, Dir. By Don Letts, 2005

Get Out, Dir. By Jordan Peele, 2017.

Chapter 3

Toward a Decolonial Paradigm of Justice

Sabelo J. Ndlovu-Gatsheni

This chapter makes a case for a decolonial paradigm of justice. It posits that justice, just like other important aspects of human life, underwent encryption to the extent that its very conceptions became aligned with the transcendental model of power called coloniality. Therefore, a decolonial paradigm of justice is predicated on considerations of geneses and genealogies of systems, structures, and institutions producing and reproducing injustices. It also requires a deliberate shift in the geography of reason/knowledge from hegemonic Eurocentric epistemologies to the reparative epistemologies of the South (see the motto of Caribbean Philosophical Association (CPA); Santos 2014, 2018; Ndlovu-Gatsheni 2018, 2023). Such a decolonial paradigm of justice entails shifting the biography of knowledge from predominantly white privileged bourgeois men to underprivileged women specifically and the subaltern in general, from the colonizers to the colonized; from settlers to Indigenous people and Indigenous academics, intellectuals, and activists (Anzaldua 1987; Ndlovu-Gatsheni 2018). These shifts must not be read as a drawing of a binary but as aimed at the recovery of subjugated knowledges and the constitution of ecologies of knowledges. These epistemic shifts are also very necessary because epistemic injustices are traceable to the very problematic conceptions of being human and articulations of the social from a Eurocentric racial and patriarchal perspectives.[1] This reality is highlighted by Joao H. Costa Vargas and Moon-Kie Jung: "The Human is to the humanities what the Social is to the social sciences: their foundational concept, the declared and assumed universality of which is ultimately belied and bounded by its 'full stop' antiblackness. The Human, the modern human, defines itself in opposition to the Black (alleged) nonbeing" (Jung 2021, 5).

What this argument points to is that perhaps the idea and concept of justice as it emerges from the Western tradition of thought might be born tainted from the beginning. The sources of taintment include the very conception of being human, racism, and sexism. This argument is buttressed by Rinaldo Walcott with reference to the origins of anti-Black racism:

> What it means to be Human is continually defined against Black people and Blackness. The very basic terms of social Human engagement are shaped by anti-Black logics so deeply embedded in various normativities that they resist intelligibility as modes of thought and yet we must attempt to think them. . . . This global anti-black condition produced in the post Columbus era, still and again manifests itself in numerous ways that have significantly limited how Black people might lay claim to human-ness and therefore how Black people might impact on what it means to be Human in a post Columbus world. (Walcott 2014, 93)

What Vargas, Jung, and Walcott are highlighting is a possible ideal starting point for a decolonial paradigm of justice with its foundations on anti-racist storytelling. At the center of this ideal starting point is the Global South as a locus of enunciation of rich pre-colonial conceptions of justice founded on such visions of life as *Ubuntu* (Africa), *Pachamama,* and *Buen vivir* (Latin America), and *Tianxia* (China) as well as the current anti-racist storytelling (Mignolo 2021). The Global South invoked here is not a geography but a site rich with pre-colonial and anti-racist stories of re-existence emerging from existential challenges, struggles, revolts, and resistances against racism, enslavement, colonialism, imperialism, capitalism, heteropatriarchal sexism, pauperization, destitution, underdevelopment, dismemberment, and dehumanization (Du Bois 1903; Cesaire 1955 [2000]; Rodney 1972; Fanon 1963; Wynter 1991, 2001, 2003; Ngugi wa Thiong'o 2009a, 2009b; Santos 2018; Dabashi 2019; Mignolo 2021).[2] The Global South has been the locus of literatures emerging from what Hamid Dabashi (2019) termed "battlefields of history"—texts that are "written in tears and blood." The typical example of texts "written in tears and blood" includes the books written by Frederick Douglass such as *Narrative of the Life of Frederick Douglass, an American Slave* (1845); *My Bondage and My Freedom* (1855), and *The Life and Times of Frederick Douglass* (1881). These texts are signatures of vivid practices of brutality, violence, dehumanization, and dismemberment, which must form a departure point for any genuine search for justice.

It is also from the Global South that the "insurgent universality" and alternatives to Euro/North American-centric modernity are emerging, articulated, and constituted (Tomba 2019). It is through the embracement of decolonial/postcolonial and feminist thinking and sensing of the world that justice framings for anti-racist storytelling can be effectively done. This is because: "The force of postcolonial thinking thus overcomes the blind spots of European modernity and postmodernity and faces the colonial consequences of

European instrumental reason" (Dabashi 2019, 129). Even the Global South within the Global North has been awakened to rise against racism as well, to protest and highlight the injustices they are facing. The multi-classness and the interracial character of the protesters perhaps demonstrate that decolonial consciousness is indeed assuming a planetary scale in its resonances. Priyamvada Gopal (2019) expressed how anti-colonial resistance influenced British dissent over the empire. This is how she put it: "We might even ask whether the idea of Britain's uniquely liberal Empire, which was humanitarian in conception and had the liberation of its conquered subjects as its ultimate goal, might itself have been, at least in part, a response to the claims of humanity, freedom and self-determination made by those very subjects" (Gopal 2019, 6). Therefore, what is attempted here is not thinking against Europe *per se* but thinking beyond Europe as part of offering justice framings for anti-racist storytelling to break from debilitating oscillation "between the world Europe has enabled and the world we wish to enable after-Europe" (Dabashi 2019, 1).

THE PRESENT CONJUNCTURE AS AN ENTRY POINT TO JUSTICE FRAMINGS

At the present conjuncture, the modern world is at a crossroads—the world of domination remains resilient, and the world of liberation is struggling to emerge triumphantly. The modern civilizational project (1492–2023), the U.S. hegemonic project (1945–2023), and the neoliberal project (1973–2023) are revealing their exhaustion and are besieged by crises (Mignolo 2023; Ndlovu-Gatsheni 2023). Dominant ideas, norms, concepts, theories, systems, structures, epistemologies, knowledges, and institutions are exposed to uncertainties and heavy questioning. The symptomatic signatures and indeed the surface manifestations of these crises include global warming; global financial crises; increased human migrations and global human entanglements; deepening material inequalities and pauperization; mass unemployment; rising global and national polarizations; the rise of racist, authoritarian, xenophobic, and sexist regimes; the risk of nuclear conflagrations; pandemics; increasing rates of femicides and suicides; intensifying epistemic and intellectual contestations over truth and indeed "knowledge of knowledge itself"; and other sources of injustices and human precarity (Ndlovu-Gatsheni 2018, 2020; Mignolo 2023). The current neoliberal global order is failing to hold the center as the peripherized world is refusing to follow the dictates of coloniality of internationalism (Ndlovu-Gatsheni 2022b, 2023). This analysis dovetails with that of Christian Reus-Smit and Ayşe Zarakol, who posited that: "The post-1945 international order is in crisis. . . . It is condemned for its economic inequalities, social hierarchies, institutional unfairness, intergenerational inequities, historical injustices and, accentuating all of these, its normative and epistemic biases: the privileging of Western—often 'white'—values and knowledge systems" (Reus-Smit and Zarakol 2023, 1).

Even though the post-1945 era was an age of construction of multilateralism, building of global normative standards as well as articulations of human rights and human well-being, the world has reached a stage where sharp and very critical questions are posed regarding the promises of Euro-North American modernity—promises of a brave modern world in which rationality, science, technology and work ethics enabled by modern bureaucratic institutions were expected to solve problems inhibiting human flourishing (see Weber 1905; Giddens 1991 on celebrations of modernity). Such scholars as Arturo Escobar (2004) posited that the modern world is framed by a modernity that has created numerous modern problems of which it is incapable of providing modern solutions. What is more visible are three main fault-lines of hegemonic, legitimacy, and institutional crises haunting the present conjuncture (see Santos 2017). There is also the ecological crisis provoked by rampaging global capitalism. It has forced the planet to "pass the threshold of the Holocene and entered a new geological epoch altogether" known as the Anthropocene characterized by an entanglement of "geological and biological timescales, something that has never happened before in the history of humanity" (Chakrabarty 2021, 7). The climate crisis accompanied by ecological disasters linked to extractive racial capitalism is one of the big elephants in the room. Taken together, the contemporary crises have the effect of holding "a giant mirror to society and in this case to the world at large, exposing its underlying structural deformities and dysfunctions" (Zeleza 2021, vii).

At the end of the Second World War, three visions of development and the future dominated the world: (a) the welfare society in the West, (b) the socialist/communist revolutionary society in the East, and (c) the popular Bandung-inspired nationalist projects in the south. All of them have fallen into crisis. At the hegemonic level, the existing conceptions of the human, power, justice, knowledge, order, and all other important aspects of modern life are at one level lagging behind the changed realities on the ground, and at another, they are confronted by new conceptions emerging mainly from the Global South (see Quijano 2000; Mignolo 1995, 2000, 2011; Wynter 2003; Santos 2018). As noted in the first section of this literature review, the Global South is not a mere physical geography. It is a geography of poverty, where destitution happened as a result of racism, enslavement, colonialism, imperialism, racial capitalism, and heteropatriarchal normative sexism (Robinson 2000; Ndlovu-Gatsheni 2013, 2018, 2020, 2022a; Santos 2018; Tamale 2020; Mignolo 2021). It is a positionality within an asymmetrical modern global power structure. It is a majority world. The limits of Euro-North American-centric modernity revealed its negative underpinnings in the Global South.

Today, in the words of Jean Comaroff and John L. Comaroff (2012, 1), "it is the global south that affords privileged insight into the workings of the world at large." The upsurge of epistemologies of the Global South, decolonial/postcolonial theories, the resurgence of Indigenous knowledge, the spreading feminist and gender analysis and theories, as well as the increasing embrace of theories from the Global South—all these directly challenge the previous conceptions of knowledge, justice, power, and others coming from Europe and North America. For example, feminists and gender scholars of the Global South have mounted a strong critique of what they have termed "civilizational feminism" and they have introduced "decolonial feminism" (See Lugones 2007, 2008, 2010; Verges 2021, 2022).

The limits of "civilizational feminism" are many. They include that it "borrows the vocabulary and objectives of the colonizing mission" (Verges 2021, vii). It is part of Eurocentric modernizing agendas and neoliberal philosophies. The only form of power that is targeted is patriarchy, and it ignores racism, enslavement, colonialism, imperialism, and capitalism. But patriarchy works in tandem with other forms of systemic and structural oppression. This is why Francoise Verges (2022, vi) identified "neoliberal capitalism, racism, imperialism, white supremacy and patriarchy, homophobia and transphobia" as structural and systemic violence that "are showing their insatiable appetite for domination and oppression." "Civilizational feminism is also complicity in 'criminalising the veil and Islam'" (Verges 2021, vii). At the center of "civilizational feminism" lurks racism. This critique of "civilizational feminism" led Verges (2021, 2022) to embrace "decolonial feminism" as a progressive feminism that considers entanglements and intersectionality of multiple oppressions and injustices affecting women. The concept of intersectionality was introduced by Kimberlé Crenshaw (1995), and it has successfully deepened the understanding of the multiplier effects of oppression on women. Decolonial feminism draws from it. This is how she articulated decolonial feminism: "The decolonial feminism I defend seeks to bring to light a kaleidoscopic narrative encompassing broad swathes of time and territory and to valorize the unstoppable struggles that challenge the legacies of colonial slavery and racism amid a new age of endless wars" (Verges 2021, ix).

Verges elaborated that:

> To call one a decolonial feminist, to defend feminism with decolonial politics today, is not only to tear the word "feminism" out of the greedy hands of reactionaries' empty ideologies. It is also to affirm our fidelity to the struggles of the women of the Global South who have come before us. It is to recognize their

> sacrifices, honour their lives in all their complexity, the risks they took, and the difficulties and frustrations they experienced; it is to receive their legacy. On the other hand, it means recognising that the offensive against women that is now openly justified and acknowledged by state leaders is not simply an expression of a brazen, masculinist dominance, but a manifestation of the destructive violence generated by capitalism. Decolonial feminism leads to de-patriarchizing revolutionary struggles. In other words, feminists with decolonial politics contribute to the struggle, undertaken for centuries by part of humanity, to assert it right to existence. (Verges 2021, 10)

It is these struggles, interventions, and initiatives that have opened a hegemonic crisis within the transcendent model of power called coloniality. Previous conceptions of the modern world emerging from above (from elites at the center) have locked horns with new conceptions emerging from the subaltern and from the margins. Failure to reconcile these contradictions has generated a hegemonic crisis (Santos 2017, 175–76). The hegemonic crisis has produced a legitimacy crisis, with institutions such as the university ceasing "to be a consensual institution in view of the contradiction between the hierarchization of specialized knowledge through restrictions of access and credentialing of competences, on the one hand, and the social and political demands for a democratized university and equal opportunity for the children of the working class and other social groups historically excluded from higher education, on the other" (Santos 2017, 176). The legitimacy crisis has led to an institutional crisis, with modern institutions caught up between neoliberal demands for corporatization, commercialization, efficiency, productivity, and dollarization of everything on the one hand; and on the other the decolonization demands for social relevance, social responsibility, epistemic justice, gender justice, restorative justice, environmental justice, and many others. Adebayo Olukoshi and Paul Tiyambe Zeleza captured the crisis very well as it manifests itself in African higher education where challenges of reconciling contradictions have become very sharp, complex, and difficult: "How to balance autonomy and viability, expansion and excellence, equity and efficiency, access and quality, authority and accountability, representation and responsibility, diversification and differentiation, internationalization and indigenization, global presence/visibility and local anchorage, academic freedom and professional ethics, privatization and public purpose, teaching and research, community service/social responsibility and consultancy, diversity and uniformity, the preservation of local knowledge systems and the adoption of global knowledge systems, knowledge production and knowledge dissemination, the knowledge economy and the knowledge society?" (Olukoshi and Zeleza 2004, 3).

While Olukoshi and Zeleza were specifically concerned about the contradictions within higher education in Africa, their analysis and distillation of contours of contradictions apply to many other modern institutions, modern constitutions, and judiciary systems that are expected to deliver justice. The resurgent and insurgent decolonization of the twenty-first century has led to the accentuation of the contradictions, with modern institutions resorting to the time-tested strategy of posturing as though they were undergoing decolonization when in fact, they were defanging it, disciplining it, re-colonizing it, and resubordinating it to the orthodoxies and the usual ways of functioning of modern institutions. This analysis of the present conjuncture takes us to a critique of the conventional Western conceptions of injustices and justice as they emerged from Europe and North America.

A CRITIQUE OF CONVENTIONAL WESTERN CONCEPTIONS OF JUSTICE

The "West," which is today called the Global North, just like the Global South, is not a denotation of a physical geography but a locus of enunciation of particular ideas and conceptions of the world and indeed a geography of opulence. This is why Walter D. Mignolo (2015, xxv–xxvi) wrote: "What constitutes the West more than a geography is a linguistic family, a belief system, and an epistemology. It is constituted by six modern European and imperial languages: Italian, Spanish, and Portuguese, and English, French and German, which have been dominant since the Enlightenment." Like the Global South, the Global North has its own internal divisions and contestations, but they all amount to what Immanuel Wallerstein (1997) termed "anti-Eurocentric Eurocentrism." This concept of "anti-Eurocentric Eurocentrism" speaks to internal ructions and critiques within Eurocentrism but which do not burst its core epistemic and systemic configurations and architecture.

The emerging pattern in reading Western evolution of thought on injustices and justice—from the time of the Sophists right up to the current crisis-ridden neoliberal conceptions—is a running thread of the story of justice linked to ideas of particular philosophers, giving the story of justice and injustice an abstract philosophical orientation. For example, Kant advanced the idea of moral principles that individuals should always act in a way that they would want others to act in similar situations, and he strongly advocated for justice defined through universal principles. This formed the basis of deontology (Kant 1963). The problem was that the conception of the universal itself was very narrow because of a limited understanding of the world. Even today, universalism remains an aspiration rather than a reality. Plato (1981) articulated a justice informed by a Socratic method and labored in search of working definition of justice. What emerges is a powerful idea and concept of justice that is driven by a particular epistemology, producing a hegemonic Western storytelling of justice and injustices. The Global South storytelling shifts from abstractions to empirical systems, structures, institutions, histories, and processes of production and reproduction of injustices such as racism, enslavement, colonialism, imperialism, racial capitalism, heteropatriarchal sexism, narrow nationalism, and underdevelopment (Du Bois 1903; Cesaire 1955 [2000]; Fanon 1963; Rodney 1972; Chinweizu 1975; Quijano 2000; Mignolo 2000, 2021; Ndlovu-Gatsheni 2013, 2022a).

In Western storytelling of justice and injustice, even the subjects of enslavement, gender, and war are brought in an abstract philosophical manner to the extent that the discussion in classical philosophy becomes about whether their slavery and gender differences were a natural basis for discrimination as well as whether they are right or wrong. However, John S. Mill (1997) offered a critique of the gender inequalities within European gender norms and advocated for a right to vote for both men and women. But he was of the opinion that the uneducated have to be excluded from voting. Mill was also the first among the utilitarian philosophers to link justice and the happiness of society. But what is also noticeable at the center of philosophical contestations within the Western theories of justice is the abstraction of justice into philosophical matters of morality and virtue rather than a product of concrete historical processes of dehumanization, oppression, and exploitation (Waterfield 2000). This is why one finds scholars and theorists from the Global South such as Ricardo Sanín-Restrepo and Gabriel Méndez-Hincapíe (2015, 29) questioning any idea and concept of justice which constructs "a theory outside the complex frame of coloniality makes the theory vulnerable to severe hindrances." At another level, the Western story of justice either begins with the theological notion of sin at the center or philosophy with the Sophists (wise-men) of fifth century ancient Greece with their "dialogues" forming the genealogy and genesis of justice as an idea, a concept, a theory, and a system (Kant 1999). See table 3.1.

There are various matters arising from table 3.1. The first is the clear fact of the difficulties encountered by philosophers in defining justice and articulating its principles, without fully considering systemic, structural, institutional, epistemic, and indeed concrete historical and manifest injustices. This difficulty was compounded by the fact that the story is told by entitled white male philosophers, which made them to produce a reductive and at times even fictional history from which to construct ideas, concepts, theories, and principles of justice (Sanín-Restrepo and Méndez-Hincapíe 2015; Parnami 2019). The second matter is the problematic nature of the search for a departure point to philosophize about justice and injustice. This problem led Thomas Hobbes to construct what he termed "the state of nature" where life

Table 3.1 Summary of Western Conceptions of Justice

Time	*Thinkers*	*Notions of Justice*
Ancient Greece	Sophists, Socrates, Plato, Aristotle	Nature (physis), custom (nomos), telling truth, payment of debts, prevention of harm/impunity, giving what is due, goodness/good society/good character (wisdom, courage, temperance, and justice), virtue, ethics, order, morality, distributive justice, corrective justice, rational compromise between extremes/mean between getting too much and getting too little, natural justice, equality, meritocracy, common good
Medieval Christianity	Thomas Aquinas, Augustine	Divine justice(sin), righteousness, God's justice, prudence/wisdom, fortitude/courage, temperance, law of God vs law of the state/civil law, unjust law is not law, rule of the just not the powerful, just war, equality, natural justice, natural law, natural right, legal justice, particular justice, distributive justice, commutative justice, reciprocity
Early Modernity	Thomas Hobbes, David Hume, John Locke, Jean-Jacques Rousseau, Mary Wollstonecraft	Monism, state of nature (will to power, survival, self-interest and egoism), interpersonal antagonism, no morals, war of every man against every man; social contract (shift from state of nature to civil society), rules/principles of justice, sovereign authority, birth of government, punishment (corporal/pecuniary, ignominy, imprisonment, exile), birth of political society, general will (common good enforced by government), property rights, public utility
Recent Modernity	Immanuel Kant, John Stuart Mill	Deontology (science of duty), pure practical reason, political virtue, moral virtue, ethical system, doctrine of right, doctrine of justice, doctrine of law, freedom of the will, property rights, crime and punishment, abilities and needs, liberal utilitarianism (great happiness principle), legal rights, moral rights, deserving, non-breaking of faith of others, impartiality in judgment, liberty (self-protection from harm, freedom of thought, freedom of expression, freedom of personal lifestyle, freedom of association), equal opportunity for women
Contemporary Times	John Rawls	Notion of original position/state of nature (veil of ignorance); revival of social contract, justice as fairness; liberty and equality for all citizens, civil rights (constitution, free speech, freedom of assembly, freedom of conscience, the right to private property, right to vote and hold public office, freedom from arbitrary arrests and seizure), principles (equal civil liberties is the first; social and economic inequalities have to be to everyone's advantage and attached to positions; and fair equal opportunity must be connected to positions to which all members of society could have access), tolerance of diverse ideas, just war
Post-Rawls Times	Robert Nozick, Kai Nielsen, Michael J. Sandel, Thomas W. Pogge, Martha Nussbaum, Amartya Sen	Libertarianism (individual liberty, minimal state, distributive justice, property rights, against taxing of the rich for the benefit of the poor), socialism (equality, self-determination, political participation, egalitarian concept of justice); communitarianism (well-being of community); globalist (international justice, international law, Global Resources Tax (GRT)); capabilities (feminism, equality for women, human rights, body health and integrity, exercise of practical reason, concern for nature)

Source: Drawn by the author; it is illustrative.

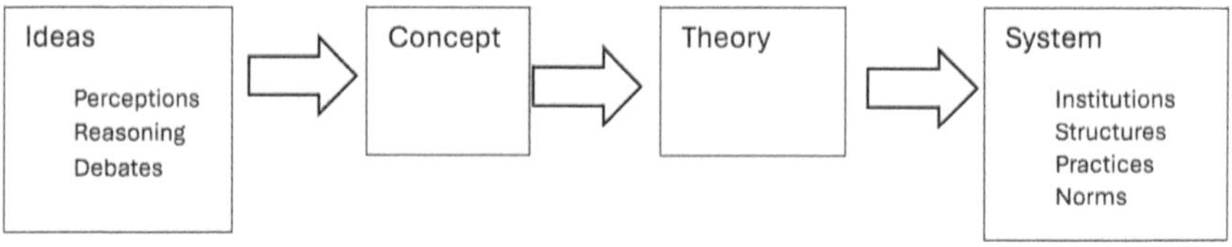

Figure 3.1 Summary of the Evolving Idealist Trajectory of Thinking on Justice. *Source*: Drawn by the author.

was brutal, short, and nasty; and John Rawls followed suit to invent what he termed "the original position," which was enveloped by a "veil of ignorance" (Hobbes 1994; Rawls 1971). In Leviathan, Hobbes posited that human beings were motivated by self-preservation and self-interest. He became worried about a society where there was no common center of power, no laws—and he articulated an argument for common laws and common power governing society.

What emerges poignantly from reviewing Western literature is its linear conception of the evolution of justice from ideas to concepts to theory to principles and then finally to a system of justice (see figure 3.1). Of course, there were internal contestations and divergences over individual and communal bases of justice.

This linearity is made possible by the fact that in the Western context, the question of justice emerges more as a philosophical idea and a preoccupation of philosophers (see figure 3.1). Consequently, credit for developing justice from an idea to a theory and to practice goes to some "enlightened individual" philosophers.

But what is highly problematic about this Western foundational story of justice and injustice is that it creates a temporality in which humans were like animals. They had no morals. They were driven by instincts. They were enveloped by a "veil of ignorance." Violence was the state of affairs. There was no respect for life. There were no institutions including family institutions. This sounds like a concocted philosophical fairy-tale, which was created to fulfill the idea of "original position." There is no such temporality in the conceptions of humanity and justice from the Global South (see next section). The problem in Western conceptions of justice is its idealistic departure point. Even though Karl Marx and other Marxists after him sharply critiqued idealism and postulated a materialist conception of justice, idealism has survived the critique and is very alive within contemporary neoliberalism (see Ndlovu-Gatsheni 2022b). However, the materialist conception of justice enables engagement with systems, structures, and institutions that produced and reproduced injustices with capitalism as the main one. Five classifications of justice are discernible from table 3.1:

- Natural justice: derived from assumed innate qualities of human being of being fair and from ideas of natural law.
- Political justice: derived from the notions of equal political rights administered and delivered by a sovereign authority (the state).
- Economic justice: derived from two opposed notions of the capitalist right to private property on the one hand and on the other the socialist ideas of equal distribution of economic resources.
- Social justice: derived from justice as fairness entailing equitable division of resources, opportunities, and privileges in a society. It is also known as "distributive justice."
- Legal justice: derived from linking justice and law to give justice coherence and expression institutionally.

What must be noted is that as an idea and a concept, justice has been evolving from ancient times to the present and simultaneously branching into various classifications. The snowball evolution of the idea and concept of justice has a direct correlation with expanding principles of justice such as access, equity, diversity, racial equality, gender equality, LGBTQIA+1 equality, and many others depending on the concrete situation and legal frameworks in place.

An important third matter that arises from table 3.1 is that from the time of the Sophists to the contemporary time of the neoliberals, there is a discernible thread of what Ricardo Sanín-Restrepo (2016) termed "encryption of power," with philosophy working as an encrypting force to lay a foundation for the construction of what Anibal Quijano (2000) depicted as "coloniality." In the name of justice, power as "potentia" (something available to people and an enabler of doing things by the people as free agents) is gradually snatched from them and re-deployed as "potestas" (entailing the subjection of the people to power as domination) (Sanín-Restrepo 2016, 1–2). The very fact that scholars like Saurabh Dube could write such books as *Subjects of Modernity* (2017) gives us a hint of how the reality of human subjection to modern power has become accepted and normalized. At the center of modernity is an invented transcendent model of power to which all aspects of modern life are subordinated.

While Western philosophers like Thomas Hobbes, Jean-Jacques Rousseau, and even John Rawls sugar-coated this process using the concept of voluntary surrendering of power by the people to a sovereign authority in a process known as social contract, there is much that is lost, and the brick-by-brick total subjection of the entire world population to a "transcendent model of power" (coloniality) is traceable to how Western philosophers conceived justice and justified the construction of what Amartya Sen (2009) termed "transcendental institutionalism." Table 3.2 provides a clear picture of the transcendent model of power within which injustices were naturalized and authorized as subjection and subjectivation, at a planetary scale.

Table 3.2 Summary of Transcendental Model of Power (Global Coloniality)

Hierarchy	*Elaboration*
Global class formation	Bourgeois, worker, peasant, lumpen-proletariat, and so on
Global international division of labor	Racial capitalism with the periphery characterized by race, gender, and coercive labor regimes and practices
Global inter-state system	Unequal sovereignties and hierarchized hidden and visible power structures within the so-called "united nations"
Global racial/ethnic social system	Racialized, gendered, classed social pyramid with those who are designated as white at the top and those designated as black at the bottom
Global gender hierarchy	Privileged men privileged and underprivileged women mediated by patriarchy and sexism
Global sexual hierarchy	Privileged heterosexuals over all other forms of sexual orientation, mediated by misogynistic masculine behavior and homophobic ideologies
Global spiritual hierarchy	Christianity is privileged to some extent over Islam and other religions and spiritualities, with conversions authorized
Global epistemic hierarchy	Eurocentric epistemology, knowledge, and cosmology are privileged within universities, and "written" is privileged over "oral" knowledges
Global linguistic hierarchy	Privileged and universalized European colonial languages and their adoption as official languages, displacing other languages like, for example, Indigenous languages
Global aesthetic hierarchy	Art is hierarchized into high (modern/superior) and low (primitive) within museums, art galleries, and art markets. Standardization and normalization of European conceptions of beauty
Global pedagogical hierarchy	Privileging of particular forms of learning and teaching over others
Global media/ informational hierarchy	Monopoly and control of media and communication channels and its technologies so as to manage the flow of information and ideas
Global age hierarchy	Ageism whereby ages (15–65 years) are privileged as productive, and those from 65 and beyond are deemed to be unproductive in contradiction with other civilizations where old age is valued for experience and wisdom
Global ecological hierarchy	Dualism of nature–human/nature–-culture resulting in objectification of nature into natural resource
Global spatial hierarchy	Center-periphery, rural-urban divisions

Source: Drawn by the author based on ideas of Grosfoguel (2011, 16–17); see also Ndlovu-Gatsheni (2023).

Table 3.2 provides a detailed sample of the content of a global cartography of power and highlights the complex hierarchies, if not hetararchies that underpin it. These hierarchies and heterarchies of power are constitutive of the contemporary post-1945 global order of power. What happened after 1945 in general and what emerged after 1989 in particular is well captured by Catherine Lu:

> Consequently, the political productivity of changes in the foundational organizing of principles of successive international orders—from empire to statehood, from civilization to self-determination, from hegemony to multilateralism, from modernization to development, from sovereignty to human rights, from colonial law to rule of law, and from exclusion to inclusion—has yielded new disciplinary practices against historically marginalized and oppressed groups, while maintaining their structural disadvantages, and doing little to check domination, exploitation, and uses of imperialism, colonialism, global capital and white supremacy. (Lu 2023, 143)

This reality of encryption of power and its pretenses of considering the structural, systemic, and institutional as well as historical injustices takes us to a reconsideration of the ideas and theories of justice by Amartya Sen (2009). Sen's work is reviewed here as one which enables a transition from Western conceptions of justice to other conceptions of justice. Sen attempted a spirited critique of John Rawls' widely accepted idea, conception, and theory of justice. He criticized what he depicted as the transcendental concept of justice and institutional transcendentalism, whereby alternative ideas, concepts, and theories are ignored if not destroyed so as to construct a singular transcendental model (Sen 2009).

While Sen's argument is not radical enough to assume a decolonial framing of justice, it is used as a transition and a bridge from conventional Western conceptions of justice to the decolonial paradigm of justice. Sen is very critical of ideas and conceptions of justice that privilege institutions and are predicated on a search for a perfect and just society as a departure point. He proposes "manifest injustice" as a starting point, and this is how he puts it:

> It is fair to assume that Parisians would not have stormed the Bastille, Gandhi would not have challenged the empire on which the sun used not to set, Martin Luther King would not have fought white supremacy in "the land of the free and the home of the brave," without their sense of manifest injustices that could be overcome. . . . The identification of redressable injustice is not only what animates us to think about justice and injustice, it is also central, I argue in this book, to the theory of justice. In the investigation presented here, diagnosis of injustice will figure often enough as the starting point for critical discussion. (Sen 2009, vii–viii)

While Sen's take on "manifest injustices" as a departure point is well taken here, his theory of justice remained trapped within liberal thinking. This means that his theory of justice failed to consider deeper questions of racism, colonialism, capitalism, heteronormative sexism, and even liberalism as constitutive of modernity and as signifiers of coloniality. Sen became linked with such thinkers as Rawls, who failed to understand the injustices that are encrypted into modern power configurations and institutionalization within which emerges the modern nation-state enjoying not only the monopoly of violence but also the prerogative of "state secrets" (Sanín-Restrepo and Méndez-Hincapíe 2015, 33). Coming from the vantage point of the theories of encryption and decryption of power as part of struggles for justice, Sanín-Restrepo and Méndez-Hincapíe (2015, 33) proposed a third principle of justice—the "principle of publicity" as an addition to the principles of freedom and equality of opportunities. The importance of the principle of publicity is that it targets the encryption of power and the concealment of information as constituent parts of injustices.

Sanín-Restrepo and Méndez-Hincapíe (2015, 29) expected Sen to consider what they termed "the duality (modernity/coloniality)" as it produced "a twofold but interdependent reality: for western world it means the achievement of values such as liberty and prosperity; for the non-western world, racism, extraction and exclusion." Because of this failure by Sen to consider the reality of "modernity/coloniality," he fell into the trap of embracing liberal democracy, which is in bed with capitalism—a systemic generator of inequalities and injustices (Sanín-Restrepo and Méndez-Hincapíe 2015, 33). This is why I consider the work of Sen as standing at the transition from the Western theory of justice to the decolonial paradigm of justice.

TOWARD A DECOLONIAL PARADIGM OF JUSTICE

At the center of a decolonial paradigm of justice are four overarching issues: (a) existential issues (of denied humanity/coloniality of being); (b) material issues (denied development/uneven development/destitution); (c) epistemic issues (theft of history and epistemicides); and (d) leadership for liberation emerging from the ranks of the oppressed (Ndlovu-Gatsheni 2018, 2020). The existential question was well-expressed by William E. B. Du Bois when he posed the challenge of how it felt to be defined as a problem (Du Bois 1898, 1899). Being defined as a problem entails reduction to that which is unwanted. Elimination/genocide was considered as the final solution. The existential issue for those people who were designated as Black and native was also articulated by Aime Cesaire in terms of three tormenting questions:

who am I, who are we, and what are we in an anti-black world (Cesaire in Thiam 2014). Lewis R. Gordon (2021, 7–8) explained that these existential questions arose within the context of "black people's relation with Euro-modernity" and he posed the questions this way: What does it mean to be human? What is freedom? How are justificatory practices justifiable in light of the historic and continued challenges to reason posed by colonialism, enslavement, racism, and cultivated dependency not only as material and political projects but also as intellectual enterprises? Whether material questions entail epistemic ones? What could be done about reason when colonialism produced colonial forms?

It is the existential questions that provoked the emergence of what Cedric Robinson (2000) termed the "Black Radical Tradition" and what Gordon (2000) depicted as "Africana existential thought." At the center of the "Black Radical Tradition" are the struggles and initiatives for re-existence and self-determination. The struggles and initiatives range from Ethiopianism (claiming Africa as home and retracing African roots by survivors of enslavement and their descendants), Garveyism (back-to-Africa movement, Black struggles for power and economic liberation); Negritude (re-articulation of Black/African cultures/re-constructions of African personality); Indigeneity (claims of land and self-definition by survivors of genocides and their descendants); Black Marxism (redemption from class, race, gender, and colonial oppressions); African Renaissance (rebirth of Africa) to decolonial feminism (see Verges 2021, 2022; Ndlovu-Gatsheni 2023).

The other name for it is African existential thought, of which Gordon (2000, 1) explained that "Africana thought also refers to the set of questions raised by the historical project of conquest and colonization that has emerged since 1492 and the subsequent struggles for emancipation that continue to this day." Sylvia Wynter (2003) and Nelson Maldonado-Torres (2007) articulated the existential question in terms of the coloniality of being, which took the form of social classification of human populations accompanied by racial hierarchization. Today, the existential question animates what has come to be known as the Black Lives Matter movement.

In a profound sense, the existential question is inextricably intertwined with the material and epistemic questions. For example, being denied humanity was linked to genocides and the unfolding of settler colonialism with its dispossession, displacements, and destitution of its targets (see table 3.3). At another level, the denial of humanity was accompanied by theft of history, denial of history, and of knowledge which led Sabelo J. Ndlovu-Gatsheni (2018, 3) to link the "colour line and the epistemic line" to make a strong case for "epistemic freedom" and epistemic justice. This analysis is in tandem with that of Gordon (2000, 63) who explained that:

"The colour line is also a metaphor that exceeds its own concrete formulation. It is the race line as well as the gender line, the class line, the sexual orientation line, the religious line—in short, the line between 'normal' and 'abnormal' identities."

Basically, a decolonial paradigm of justice is characterized by a deliberate strategy of making linkages across domains of oppression and indeed embracing the intersectionality of multiple forms of oppression as it seeks to break "the walls of very strictly guarded, normed, repressive domains" (Lugones 2003, 1). Thus, a decolonial paradigm of justice responds adequately to Sylvia Tamale's (2020, 9) question: "Who will connect the ideological dots of racism, colonialism, capitalism, sexism and heterosexism in ways that our children understand?" It clearly links existential, material, and epistemic questions while indicating the contexts from which they emerge. It, thus, takes seriously the contexts of history and power dynamics. For example, the modern history of racism, enslavement, imperialism, colonialism, capitalism, and heteronormative patriarchy are given as foundational structures and systems generating injustices. Natalie Etoke also helps in making connections of existential, material, epistemic, and subjectivity issues that generate injustices:

> In a world where thought closes itself in language that strives to erase the sensitivity of existence, how can we make sense of Sub-Saharan or Afrodiasporic life experiences rooted in suffering born of social, economic, cultural, and historical structures dominated by unequal power relations? How can we examine the encounter with the Other? How can we understand a path towards freedom forged through pain inflicted on the body, pain that penetrated the soul? How can we describe a subjectivity in which self-destruction and reconstruction arise from traumatic experience? People who were excluded from the universal family must face these questions. . . . My process breaks with the habits that would have me speak of myself and mine as if I speak of another, step out of myself for the sake of objectivity, regurgitate the Other's way of thinking in the Other's rhetoric that I have learnedly digested. In all frankness, I take the risk of injecting subjectivity into my words. (Etoke 2019, xix–xxi)

Verges also demonstrates the value of connecting the dots for a clear understanding of multiple oppressions and injustices using violence as an entry point:

> Violence is consubstantial to racial capitalism; it is not something that comes afterwards, the act of some extreme groups. Ecosystem degradation is accelerated by capitalism, which intensifies pollution and waste, land-use change and exploitation, and carbon-driven energy systems. Rape, land theft, genocides,

> massacres, assassinations, destruction of public services, processes of enslavement, creation of private militias, torture, censorship, have always been tools of colonialism and capitalism disguised as civilizing missions or humanitarian interventions. Imperialist wars leave behind ruins, pollution, devastation and misery and their "end" means that war is pursued through other means. (Verges 2022, vii)

It is, therefore, not surprising that a decolonial paradigm of justice presented here highlights what the Latin American decolonial theorists have termed the "modernity/coloniality" power structure within which some were elevated to superiority and full being and others were degraded to inferiority and subhumanity (Quijano 2000; Mignolo 2000; Lugones 2008). What emerges poignantly as a useful decolonial thesis is the idea of a two-faced modernity with coloniality as its underside or negative side. It was Anibal Quijano (2000) who, in the middle of the triumphalism of neoliberalism and its celebrated notions of democracy, human rights, and rule of law in the 1990s, introduced the concept of "coloniality of power" and "colonial matrices of power" as he launched a decolonial critique of the architecture and configuration of a hegemonic and modern transcendental model of power. Table 3.2 provides a good summary of the operations of this transcendental model of power (see also table 3.3).

Coloniality of power is a reference to a modern transnational power structure which subjects all aspects of human life. The ways of subjecting all aspects of human and even non-human life to power constitute a modern foundational injustice. The concept of coloniality enables a clear understanding of modernity as constituted by two sides: the positive and negative sides (Mignolo 2011). The positive side is characterized by the achievement of values of liberty, prosperity, equality, fraternity, emancipation, regulation, tolerance, and rule of law in Europe and North America. The negative side enabled racism, enslavement, genocides, colonialism, capitalism, heteronormative sexism, and underdevelopment of other parts of the world (Quijano 2000; Mignolo 2011, 2021). What divides the positive side and the negative side in modernity has been variously named as the "colour line" by William E. B. Du Bois (1903); zone of being and zone of nonbeing by Frantz Fanon (1968); and "abyssal thinking" by Boaventura de Sousa Santos (2007) (see Santos 2017). Table 3.3 outlines a link between systems and structures of oppression with the injustices they produced as well as with the grammars/principles of justice that they provoked.

What appears in table 3.3 as structures and systems of domination are also known as "colonial matrix of power." Walter D. Mignolo and Catherine Walsh (2018, 142) depicted the colonial matrix of power as a "complex

Table 3.3 Structures and Systems of Injustices

Structures/Systems of Domination	*Forms/Types of Injustices*	*Grammars/Principles of Justice*
Racism	Discrimination Dismemberment Dehumanization Dispossession Feminization	Deracialization Egalitarianism Equality Re-membering Rehumanization Decolonization Decoloniality Human Rights Decolonial feminism Depatriarchization
Enslavement	Dehumanization Thingfication Violence Dispensability Exploitation Dismemberment	Abolition Reparations Rehumanization Re-membering Black Lives Matter Liberation Will to live
Colonialism	Conquest Genocides Dispossession Displacement Looting Pauperization	Decolonization Decoloniality Decolonial feminism Dewesternization Democratization Deracialization Depatriarchization Delinking Self-determination Empowerment Indigenization Land reclamation Recognition Restitution Reparations
Capitalism	Extractivism Exploitation Proletarianization Peasantization Destitution Underdevelopment Commodification Commercialization Dollarization	Socialism Communalism Decorporatization Trade unionism Labour rights Autonomous self-development Delinking Self-reliance De-dollarization De-growth Ecological movements
Patriarchy	Feminization Sexism Domestication Homophobia	Feminism Womanism Decolonial feminism Black feminism Equality Empowerment Inclusion LGBTQIA+1 Depatriarchization

Source: Drawn by the author.

structure of management and control composed on domains, levels and flows." As outlined in table 3.2, they operate at all levels and domains of modern human life. Sanín-Restrepo (2016) introduced the concepts of encryption of power and decryption of power to help us understand how the injustices listed in tables 3.2 and 3.3 were committed and how struggles for justice can be articulated.

On the one hand, the theory of encryption of power helps us to understand how a modern transcendent model of power called coloniality was constructed through the encryption of language to destroy communication, the transformation of knowledge to expertise, human beings from agents to subjects, the simulation of democracy to wilt it down into a low-intensity version, turning law into a means to hide power and meaning, and making constitutions temples of encrypted and solidified power as domination (Sanín-Restrepo 2016). Encryption also couples together power, capital, and knowledge for the sake of domination. The theory of decryption of power is a means to confront the encryption of power and reimagine a world of liberation, justice, and freedom.

Sanín-Restrepo and Machado-Araujo recently provided this definition of the encryption of power:

> The encryption of power . . . is the imposition of institutional simulations of difference that condition, neutralize or prohibit political agency, reducing difference to static and solid models of identity that pose as the only form of power. As any abstraction this one may be difficult to grasp, but it contains many of the building blocks of a definition. We could choose another set of words and yet another angle: to encrypt (power) is to simulate power (democratic, constituent) and to prohibit or condition being while collapsing political agency (constituent power, resistance) into fixed, final, transcendent, and solid structures (constituted power, law). (Sanín-Restrepo and Machado-Araujo 2020, 19)

This analysis takes us to the eight principles of the Bamako Appeal of 2013 formulated by the World Forum for Alternatives (WFA), which gives life to a decolonial paradigm of justice. Table 3.4 provides details.

These eight principles of the *Bamako Appeal* not only align with a decolonial paradigm of justice but also link very well with current struggles for environmental justice and cognitive justice. This construction of a decolonial paradigm of justice through the review of literature takes us to the examples of epistemic and environmental (in)justices. The epistemic and environmental (in)justices are inextricably intertwined.

Table 3.4 The Bamako Appeal Principles

Principle	*Articulation*
1. Construction of a world founded on the solidarity of human beings and peoples	Shift from competition to solidarity
2. Construction of a world founded on full affirmation of citizenship and equality of sexes	Active citizenship and eradication of all forms of patriarchy
3. Construction of a universal civilization offering all areas full potential of creative development to all its diverse members	Recognition of diversity as the basis of the spread of the best human qualities
4. Construction of socialization through democracy	Shift from socialization through markets to sociality as the principle of democratization
5. Construction of a world founded on recognition of the non-market-driven law of nature and of the resources of the planet and its agricultural soil	Liberation of life from commodification, privatization, and marketization as their threat to nature and life on the planet earth
6. Construction of a world founded on recognition of cultural products and scientific acquisitions, education, and of health care	Liberation of cultural products, knowledge, food, and health care from commodification and privatization
7. Promotion of policies informed by democracy and affirmation of autonomy of nations and peoples	Rescuing democracy from neoliberalism and affirmation of a democracy amenable to the autonomy of nations and peoples and their equality
8. Affirmation of the solidarity of peoples of the North and the South in the construction of an internationalism on an anti-imperialist basis	Shift from divisions imposed by racism, sexism, and classism to anti-imperialist front opposed to victimization by capitalism, imperialism, and militarism

Source: Drawn from the work of Amin (2019, 443–45).

THE EXAMPLES OF EPISTEMIC AND ENVIRONMENTAL (IN)JUSTICES AS FRAMING FOR ALL OTHER FORMS

The Indian psychologist Ashis Nandy (1983, 3) posited that "Perhaps that which begins in the minds of men must also end in the minds of men." This argument means that knowledge frames reality and, by extension, injustices are conceived epistemically before they are committed practically. For example, before genocides (killing of people), there are epistemicides (denial and killing of knowledges, cultures, and histories). The foundations of genocides are laid through the denial of humanity of the targets of genocides in the minds of genocidaires. Enslavement of a people is preceded by their denial of humanity in the minds of enslavers. The idea of Black people as natural slaves, born of a racial epistemic imaginary, enabled the hunting, kidnapping, and trafficking of African people as slaves across the Atlantic Ocean to work in the mines and plantations in the Americas. Without the coloniality of being (see Wynter 2003; Maldonado-Torres 2007) and its social classification and racial hierarchization of human population in accordance with differential ontological densities, the genocides of the native peoples would have been avoided (see Ndlovu-Gatsheni 2018).

The colonization of Africa, for example, was informed by a prior epistemic notion of their sub-humanity and assumed inferiority that had previously justified the enslavement of Africans. Philosophers as George Wilhelm Friedrich Hegel (1770–1831) in his *Lecturers on the Philosophy of World History* not only questioned the humanity of African people, depicting them as barbarians stuck in a state of nature, but also denied Africa space in his idea and philosophy of history (see Tibebu 2011). The Regius Professor of History at the University of Oxford, Hugh Trevor-Roper, as recently as the 1960s, could still deny the existence of African history, positing that before the arrival of Europeans there was nothing but "darkness" and that darkness was not a subject of history (Trevor-Roper 1965, 1969). These racist notions were used to justify colonialism as a civilizing mission. The paradigm of discovery, the claims of the discovery of "a new world," and the subsequent commission of genocides, conquest, and colonization of Latin America were driven by a prior notion of "empty lands" outside of Europe (see Blaut 1993). Capitalist extractivism is enabled by a conception of nature and humanity as natural and human resources available for exploitation. This is where the challenges of climate breakdown and biodiversity loss originate. This epistemic idea of natural resources available for humans to exploit was accompanied by the decoupling of the human from nature and the elevation of the human above nature. The result has been the current problematic age of the Anthropocene (see Chakrabarty 2021), which has provoked numerous environmental justice movements. Environmental (in)justices reflect the convergence of multiple systemic, structural, epistemic, and institutional forms of oppression.

THE SPECIFIC EXAMPLE OF ENVIRONMENTAL (IN)JUSTICES

The South African economist Sampie Terreblanche (2014) posed two important arguments about contemporary inequalities. The first is that the contemporary challenges of inequality and poverty cannot be understood "without understanding the ways in which 500 years of Western empire building, often with the complicity of the elites of the Restern world, have shaped our world into the deeply unequal and gratuitously unjust place that it is today" (Terreblanche 2014, 3). The second is, "We cannot hope to remedy the brokenness of our modern economic system without understanding the economic, social and political drivers that have brought us here, and that continue to dictate the narrative of institutionalized poverty and globalized inequality" (Terreblanche 2014, 3). The decolonial paradigm mapped above is founded on this logic. The environmental (in)justices are reflective of what Terreblanche terms the "brokenness of our modern economic system," and how this is harming the planet earth. The epistemology of extractivism driving the racial capitalist exploitative system is responsible for environmental injustices. Maria Lugones explained the cognitive needs of capitalism in these revealing words:

> The cognitive needs of capitalism include measurement, quantification, externalization (or objectification) of what is knowable with respect to the knower so as to control the relations among people and nature and among them with respect to it, in particular the property in means of production. This way of knowing was imposed on the whole capitalist world as the only valid rationality and as emblematic of modernity. (Lugones 2008, 8)

The consequence of this epistemology of extractivism, which is also the capitalist epistemology, has resulted in a new geological epoch (Anthropocene) characterized by the collapsing into each other of "human and non-human scales" (Chakrabarty 2021, 8). On the ground, a floodgate of battles and struggles over land rights, sacred sites, food security, local knowledge, and the right to health ensued (Schlosberg 1999, 2007; Schlosberg and Carruthers 2010). The most affected and indeed victims of environmental injustices are the First Nations/Indigenous Peoples, who have already been pushed to a high level of vulnerability as survivors of genocides, enslavement, dispossession, displacements, and racial capitalist exploitation (Ndlovu-Gatsheni 2020, 2023).

The example of the Mapuche of Southern Chile is very revealing of the dimensions and dynamics of environmental injustices and struggles for environmental justice. The Mapuche's life of struggles against Spanish colonialism and postcolonial Chilean governments in cohorts with multinational corporations has been long and is continuing. Like many Indigenous People across the modern world, the Mapuche have been victims of modernist discourses of "development" imposed by colonial and postcolonial governments. Loss of land through imposed reservations and redistributions of Indigenous lands to non-indigenous elites with commercial interests has resulted in the Mapuche remaining with 5% of their original territory

(Schlosberg and Carruthers 2010, 24). Under the 17 years of dictatorial military government of General Pinochet, which began concurrently with the global neoliberal project, the Mapuche territory was subjected to privatization, with mining and timber companies invading the land. These interventions provoked the Mapuche to mobilize themselves to fight for their existence.

The megaprojects such as the building of the Ralco Dam in the Upper Bio Bio River Basin at the heart of Mapuche territory resulted in the dispossession, displacement, and forced relocation of hundreds of Pehuenche families from their ancestral lands (Schlosberg and Carruthers 2010, 25). The contours of conflicts were not only about different interpretations of law but also about differing conceptions of development. These clashes were well captured by Domingo Namuncura, who said, "we don't want your progress to rob our culture" (Schlosberg and Carruthers 2010, 27). The Mapuche were angered by why their territory was targeted and interpreted these so-called development initiatives as amounting to "ethnocide." Timber acquisition by multinational companies in Arauco and Traiguen amounted to another intervention on the territory of the Mapuche. A Mapuche political prisoner Patricia Troncoso who embarked on a long-hunger strike wrote an open letter to the government in January 2008 stating: "From here, I want to encourage you to continue defending us from this predatory economic system that is seeking to pillage the little bit of nature we have left, and it is inhumane, because any economic project in our Mapuche territory is considered more valuable than we are, and immoral because the only human goals it leaves us are money and consumerism" (quoted in Schlosberg and Carruthers 2010, 29).

In the long-standing struggle of the Mapuche, it is clear how environmental justice encompasses land rights, sacred places rights, healing rights, recognition rights, religious rights, health rights, and indeed the very existence of an Indigenous people. Basically, environmental justice is about preservation and protection of the earth, ecological relationalities, interdependencies of all beings and selves (all species), and prevention of ecological destruction from "market colonization of society" (see Gordon 2021, 58).

What is hidden behind the environmental degradation of Indigenous people's territories is the denial of Indigenous people's knowledge of themselves and Indigenous ecological knowledge. What a decolonial paradigm of justice underscores is the connections of epistemicide and ecocide. Before any ecocide (destruction of conditions that sustain life), there is epistemicide (repudiation of Indigenous people's meaning-formations) (Karmakar and Chetty 2023, 1). This is why there is a need to understand that the threat to Indigenous people's lives and territories must be traced to the very arrival of "the Anthropoi" "from a land very far away" (see Gosh 2022, 10; Karmakar and Chetty 2023, 7).

This is why a decolonial paradigm of justice highlights the necessity of critical epistemic and political decolonial consciousness as an essential basis for any struggle and initiative aimed at advancing the case for any justice. The decolonial consciousness has to enable unlearning what was imposed by colonialism. It also entails openness to relearning for the purposes of advancing struggles and initiatives for justice. Building on this thinking, Sabelo J. Ndlovu-Gatsheni (2018) posited that for any sustainable justice to be achieved, there is a need to "seek epistemic freedom first." This means "casting light at last onto subjugated peoples, knowledges, histories and ways of living" and the transformation of "passive analysis into a generative force that valorizes and recreates life for the previously museumized" (Hoppers and Richards 2012, 8). At the center of the advancement of epistemic justice as an essential prerequisite for understanding other forms of injustices is rethinking thinking and unthinking thinking. Odora C. Hoppers and Howard Richards deliver the point clearly: "The task for rethinking thinking is therefore precisely this: to recognize the cultural asphyxiation of those numerous 'others' that has been the norm and work to bring other categories of self-definition, of dreaming, of acting, of living into the commons as a matter of universal concern" (Hoppers and Richards 2012, 8).

In a nutshell, the epistemic intervention forms the basis for understanding and indeed identification of which systems, structures, and institutions form an infrastructure of oppression, repression, and injustices and sustain racism, afterlives of enslavement noticeable in present-day exploitative labor regimes, postcolonial politics of inclusion, and exclusion which cause migrations, unequal distributions of opportunities and material resources, patriarchy, and sexism. It is racism, enslavement, colonialism, capitalism, and patriarchy which concentrated power, resources, and opportunities in the hands of a few. The epistemic intervention also goes straight to the task of cultivation of new consciousness amenable to intercultural understanding consonant with a world characterized by increased global human entanglements. Finally, new relationalities cannot be built with the knowledge which set afoot the present racisms and sexisms. There is a need for radical change at the epistemological level if a new coherent justice narrative for the IIED is to be rolled out (see table 3.4). This is why Verges posited that:

> The struggle for epistemic justice, which is to say, a struggle that demands equality between knowledges and contests the order of knowledge imposed by the West, is central. Decolonial feminisms are part of the long movement of scientific and philosophical re-appropriation that is revising the European narrative of the world. they contest the Western-patriarchal economic ideology that turns women, Black people, Indigenous people, and people from Asia and Africa into inferior beings marked by absence of reason, beauty, or a mind capable

> of technical and scientific discovery. The ideology has provided the basis for development policies that essentially say: "You are underdeveloped, but you can be developed if you adopt our technologies, our ways of solving social and economic problems. You must imitate our democracies, the best system, because you do not know what freedom, respects for the law, or separation of powers is." (Verges 2021, 13)

What Verges articulates is epistemicide as a precondition of ecocide. The most urgent task is how to roll out a well-conceived program for environmental justice. The starting point is to consider how to roll back epistemicides through the promotion of ecologies of knowledges (Santos 2007). The second is to identify the archives that carry knowledge for life rather than knowledge for profit. Indigenous Knowledge Systems (IKS) have to be recovered and promoted because they do not privilege extractive tendencies. In the first instance, it is in the African archive, which includes the myths of foundation and what was dismissed as animism, that one finds distributed agency among diverse beings and selves, without the human being monopolizing vital forces of life (Mbembe 2023).

The African metaphysics and those of other Indigenous peoples, there is no dualism of inert/passive/lifeless versus active/full of life, in the ecosystem (Mbembe 2023). The earth is conceived as a home for all species, and it is from this archive that a new general idea of ecology informed by a will to live of all beings and selves can be constructed (Mbembe 2023). The final point is that any genuine struggle and initiative for justice informed by anti-racist storytelling must not be "focused on symptoms of racism that we ignore the systemic problem" (Andrews 2019, 5). If one reads this intervention and does not feel uneasy and if it does not lead one to question the current world order and present ways of doing things, then I have failed. But if it makes you uneasy and provokes rethinking and unthinking, I have succeeded.

NOTES

1. Of course, even within Europe, there emerged other conceptions of being human that were opposed to the dominant ones pushed by scholastic elites and which buttressed the church doctrines. But these were not just a minority, they also remained just an opposition within Eurocentrism. The second issue to raise is that there was also "colonization" within Europe such as that of the British colonization of the Irish, where the Irish were subjected to inferiorization. However, these realities do not in any way diminish the need to shift to reparative epistemologies—away from dependence on knowledge based on philosophies from privileged white men to knowledges from the subaltern including women so as depatriarchize knowledge itself.

2. This invocation of the Global South is not oblivious of hierarchies of power, caste, gender, ethnicity, and others that existed some even before colonization within the Global South. However, the concept of the Global South makes even more sense now than before because of the way the countries of Africa, Asia, and Latin America (the Global Africa and the Global East) have expressed their desire for autonomous agency even within international affairs vis-à-vis the Russia–Ukraine War, which broke out on February 22, 2023. The Global South's push for a mediated solution to the war has stood out. There is also clear evidence of an emerging Global East led by China, which is poised to create solidarities with the Global Africa (Global East + Global Africa), making the idea of the Global South very meaningful.

BIBLIOGRAPHY

Amin, Samir. 2019. *The Long Revolution of the Global South: Towards a New Anti-Imperialist International.* New York: Monthly Review Press.

Andrews, Kehinde. 2019. *Back to Black: Black Radicalism for the 21st Century.* London: Zed Books.

Anzaldua, Gloria. 1987. *Borderlands La Frontera: The New Mestiza.* San Francisco, CA: Aunt Lute Books.

Blaut, J. M. 1993. *The Colonizer's Model of the World: Geographical Diffusion and Eurocentric History.* New York: Guilford Press.

Cesaire, Aime. 1955 [2000]. *Discourse on Colonialism.* New York: Monthly Review Press.

Chakrabarty, Dipesh. 2021. *The Climate of History in a Planetary Age.* Chicago, IL and London: The University of Chicago Press.

Chinweizu, Ibekwe. 1975. *The West and the Rest of Us: White Predators and Black Slavers and the African Elite.* New York: Random House.

Comaroff, J. and J. L. Comaroff, 2012. *Theory from the South Or, How Euro-America is Evolving Towards Africa.* Boulder, CO and London: Paradigm Publishers.

Crenshaw, Kimberle. 1995. "Mapping the Margins: Intersectionality, Identity Politics and Violence against Women of Colour." In K. Crenshaw, N. Gotanda, G. Peller and K. Thomas (eds.) *Critical Theory.* New York: The New Press, pp. 282–313.

Dabashi, Hamid. 2019. *Europe and Its Shadows: Coloniality After Empire.* London: Pluto Press.

Douglass, Frederick. 1845. *Narrative of the Life of Frederick Douglass, an American Slave.* Boston, MA: Anti-Slavery Office.

Douglass, Frederick. 1855. *My Bondage and My Freedom.* New York: Miller, Orton, and Mulligan.

Douglass, Frederick. 1881 [2008]. *The Life and Times of Frederick Douglass.* Radford, VA: Wilder Publications.

Du Bois, W. E. B. 1898. The Study of the Negro Problem." *Annals of the American Academy of Political and Social Science*, XI, January, pp. 1–23.

Du Bois, W. E. B. 1899. *The Philadelphia Negro: A Social Study*. Philadelphia, PA: University of Pennsylvania.

Du Bois, W. E. B. 1903. *The Souls of Black Folk*. New York: Dover Publications.

Dube, Saurabh. 2017. *Subjects of Modernity: Time-Space, Disciplines, Margins*. Manchester: University of Manchester Press.

Escobar, Arturo. 2004. "Beyond the Third World: Imperial Globality, Global Coloniality and Anti-Globalization Social Movements." *Third World Quarterly*, 25(1), pp. 207–30.

Etoke, Nathalie. 2019. *Melancholia Africana: The Indispensable Overcoming of the Black Condition*. Translated by Bill Hamlett. London and New York: Rowman & Littlefield International.

Fanon, Franz. 1963. *The Wretched of the Earth*. New York: Grove Press.

Ghosh, Amitav. 2022. *The Living Mountain*. New Delhi, India: Fourth Estate.

Giddens, Anthony. 1991. *The Consequences of Modernity*. London: Blackwell Publishers.

Gordon, L. R. 2000. *Existentia Africana: Understanding African Existential Thought*. New York: Routledge.

Gordon, L. R. 2021. *Freedom, Justice, and Decolonization*. New York and London: Routledge.

Gopal, Priyamvada. 2019. *Insurgent Empire: Anticolonial Resistance and British Dissent*. London and New York: Verso Books.

Grosfoguel, Ramón. 2011. "Decolonizing Post-Colonial Studies and Paradigms of Political-Economy: Transmodernity, Decolonial Thought, and Global Coloniality." *Transmodernity: Journal of Peripheral Cultural Productions of the Luso-Hispanic World*, 1(2), pp. 1–38.

Hobbes, Thomas. 1994. *Leviathan*. Indianapolis, IN: Hackett.

Hoppers, C. O. and H. Richards. 2012. *Rethinking Thinking: Modernity's "Other" and the Transformation of the University*. Pretoria: UNISA Press.

Kant, Immanuel. 1963. *Lectures and Ethics*. Translated by Louis Infield. New York: Harper & Row.

Kant, Immanuel. 1999. *Metaphysical Elements of Justice*. Translated by John Ladd. Indianapolis, IN: Hackett.

Karmakar, Goutam and Rejendra Chetty. 2023. "Episteme and Ecology: Amitav Ghosh's The Living Mountain and the Decolonial Turn." *South Asia Review*. https://doi.org/10.1080/02759527.2023.2206307.

Lu, Catherine. 2023. "Progress, Decolonization and Global Justice: A Tragic View." *International Affairs*, 99(1), pp. 141–59.

Lugones, María. 2007. "Heterosexism and the Colonial/Modern Gender System." *Hypatia: Journal Feminist Theory*, 22(1), pp. 186–209.

Lugones, María. 2008. "The Coloniality of Gender." *Worlds & Knowledges Otherwise*, Spring, pp. 1–17.

Lugones, María. 2010. Towards Decolonial Feminism." *Hypatia: Journal of Feminist Theory*, 25(4), Fall, pp. 742–59.

Lugones, María. 2003. *Pilgrimages/Peregrinajes: Theorizing Coalition Against Multiple Oppressions*. Lanham, MD: Rowman & Littlefield Publishers, Inc.

Mbembe, Achille. 2023. "The Earthly Community." Keynote Presentation Delivered at "The Changing African Idea of Africa and the Future of African Studies" Monthly Seminar Series, University of Bayreuth, Bayreuth, 20 April.

Mignolo, Walter. 1995. *The Darker Side of the Renaissance: Literacy, Territoriality and Colonization.* Ann Arbor, MI: University of Michigan Press.

Mignolo, Walter. 2000. *Local Histories/Global Designs: Coloniality, Subaltern Knowledges and Border Thinking*. Princeton, NJ: Princeton University Press.

Mignolo, Walter. 2011. *The Dark Side of Western Modernity: Global Futures, Decolonial Options*. Durham, NC and London: Duke University Press.

Mignolo, Walter. 2015. "Foreword: Yes, We Can." In Hamid Dabashi (ed.) *Can Non-Europeans Think*? London: Zed Books, pp. viii–xiii.

Mignolo, Walter. 2021. *The Politics of Decolonial Investigations.* Durham, NC and London: Duke University Press.

Mignolo, Walter. 2023. "It is a Change of Era, No Longer the Era of Changes." https://postcolonialpolitics.org/it-is-a-change-of-era-no-longer-the-era-of-changes/ (Accessed 23/03/2023).

Mignolo, Walter and Catherine Walsh. 2018. *On Coloniality: Concepts, Analytics, Praxis*. Durham, NC and London: Duke University Press.

Mill, J. S. *The Subjection of Women.* Mineola, NY: Dover Publishers.

Nandy, Ashis. 1983. *The Intimate Enemy: Loss and Recovery of Self under Colonialism.* Oxford: Oxford University Press.

Ndlovu-Gatsheni, Sabelo J. 2013. *Empire, Global Coloniality and African Subjectivity*. Oxford and New York: Berghahn Books.

Ndlovu-Gatsheni, Sabelo J. 2018. *Epistemic Freedom in Africa: Deprovincialization and Decolonization*. London and New York: Routledge.

Ndlovu-Gatsheni, Sabelo J. 2020. *Decolonization, Development and Knowledge in Africa: Turning Over a New Leaf.* London and New York: Routledge.

Ndlovu-Gatsheni, Sabelo J. 2022a. *Coloniality of Power in Postcolonial Africa: Myths of Decolonization: Second Edition*. Dakar: CODESRIA Books.

Ndlovu-Gatsheni, Sabelo J. 2022b. "Triple Internationalism: Imperialism, Marxism, and Decolonization." In Sabelo J. Ndlovu-Gatsheni and Morgan Ndlovu (eds.) *Marxism and Decolonization in the 21st Century: Living Theories and True Ideas*. London and New York: Routledge, pp. 89–108.

Ndlovu-Gatsheni, Sabelo J. 2023. *Beyond the Coloniality of Internationalism: Reworlding the World from the Global South*. Dakar: CODESRIA Books-In Press.

Ngugi wa Thiong'o. 2009a. *Re-membering Africa*. Nairobi: East African Publishers Ltd.

Ngugi wa Thiong'o. 2009b. *Something Torn and New: An African Renaissance*. New York: Basic Civitas Books.

Olukoshi, Adebayo and Paul Zeleza. 2004. "Introduction: The Struggle for African Universities and Knowledges." In Paul Tiyambe Zeleza and Adebayo Olukoshi (eds.) *African Universities in the Twenty-First Century. Volume one: Liberalization and Internationalism.* Dakar: CODESRIA Book Series, pp. 1–18.

Parnami, Komal. 2019. "Concept of Justice: Difficulties in Defining Justice." *International Journal of Law Management & Humanities*, 2(5), pp. 1–7.

Plato. 1981. *Five Dialogues*. Translated by G. M. A. Grube. Indianapolis, IN: Hackett.

Quijano, Anibal. 2000. "The Coloniality of Power and Social Classification." *Journal of World-Systems Research*, 6(2), Summer/Fall, pp. 342–86.

Rawls, John. 1971. *A Theory of Justice*. Cambridge, MA: Harvard University Press.

Reus-Smit, Christian and A. Ayşe Zarakol. 2023. "Polymorphic Justice and the Crisis of International Order." *International Affairs*, 99(1), pp. 1–22.

Robinson, Cedric J. 2000. *Black Marxism: The Making of Black Radical Tradition*. Chapel Hill, NC: University of North Carolina Press.

Rodney, Walter. 1972. *How Europe Underdeveloped Africa*. London and Dar es Salaam: Bogle-L'Ouverture Publications and Tanzania Publishing House.

Sanín-Restrepo, Ricardo. 2016. *Decolonizing Democracy: Power in a Solid State*. London and New York: Rowman & Littlefield International.

Sanín-Restrepo, Ricardo and Marinella Machado-Araujo. 2020. "The Theory of Encryption of Power: Itinerary of an idea." *Revista da Faculdade Mineira de Direito*, 23(45) 1833.

Sanín-Restrepo, Ricardo and Gabriel Méndez-Hincapíe. 2015. "Manifest Injustice from the (De)colonial Matrix: The Reversal of the Panoptic." *Philosophy and Social Criticism*, 41(1), pp. 29–36.

Santos, Boaventura de Souza. 2007. "Beyond Abyssal Thinking: From Global Lines to Ecologies of Knowledges." *Review*, XXX(1), pp. 45–89.

Santos, Boaventura de Souza. 2014. *Epistemologies of the South: Justice Against Epistemicide*. Boulder, CO and London: Paradigm Publishers.

Santos, Boaventura de Souza. 2017. *Decolonizing the University: The Challenge of Deep Cognitive Justice*. Newcastle upon Tyne: Cambridge Scholars Publishing.

Santos, Boaventura de Souza. 2018. *The End of the Cognitive Empire: The Coming of Age of Epistemologies of the South*. Durham, NC and London: Duke University Press.

Schlosberg, David. 1999. *Environmental Justice and the New Pluralism: The Challenge of Difference to Environmentalism*. Oxford: Oxford University Press.

Schlosberg, David. 2007. *Defining Environmental Justice*. Oxford: Oxford University Press.

Schlosberg, David and David Carruthers. 2010. "Indigenous Struggles, Environmental Justice, and Community Capabilities." *Global Environmental Politics*, 10(4), pp. 12–35.

Sen, Amartya. 2009. *The Idea of Justice*. Cambridge, MA: The Belknap Press of Harvard University Press.

Tamale, Sylvia. 2020. *Decolonization and Afro-Feminism*. Ottawa: Daraja Press.

Terreblanche, Sampie. 2014. *Western Empires: Christianity, and the Inequalities Between the West and the Rest 1500–2010*. Johannesburg: Penguin Books.

Thiam, Cheikh. 2014. *Return to the Kingdom of Childhood: Re-Envisioning the Legacy of and Philosophical Relevance of Negritude*. Columbus, OH: Ohio University Press.

Tibebu, Teshale. 2011. *Hegel and the Third World: The Making of Eurocentrism in World History*. Syracuse, NY: Syracuse University Press.

Tomba, Massimiliano. 2019. *Insurgent Universality: An Alternative Legacy of Modernity*. Oxford: Oxford University Press.

Trevor-Roper, Hugh Redwald. 1965. *The Rise of Christian Europe*. London: Thames and Hudson.

Trevor-Roper, Hugh Redwald. 1969. "The Past and the Present: History and Sociology." *Past and Present*, 42, pp. 3–17.

Vargas, Joao H. and Moon-Kie Jung. 2021. "Antiblackness of the Social and the Human." In Moon-Kie Jung and Joao H. Cast Vargas (eds.) *Antiblackness*. Durham, NC and London: Duke University Press, pp. 1–14.

Verges, Françoise. 2021. *A Decolonial Feminism*. London: Pluto Press.

Verges, Françoise. 2022. *A Feminist Theory of Violence*. London: Pluto Press.

Walcott, Rinaldo. 2014. "The Problem of the Human: Black Ontologies and 'the Coloniality of Our Being." In Sabine Broeck and Carsten Junker (eds.) *Postcoloniality—Decoloniality—Black Critique: Joints and Fissures*. Frankfurt and New York: Campus Verlag, pp. 93–108.

Wallerstein, Immanuel. 1997. "Eurocentrism and Its Avatars: The Dilemmas of Social Science." *New Left Review,* 226(November–December), pp. 93–104.

Waterfield, Robin. 2000. *The First Philosophers*. New York: Oxford University Press.

Weber, Max. 1905. *The Protestant Ethic and the Spirit of Capitalism*. London: Penguin Books.

Wynter, Sylvia. 1991. "Columbus and the Roots of the Propter Nos." *Annals of Scholarship*, 8(2), pp. 251–86.

Wynter, Sylvia. 2001. "Towards the Sociogenic Principle: Fanon, Identity, the Puzzle of Conscious Experience." In Mercedes F. Duran-Cogan and Antonio Gomez-Moriana (eds.) *National Identities and Socio-Political Change in Latin America*. New York: Routledge, pp. 30–66.

Wynter, Sylvia. 2003. "Unsettling the Coloniality of Being/Power/Truth/Freedom: Towards the Human, after Man, Its Overrepresentation: An Argument." *New Centennial Review,* 3(3), pp. 257–337.

Zeleza, Paul Tiyambe. 2021. *Africa and the Disruptions of the Twenty-First Century*. Dakar: CODESRIA Books.

Chapter 4

The Communal Practice of *Quilombismo* as a Technique of Decryption

Forms of (R)existence through the Subversion of Colonial Encryption

Bethania Assy and Rafael Rolo

"Our laws are not generally known; they are kept secret by the small group of nobles who rule us," says a mysterious Kafkian narrator at the beginning of the short story entitled "The Problem of Our Laws" (Kafka 1946). The beauty of Kafkian stories lies precisely in the fact that the situations presented are never so far away from an experience which is somewhat problematically universal, radically transcendental, and embedded in a sort of familiarity which simply makes the reader feel uneasy, in a state of *Unheimlichkeit* (Freud 2019).[1]

That the laws are not generally known to us means that they are encrypted. The few ruling men, in order to maintain their rule over the many, have a way of making apparent just enough to keep all of those who do not share the same traits as them (be it a so-called virtue, be it property, be it the color of the skin, or the gender one performs) away from that relevant public space in which influence is tipped, where decisions are made, and over which opinions count.

In this way, encryption is deemed a technique that ascertains a sort of "bastard" power (a *potestas* in the sense of Sanín-Restrepo's [2018] contribution). This *potestas* is termed "bastard" in the sense that it is decoupled from power's effective origin, which never lies immediately in a specific state apparatus, such as the police, a specific branch of government, or a specific privileged stratum of noblemen, but in the very fact of the multitude. Democracy, in this sense, albeit being the immanent reality of every political system, is not always "*at hand*" (in the Heideggerian double sense of being *Vorhand/Zuhand*, that is, of being actually available "for grabbing").

Said technique of encryption separates the political system from its supposed teleology and institutional meaning. To decrypt *potestas* means to approximate political institutions to the origins of power, an origin which is never "past," which is never merely a case of documented history in the Athenian constitution or other specific historical experience, but which is ever so present, as a specific dimension of the Machiavellian *virtù*, as a virtual dimension for political chance. Revolutions tend to make this otherwise merely gleaming chance their actuality to impose real change.

But, for change to thrive, it needs to encrypt new forms of life and of government. Therefore, a new moment for encryption comes into play. Is it possible to present encryption differently than as a technique to ascertain a *potestas*? Is it possible to think of decryption not only as an emancipatory tendency? These new questions pose a different topology for consideration. Instead of a binary contraposition, we present a more nuanced picture in which encryption and decryption are not judged simply by what they might abstractly mean, but by how they actually function.

Racism, patriarchy, and heteronormativity are common ways in which power is concealed and exerted, akin to a form of encryption. These systems not only mask power but also interpret and categorize differences in a dangerous and detrimental way, as to define an "internal enemy" or an "absolute Other," contributing to the unjust ideas that some lives are less valuable or even disposable. This process is akin to making certain individuals or groups appear as mere objects or targets, undermining their humanity and rights. Encryption is never radical and absolute in the sense of not admitting some form of decryption from the outset. Otherwise, it would tend to pure entropy and communication would be all but impossible; it would be pure chaos, which would be antithetical to any political form of government. Thus, the real question must be then which form of "*en/de-cryption*?"

Another example, this time on the side of legitimacy, is that of those minor languages, of slangs, of streetwise, of *l'argot*. Think of verlan, *pretuguês*, or the way young, often poor, and black communities tend to radically appropriate the official language to encrypt their particular meanings so that others are truly refrained from even understanding a word of what is being said. Encryption is not merely a technique for the institution of potestas, this decoupled and illegitimate form of power, for it might also be deemed a technique of and for resistance (or, as will be put forward, of "[r]existance"). Encryption and decryption, in this sense, are not merely techniques for creating a bastard form of power, but also for resisting that very form of *potestas*. Once again, the real question is which form of "*en/de-cryption*?"

The following essay will deal with the notion of "*quilombismo*," a hardly translatable term which means a specific sort of technique for "counter-colonization," that is, of (R)existance against that potestas which obnubilates racial difference. This essay intends to present some guidelines to what is termed as a conducting question concerning the matter of the "decryption of justice," which is: How does the practice of *quilombismo* subvert the hegemonic form of encryption of power (in the form of Sanín-Restrepo's potestas) by instituting a communal sphere of resistance through new territorial and social filters which tend to contrapose the project of coloniality in order to ascertain new ways of being and of life?

To address the proposed issue, this essay is divided into three sections. First, it will consider the presentation of the issue of "en/de-cryption," in the sense of Sanín-Restrepo (2018), as already advanced in this brief introduction. Second, the literature on the phenomenon of "*quilombismo*" will be presented to respond to three basic questions: (a) what precisely is "*quilombismo*?" (b) Why "*quilombismo*?" and (c) How does "*quilombismo*" work? Third, the practices of "*quilombismo*" will be presented in the horizon of en-/de-cryption, discussing the need for the movement to build an interface with its outside, be that in the sense of a direct form of resistance or in the sense of opening up to alliances with non-members of the "*quilombismo*" movement.

EN/DE-CRYPTION: WHAT DOES IT MEAN? HOW DOES IT WORK?

First and foremost, one must consider the question: What does encryption/decryption mean? Is encryption really a new form of power *device*? Can democratic principles truly coexist with the practices of encryption?

Legal studies, as much as any form of science, have always been considered a discipline of lore as much as an exclusionary social practice. Following Bourdieu (2014, 176 ff.), legal discourse is both *esoteric* and *exoteric*. This double-edged scientific discourse, for instance, is responsible for fixing different social actors in different roles played either by experts and professionals or by laypeople and the "profane." This way, scientific discourse insulates itself from the influence of common sense and those non-initiated as much as confides the definition of its very *dynamis* to a caste of representatives who embody a recognizable noble *stratum*.

What differentiates this double dimension of scientific discourse and the phenomena of encryption? Beyond the dual esoteric-exoteric condition of traditional scientific discourse, encryption is the effect of a specific entanglement between language and a purposeful form of severance, which does not simply aim at preserving a form of discipline that protects and validates scientific truth-discourse but goes further dividing the *demos* from its very potency (its "*potential*"). Encryption, in the sense of Sanín-Restrepo and Méndez-Hincapíe (2018), instantiates a perverse form of disempowerment of the multitude, severing it from within, so that legal language is deemed the realm of the few who accumulate power (*potestas*) and therefore are able to interpret and apply it according to their own private whims, pervading any form of control from the multitude. Encryption does not simply aim at protecting and validating a scientific aspect of political discourse. Its main goal is the very severance between the *potentia* of the multitude (democracy) and the power of a select group of social agents (*potestas*).

As Sanín-Restrepo (2018) puts it, the "power of encryption goes far beyond the simple muddling or deliberate concealment of language," but "secures the smooth perfection of a predatory system, and it guarantees the destruction of democracy in its name, with all the horrors imbued in the term: colonization, famine, wars, violence of gender, racism, legal expropriation, and the Empire of Capital" (2018, xvii). Specifically, encryption is a device for "occluding politics" (Sanín-Restrepo 2018, xvii) by leveling differences and breaking communication, that is, by impeding democracy.

Sanín-Restrepo and Méndez-Hincapíe (2018) attribute this encryption scheme to the fact that capitalism cannot thrive without parasitizing the sovereign State. This parasitical dynamic produces a "porous sovereignty" (Sanín-Restrepo and Méndez-Hincapíe 2018), that is, it weaponizes sovereignty in favor of the sheer and reckless expansion of capitalism. "Porosity" in this context means basically that the a priori closed quarters of the national sovereign State are breached by the purely economic logic of Capital, colonizing every other extraeconomic asset in favor of the imperatives of that perfidious expansion, impeding democratic means to counterbalance it.

Especially in the case of democracy, when faced with the ruthless development of the Capitalist logic, this process of colonization is mainly secured by three means, which are: the privatization of the commons, the depoliticizing of social conflicts, and the failure of the promises of democracy. These three mechanisms are tributaries of the colonization of different areas of social life by the strictly economic logic of capitalism. The privatization of the commons is seen through the privatization of politics, by the reduction of political affairs to the condition of phenomena "in the market," denying democracy from effectively exerting any kind of influence. Second, by the depoliticization of social conflicts, such reduction of other social logics to that of the economy is taken a step further, in that the economy becomes "scientific," social and class struggles become pathological, and the ruling elite manages to naturalize its very privileged position over the masses. Finally, democracy fails altogether in its promises for further inclusion, rendering formal equality an axiom that enables liberal ideology to cynically assume individualism and utilitarianism as ground rationalities. Encryption is thus secured. That is, "the monopoly of a hegemonic group over reality" (Sanín-Restrepo 2018, xix) is thus instituted and fiercely protected against any form of self-criticism. It becomes literally "autoimmune" in that its very logic corrodes the very fundaments of social life.

Sanín-Restrepo and Mendéz-Hincapíe give the example of the American Constitution of 1787 and its subsequent amendments as powerful examples of an encrypting device. According to the authors, "the U.S. Constitution is the most systematic and sophisticated effort and, therefore, the most successful one to dismantle democracy and its constant threat to capitalism" (Sanín-Restrepo and Mendéz-Hincapíe 2018, 09). Despite the bold colors, the main argument is that, according to Sanín-Restrepo and Mendéz-Hincapíe, the American Constitution is a mechanism that enables the events presented above as means toward encryption, which are: the privatization of the commons, the depoliticizing of social conflicts, and the failure of the promises of democracy.

To assess the argument in its entirety, one needs to consider the fear of democracy that constitutes one of the driving forces of the American constitutional moment. This almost irrational fear is something that was thoroughly presented and discussed throughout the works and opinions published by the so-called "Founding Fathers" (Sanín-Restrepo and Mendéz-Hincapíe 2018, 09). Consider the Federalist Papers, for instance, and it is possible to see how the Republican form is so construed that it disengages any form of direct democratic stance, in that democracy is reduced to its "representative" aspect. This *coup de-main* allows the American Founding Fathers to establish and naturalize a direct relation between democracy and liberalism, delegitimizing the dangerous "factions" which might oppose the ruling elite, as well as framing social conflicts according to the considered neutral language of the Law.

By instituting the Judiciary Branch the way it did, the American Constitution operates a transformation of social conflicts into sophisticated legal arguments and procedures (Sanín-Restrepo and Mendéz-Hincapíe 2018, 12), filtering more radical approaches in favor of a sovereigntist Supreme Court, supposedly considered the "least dangerous branch" in relation to the other two branches of government, because it allegedly has no direct access to the budget or the army, but is a very effective device in favor of disempowering the *demos*.

Following the constitutional frame, Law reveals itself as radically both *esoteric* and *exoteric*, in such a way that the ways of direct democracy are simply disabled. The constitution is turned into a "purely techno-legal content" (Sanín-Restrepo and Méndez-Hincapíe 2018, 13), following the elitist legal language in the hands of few experts who are let free to interpret it the way they see fit, escaping any real possibility of democratic control outside of their own technocratic circles.

Even the supposedly transparent and accessible part of the constitution is not safe from the reach of encrypting strategies. Consider, for example, the idea of a constitution that starts with a grand and eloquent reference to "*We the people . . .*" and, not long after, instates the three-fifths rule on Article I, Section 2, Paragraph 3. Consider the fact that the fourteenth amendment establishes in its first section the due process clause in favor of all persons born and naturalized in the United States, while it excludes so-called "Indians not taxed" as well as women from representation in its following section. Consider, finally, the fact that the female vote was only authorized according to American Law in 1920, after the passing of the nineteenth amendment, but stated that Congress needed to enforce the article by proper legislation, a clause which ended by determinately postponing the access of women to the political realm and lastly postponing the actual and effective enfranchisement of African American and Native-American women, as well as other minorities.

Following Sanín-Restrepo and Mendéz-Hincapíe (2018):

> The encrypted constitution presupposes, in the first place, a progressive entanglement of language and of the interpretation not only of the constitution and the law, but of images and every information chain that "constitutes" reality, that strips away any commonsense and any possibility of common knowledge and public interaction until it becomes an exclusive capital of experts. Second, a stark shift in decision-making lines where, increasingly, decisions are not made in open political forums but rather in expert forums subtracted from the most basic rule of responsibility and public discussions. (Sanín-Restrepo 2014, 207)

To counter encryption, Sanín-Restrepo suggests the need for developing "creolization" techniques of decrypting. To be precise, it is important to keep in mind that no encryption is "absolute." Absolute encryption would be a paradox in its own terms, for it would actually constitute a mere form of murmuring, or a senseless soliloquy. Encryption plays with a cynical form of transparency. It shows something in order to hide the essential scheme behind its very nature. To advocate for the development of a strategic form of decryption means to invert (or subvert) this very logic, to bring it to the surface and instead of hiding and crippling the democratic ideal, to enable it in some manner by giving a say to those excluded from the elite of techno-legality.

If encryption means the "intentional hiding of the meaning of language," decrypting means the intentional upheaval of liberal discourse, connecting politics to its democratic immanence, in order to distribute power and not encapsulate it, to favor potentia in detriment to potestas. Decryption, according to Sanín-Restrepo, "does not produce a final result—a synthesis—but the opening of the possibility of conflict in language" (Sanín-Restrepo, 2018, xxi). It secures the terrain in which the agonic dimension of democracy might flourish. Instead of being a sort of "tabula rasa," decryption is the "razor's edge" cutting through the molded fabric of second nature reality instituted by liberalist exclusionary elites.

Sanín-Restrepo associates decryption with a "poetics of creolization" which seeks to "destroy genesis and mythical lines that support hierarchies," dissolving "absolute, binary, and defined identities, where there are two imagined origins defined in opposition" (2018, xxiv). Decryption through creolization uses language against the oppressor, encrypts the other way around to exclude the excluder from meaningful interaction, leaving him merely mumbling.

QUILOMBISMO: WHAT? WHY? HOW?

Many studies in Brazil are being conducted on the practice of "*quilombismo*," starting with Abdias do Nascimento, but traversing the academic and militant stances of Beatriz Nascimento, Clóvis Moura, Sueli Carneiro, among others.

"*Quilombismo*" is a neologism derived from the word Quilombo. Following Beatriz Nascimento (2018), the roots of the "Quilombo," as a socio-political organization of formerly enslaved African Brazilians, are traced back to the Angolan-Jagan institution of "*kilombo*." *Kilombo* is an ambiguous word in its origin. It originally referred to the warrior unity of the Imbangala (also known as Jaga), a nomadic warrior group that disrupted the Congolese Royalty at the time the Portuguese expanded human trafficking in Western Africa. *Kilombo* also refers either to the rites of initiation or to the sacred space in which these rites took place. Young adolescents from conquered groups were subjected to such rites of passage to be considered Imbangalan warriors and, therefore, to take part in the *kilombo*.[2] Either as an institution, a sacred site, or as a rite of passage designed to enlist the youth in the ranks of the Imbangala, the "*kilombo*" is a set of social and political practices in which the Jaga Nation would assimilate new members not through filiation but through intensive forms of alliances. These practices at last trespassed the Atlantic during the sixteenth and seventeenth centuries, merging in Brazil as a *Quilombo*.

In the Brazilian Northeast, in the former Capitania de Pernambuco, one of the most famous and most successful Quilombos of them all, the "Quilombo dos Palmares," coalesced. Its direct relationship with its African counterparts cannot be dismissed, even though in Palmares the idea of a Quilombo meant a sort of intermingling organization between the Angolan monarchic state-like regime and the Jaga nomadic war machine. It is for that very reason that Palmares was also called "Angola-Janga" (Nascimento 2018, 281–82). Before continuing, it is necessary to remember that with the violent dissolution of the social and political organization of the Palmares' Quilombo, in the seventeenth century, our opportunity of adequately understanding the communitarian experience which thrived and blossomed within the Palmarian society was dissolved as well. Clóvis Moura (1988, 161) begins by signaling the sheer absence of significant traces about the specificities and particularities of the Palmarian way of life. Despite the scarcity of historical records, it is still possible to formulate insights based on the documents that have survived, primarily through the Portuguese and Dutch colonial administrations. Additionally, by examining the foundational elements of the myths that envelop the phenomenon of Quilombo dos Palmares, one can appreciate its significance during its existence and thereafter. This extends into the social, political, and historical consciousness of Brazilians and their self-perception.

Palmares was as much a monarchy as an association designed with a well-distributed martial hierarchy. The constitution of Palmares as a military society is inevitably derived from the inexpungeable vicinity of its enemies, which were mainly the "*latifundiários*" (*ergo* the landowners characterized by the extensiveness of their estate) located in the region. Clóvis Moura (1988, 170) contends that the Palmarian mode of life and production fundamentally and existentially clashed with the colonial and slave-driven plantation system. Notwithstanding, Palmares resisted Portuguese and Dutch colonialism for a whole century, from 1595 until 1696, becoming an inescapable model of a viable social and political alternative to the slave system. As Deleuze and Guattari (1972, 257) would put it, Palmares "horizons" the Quilombo-form, serving as an all-encompassing model and ideal-form. Even though it is correct to assert that from a certain point of view, further historical experience and knowledge of the Quilombos in Brazilian lands tend to drift apart from the original experience of Palmares (Nascimento 2018, 282).

What differentiates the quilombos of the seventeenth century with those that come later, according to Beatriz Nascimento, is that each Quilombo, individually considered, slowly stops being considered as a danger to the instituted system of slavery (Nascimento 2018, 284). While individual Quilombos were not perceived as inherently threatening, the shadow of the Haitian Revolution cast over Brazil in the nineteenth century gave rise to the concept of "black danger" (Nascimento 2018, 284), which is going to be politically weaponized against the integration of the black community in the whole of Brazilian society in the final stages of slavery and beyond.

Deriving from the idea-force of "quilombo," Abdias do Nascimento draws the concept of "*quilombismo*." "*Quilombismo*" is first and foremost a response to colonial oppression and enslavement conducted by white

Europeans in Brazil (Nascimento 2018, 151). Nevertheless, it is still to this day an actual and much-needed form of resistance against the cynical and murderous white supremacism of the Brazilian elites, considering that the abolition of slavery in Brazil in 1888 was not followed by the full integration of the Black community into Brazilian society. Furthermore, it expresses the desire for a radical reassessment of African history in Brazil. "*Quilombismo*" is thus a political and cultural response, in the manner of a "*riposte,*" to all the sophisticated methods employed by the Brazilian elites that factually hinder black Brazilians from recognizing and embracing their ethnic, historical, and cultural heritage (Nascimento 2018, 141).

Quilombos are an undeniable part of Brazilian history and of the radical resistance established by former enslaved against the established obnoxious Colonial or Imperial State. Consequently, Abdias do Nascimento is clear when upholding that (a) neither did every Quilombo was necessarily considered illegal by the colonial and imperial state and (b) nor was the experience of *quilombismo* an exclusive Brazilian peculiarity (Nascimento 2018, 152). Since a quilombo is recognized as a form of association that originated directly from the imperative need of enslaved individuals to resist captivity (Nascimento 2018, 152), the multiplicity of its expressions entails considering every space in which African cultural and physical resistance takes place as a *quilombo*. We are referring to "brotherhoods, clubs, terreiros (houses of worship of Afro-Brazilian religion), tendas, afoches, samba schools, gafieiras, grêmios, confrarias," which might be recognized as quilombos as well (Nascimento 1980, 152). Because of this broad definition, not all quilombos were considered illegal associations. Many quilombos were tolerated to an extent by the state and church, according to Abdias do Nascimento (Nascimento 1980, 152). On the other hand, Abdias do Nascimento draws parallels between Brazilian quilombos and "the legacy of cumbes, palenques, cimarrones and maroons" (Nascimento 1980, 152), well-documented cultural expressions throughout the Americas, which also constitute forms of alternative Black political organization. This entire "complex" phenomenon is what Abdias do Nascimento terms as *quilombismo* (Nascimento 1980, 152).

If, according to Foucault, any system of oppression inherently contains within it the seeds of opposition or resistance, *quilombismo*, as understood here, is as old a phenomenon as the Portuguese and Dutch colonial and slavery systems. It is a long-standing strategy through which the Black community has historically countered and continues to counter the forces aimed against them, whether it be enslavement, colonialism, state violence, or oppression. In Abdias do Nascimento's (1980, 153) precise words:

> The Quilombist model has remained active as an idea-force, a source of energy inspiring models of dynamic organization, since the fifteenth century. In this

> dynamic, almost always heroic process, Quilombismo is in a constant process of revitalization and remodernization, attending to the needs of the various historical times and geographical environment.

To depict the force of this concept, it is useful to consider the work of Sueli Carneiro. Even though Carneiro is not known for delving into the meanders of *quilombismo* as a concept, her militant and theoretical efforts to address racial inequalities and promote social justice are aligned with the principles of resistance, resilience,[3] community, and cultural affirmation that are central to *quilombismo*. For instance, Carneiro is the founder of "*Géledés—Instituto da Mulher Negra*," a Non-Governmental Organization which stands out as a leading force in Brazilian black feminist thought, aiming at the integration of unique anti-racist and feminist conceptual frameworks with practices designed to embody the resistance against misogynistic and racist practices, systems, and structures.

In her most recent book, which is the commercial edition of her Doctoral Thesis, Carneiro (2023) discusses the concepts of the *racial dispositive*. These concepts, each in their own accord, give a special understanding of the importance of *quilombist* practice and theoretical disquiet. Carneiro's racial dispositive (2023, 33–37) is a notion derived from Charles Mills' (1997) theoretical analysis of the "racial contract." According to Mills' racial contract, a racial society, a racial state, and a racial legal system are established and organized in such a way that the racial division, between whites and nonwhites, is considered of its essence. Following Mills, the "purpose of this state, by contrast with the neutral state of classic contractarianism, is, inter alia, specifically to maintain and reproduce this racial order, securing and maintaining the subordination of nonwhites" (Mills 1997, 14). Different from classical contract theories (the "political" notion of contract), such as Hobbes, Locke, Rousseau, and Kant, and drawing an important critique of John Rawls' modern contractualism (the "moral" notion of contract), Mills' theoretical frame proposes to keep the descriptive approach of classic contract theories while considering the normative aspects of a contractualist theory that is not only in the position of considering how things must be, but is also able to explain how things have become (Carneiro 2023, 35).

The racial contract is a historical fact, for it is the world in which "we live." As such, it differs from the hypothetical contract of classical theorists as well as Rawls' theory (Mills 1997, 30). According to Mills (1997, 11):

> The Racial Contract is that set of formal or informal agreements or meta-agreements (higher-level contracts about contracts, which set the limits of contracts' validity) between the members of one subset of humans, henceforth designated by (shifting) "racial" (phenotypical/genealogical/cultural) criteria

> C_1, C_2, C_3... as "white," and coextensive (making due allowance for gender differentiation) with the class of full persons, to categorize the remaining subset of humans as "nonwhites" and of a different and inferior moral status, subpersons, so that they have a subordinate civil standing in the white of white-ruled politics the whites either already inhabit or establish or in transactions as aliens with these polities, and the moral and juridical rules normally regulating the behavior of whites in their dealings with one another either do not apply at all in dealings with nonwhites or apply only in a qualified form depending in part on changing historical circumstances and what particular variety of nonwhites is involved, but in any case the general purpose of the Contract is always the differential privileging of the whites as a group with respect to the nonwhites as a group, and the denial of equal socioeconomic opportunities to them. All whites are *beneficiaries* of the Contract, though some whites are nor *signatories* to it.

The racial device, as developed by Sueli Carneiro (2023, 30–31), is a derivative of Foucault's "power device" (1976). According to Carneiro's concept, the racial device is constituted through embedded social and political representations about black people, as developed since the colonial period, allowing discourses and practices that justified the establishment of a nefarious division between masters and slaves. Through this division, black people are relegated to a position where they are not subjects of their own bodies, history, or knowledge, but are objects in the hands of the whites.

Drawing from Foucault's ideas, knowledge and power are deeply intertwined. The type of knowledge that is valued and pursued in a society is shaped by its power dynamics. Conversely, the existing power structures influence what kind of knowledge is produced, encouraging certain types of understanding while suppressing or discouraging others. Essentially, the flow of knowledge and the nature of power are mutually reinforced, each shaping and being shaped by the other. In Brazil, the racial device has significantly contributed to the epistemicide of Black culture, reinforcing the flawed narrative of a Brazilian "racial democracy." The device also extols miscegenation and "mestizaje" for supposedly harmonizing effects, yet it simultaneously obscures the biopolitical violence against Black individuals, manifesting starkly in the favelas (Carneiro 2023).

According to Sueli Carneiro (2023, 52):

> The myth of racial democracy corresponds to the desire for a self-representation of society and a positive representation of the country in response to the "internalized and scientifically legitimized inferiority complex." It serves to construct a positive identity for a country whose concrete reality prevents the effective realization of Westernization, whether racial or cultural. As Sílvio Romero states in History of Brazilian Literature, "There's no point in arguing; we are

> mixed-race, that's a fact and that's enough! . . . If we are not mixed-race in blood, we are mixed-race in spirit."

To face these terrible odds imposed on the Black Community, Sueli Carneiro considers the necessity and importance of Black Resistance. If no device of power is instituted without making possible the insurgence of the means of resisting it, Black Resistance is no younger than the racial contract itself. According to Carneiro (2023, 139), the first barricade is instituted by mere survival.[4] For a black body to stay alive is in itself a form of resistance against the biopolitics of racism which, especially in Brazil, still advocates, as it has been doing for more than five centuries, for the dire need of a "whitening" process of society (culturally, politically as much as demographically). According to Carneiro (2023, 139), only while remaining alive does the black person might preserve their physical and cognitive abilities to understand and develop a proper conceptual as much as material criticism of the racial exclusion processes to which they are constantly subjected, pointing out paths for individual and collective emancipation.

QUILOMBISMO AS A FORM OF RADICAL EN-/DE-CRYPTION?

After this brief summary of the movement of en-/de-cryption and of the state-of-the-art in sociological and anthropological studies on the phenomena of "*quilombismo*," and following the thread of this brief study, the main question left to consider is: How does the practice of "*quilombismo*" subvert the hegemonic form of encryption of power (in the form of Sanín-Restrepo's potestas) by instituting a communal sphere of resistance through new territorial and social filters which tend to contrapose the project of coloniality in order to ascertain new ways of being and of life?

"*Quilombismo*" is a technique of (r)existance, of existing and standing in the mode of resisting oppression, a resistance that is possible only through the development of communal ways of being and living, ways that are radically at odds with those imposed by *potestas*. Just as importantly, *aquilombar-se* means an act of resisting the racial contract and the epistemicide as much as the murderous biopolitical system imposed by hegemonic *potestas* on those divergent forms of life and thinking, whether on ethical, aesthetic, academic, or juridical terms.

The racial contract implies a dynamic of securing the persistent production of social and political indigence. This is achieved through the negation of access to formal basic rights, such as health, education, and proper housing, as well as through the production of intellectual inferiorities and the many forms of delegitimization of the ways of non-hegemonic/non-dominant groups (such as black, women, LGBTQIA+, and autochthonous/Indigenous individuals). The racial divide is one of the prominent forms of illegitimate encryption, that is, of *potestas*. *Aquilombar-se*, that is, to consider the (r) existing through the practices of *quilombismo*, aims at resisting the colonizing encryption.

In short, "*aquilombar-se*" means to gather around; it means to create a safe space of mutual aid and care. It means to gather around a decolonizing project, resisting the space in which governing *potestas* has forcefully placed these heterotypical bodies and cultures, where the very affirmation of radical differences is requested in the sense that both encryption and decryption tend to be nurtured to affirm a decolonial form of life. *Aquilombar-se* is an ongoing action/process of resistance.

Sanín-Restrepo (2018, xxii) describes decryption as a "poetics of creolization," saying that "decryption is at the same time the intense use of the faculties of theoretical thinking and the critical putting to work of praxis, but poetics overflows these previous endeavors with a primordial knowledge that truth is only in the becoming of the new" (Sanín-Restrepo 2018, xxii). Poetic, therefore, is "the unfounded foundation for the emergence of the new. On the other side of the spectrum, encryption ensures that the novelty is driven back to a mechanical predictability of it in the model" (Sanín-Restrepo 2018, xxii). This poetics as "creolization" aims to destroy "genesis and mythical lines that support hierarchies," dissolving "absolute, binary, and defined identities, where there are two imagined origins defined in opposition" (Sanín-Restrepo 2018, xxiv), finally encrypting the "language of the dominator to return it poisoned" (Sanín-Restrepo 2018, xxv).

According to Abdias do Nascimento, *Quilombismo* is an Afro-Brazilian political and cultural movement that draws inspiration from the historical quilombos. Quilombos were more than just communities; they were socio-political gatherings in a broader and more varied sense and form, developed by escaped enslaved Africans in Brazil. As stated above, quilombos were not just refuges for escaped slaves but also sites of resistance against colonial oppression and slavery, embodying African cultural retention and autonomy.

The concept of *quilombismo* extends beyond the historical context of these quilombos. It is envisioned as a broader ideological and political framework that advocates for the recognition and valorization of African heritage and culture in Brazil. *Quilombismo* is a form of resistance against the ongoing racial, cultural, and social marginalization of Afro-Brazilians. It calls for the reassessment of Brazilian history from an Afro-centric perspective, acknowledging the contributions and struggles of African descendants in shaping Brazilian culture and its perception of its specificity as a nation. *Quilombismo* also serves as a critique of the myth of "racial democracy" in Brazil—a notion that suggests racial harmony and equality while ignoring the persistent racial inequalities and discrimination in society. *Quilombismo* challenges this fallacious narrative of a "racial democracy" in Brazil, highlighting the systemic issues and interdictions that Afro-Brazilians continue to face.

Furthermore, *quilombismo* is about asserting the political, social, and economic rights of Afro-Brazilians. It advocates for land rights, cultural recognition, and socioeconomic development, drawing parallels with the self-sufficient and autonomous nature of historical quilombos. According to Abdias do Nascimento's vision, *quilombismo* is not just a reflection on the past. It is also a call to action, urging Afro-Brazilians to organize, mobilize, and assert their rights and cultural identity in a society that often marginalizes them. In essence, according to Abdias do Nascimento, *quilombismo* is a transformative movement that seeks to reframe the narrative of African descendants in Brazil, advocating for their empowerment, cultural affirmation, and resistance against racial oppression. It's a movement that resonates with the global struggle for African descendant rights, cultural recognition, and social justice.

Therefore, *quilombismo* could be termed as a decrypting practice. It aims at affirming the worth of the African-Brazilian experience and its contribution to the formation of the national standard. Supposing the need and the capacity to invert the law of exclusion presupposed by the racial contract (which, as already discussed, assumes the forms of epistemicide, and the various modes of institutional and structural racism), *quilombismo* aims not merely at "opening up the place where meaning is to be decided" (Sanín-Restrepo 2018, xx), but at materially and concretely shifting the locus where politics does happen, instituting and recognizing the institutions of political spaces not entirely congruent with those of white politics, much like the case of Palmares, spaces in which nonetheless politics takes place and where an emancipation horizon is drawn in favor of black Brazilians.

CONCLUSION

In light of the intricate interplay between encryption and decryption within societal structures, this essay has navigated the realms of power dynamics, resistance, and resilience. The notion of encryption, as discussed, transcends the mere obfuscation of legal texts to embody a broader mechanism of power consolidation, where the elite's control over knowledge and influence perpetuates systemic inequities.

However, as revealed through the examination of the theories and practices regarding "*quilombismo*," decryption emerges not merely as a counterstrategy but as a profound embodiment of communal empowerment and resistance. "*Quilombismo*," rooted in the historical context of Afro-Brazilian resistance, extends beyond its historical confines to present a contemporary model of radical en/de-cryption. This model challenges the hegemonic encryption of power, fostering communal spheres of resistance that advocate for new territorial and social paradigms, thereby confronting the coloniality of power and engendering new existential and communal possibilities.

In essence, the dialogue between the encrypted structures of power and the decryptive endeavors of communities, particularly through the lens of "*quilombismo*," underscores a dynamic interplay where resistance is not merely reactive but constitutive of new forms of existence and understanding.

This dynamic invites a broader reflection on the mechanisms of power and resistance, urging new understandings of how communities can harness the principles of encryption and decryption to forge pathways toward more equitable and inclusive futures. Through this prism, the essay not only dissects the multifaceted nature of encryption and decryption but also celebrates the indomitable spirit of resistance and the unyielding quest for justice and emancipation in the face of entrenched power structures.

NOTES

1. This text constitutes an integral component of the research project undertaken by the authors. The project is oriented toward the publication of a scholarly work that delves into the philosophical and political analysis of the subject of injustice. Additionally, it seeks to develop a sophisticated grammatical framework that is equipped to encapsulate the varied nuances associated with potential responses to oppression.

2. Following Beatriz Nascimento's research (2018, 274–80), the Imbangala were anthropophagic. Especially, they did not raise children of their own, but rather assimilated the youth of other defeated groups and tribes by a ritual of initiation termed "Kilombo."

3. Although the difference between resistance and resilience cannot be further developed in this brief contribution, it is worth considering that both resistance and resilience are considered processes and subjective predispositions that respond to forms of oppression. Neither resistance nor resilience should be severed from the very oppressive context against which they emerge into social practice. Instead of relying on a naïve hierarchy that opposes either of these possibilities (in the manner of an "either . . . or . . . ," resistance *vs.* resilience), favoring an ideal of "activeness" over another ideal of "passiveness," the authors strive for a more complex structure in which resistance and resilience are both *valid* and legitimate forms of opposing oppression. Neither one is entirely "active" nor "passive" with regard to the *status quo*. Instead of a priori semantic and transcendent differentiation between the two, the authors understand that resistance and resilience are both available *tactics* and *schemes of action* set forth by different individuals in attendance to different conditions and goals (each of which might be either conscious or not). The difference between the two is not a qualitative one, such as

that presupposed by the "opposing" approach, but one of the degrees in which a determinate subjectivity is capable (either physically, mentally, ethically, morally, socially, or institutionally) of setting forth a proper response against oppression. Resistance and resilience can be understood as tactical responses that are inherently contingent upon specific contextual factors, including the concrete conditions of time and space. As tactics, they are intrinsically limited by their inability to fully anticipate or address the entire range of potential consequences that may arise from their deployment.

4. Contrary to the ordinary analysis of Walter Benjamin's text "*Zur Kritik der Gewalt*," "mere life" is not less valuable than "good life," for "good" life presupposes the much more obvious condition of being alive. It is therefore nonsensical to divide categorically between *zoé* and *bíos* in order to value *zoé* (social or political existence) as more important than *bíos* (also termed mere life, or "naked life"), instead of, as Benjamin proposes, considering the "*unshakeable aggregate state of 'the human being'*" (2021, 59).

BIBLIOGRAPHY

Benjamin, Walter. 2021. "Toward the Critique of Violence." In *Toward the Critique of Violence: A Critical Edition*, edited by Peter Fenves and Julia Ng. Stanford, CA: Stanford University Press, 39–61.

Bourdieu, Pierre. 2014. *On the State*. Edited by Patrick Champagne, Remi Lenoir, Franck Poupeau, and Marie-Christine Rivière, and translated by David Fernbach. Cambridge: Polity Press.

Carneiro, Sueli. 2023. *Dispositivo de Racialidade*. Rio de Janeiro: Zahar.

Deleuze, Gilles and Felix Guattari. 1972. *Anti-Œdipe: Capitalisme et Schizophrénie*. Paris: Minuit.

Foucault, Michel. 1976. *Il Faut Défendre la Société*. Cours au Collège de France. Paris: Seuil.

Freud, Sigmund. 2019. *O Infamiliar. Das Unheimliche. Obras Incompletas de Sigmund Freud*. Vol. 8. Translated by Ernani Chaves and Pedro H. Tavares. Belo Horizonte: Autêntica.

Kafka, Franz. 1946. "The Problem of Our Laws." In The Great Wall of China and Other Short Works, translated by Willa and Edwin Muir. London: Secker and Warburg, pp. 130–32

Mills, Charles. 1997. *The Racial Contract*. Ithaca, NY and London: Cornell University Press.

Moura, Clóvis. 1988. *Sociologia do Negro Brasileiro*. São Paulo: Ática.

Nascimento, Abdias do. 1980. "Quilombismo: An Afro-Brazilian Political Alternative." *Journal of Black Studies*, vol. 11, nº 2, Afro-Brazilian Experience and Proposals for Social Change, pp. 141–78.

Nascimento, Beatriz. 2018. *Beatriz Nascimento, Quilombola e Intelectual*. União dos Coletivos Pan-Africanos; UCPA. São Paulo: Filhos da África.

Nascimento, Beatriz. 2022. *O Negro Visto por ele Mesmo*. Alex Ratts (org.). São Paulo: UBU.

Sanín-Restrepo, Ricardo. 2016. *Decolonizing Democracy: Power in a Solid State*. London: Rowman & Littlefield International.

Sanín-Restrepo, Ricardo. 2018. "Introduction: The Meaning of the Encryption of Power as the Razor's Edge of Politics." In *Decrypting Power*, edited by Ricardo Sanín-Restrepo. London: Rowman & Littlefield International, pp. ix–xxx.

Sanín-Restrepo, Ricardo and Gabriel Mendéz-Hincapíe. 2018. "Introduction: The Meaning of the Encryption of Power as the Razor's Edge of Politics." In *Decrypting Power*, edited by Ricardo Sanín-Restrepo. London: Rowman & Littlefield International, pp. 1–23.

Chapter 5

The Justice(s) of the O'tan (Corazonar)

Tseltal Women's Experiences in the Pursuit of Self-Justice

Laura Edith Saavedra-Hernández

THE CONTEXT OF THE RESEARCH

As a first step in this chapter, it seems important to me to situate myself and my knowledge, since, as Haraway (1995) mentions, this not only helps me to maintain a critical view of what makes me uncomfortable but also allows me to question the criteria of truth built around the concepts I want to discuss in this chapter. Therefore, my analysis will be influenced by my experience, my militancy, my gender, my mestizo identity, and my class, which will surely give or take away epistemic privileges over certain discussions.

I have tried to do everything I mention, analyze, or say here in the most ethical and respectful way possible. To situate myself allows me to clarify that my intention in what follows is to foster new edges of discussion and research/action that help to make intelligible other forms of cosmoexistence, that help us move toward justice and to build "a world where many worlds fit."

Therefore, in this chapter, I present some of the findings of the research *Constructing Justice(s) Beyond the Law: The Experiences of Indigenous Women Participating in the Women's Rights Center of Chiapas A.C.*[1] Later published in the book *Corazonar las justicias. Los saberes de las mujeres tseltales sobre violencias, justicias y derechos humanos.*[2] The main objective of this research was to analyze the gap and tensions that exist between the meanings of the hegemonic concepts of Westernized theory and the meanings of the different ways of life that exist in concrete realities and that have been made invisible regarding violence, justice, and human rights. For this reason,

I have taken on the task of making intelligible the knowledge and wisdom of Tseltal and Tsotsil women from the Highlands of Chiapas, Mexico, focusing on Tseltal philosophy.

I understand hegemony as "coercion, the use of force, persuasion, the ability to bend contrary or simply divergent opinions, as well as what is not questioned out of habit, acceptance or weakness" (Gargallo 2010, 157). Moreover, from a Foucauldian perspective, it is a positioning of the exercise of power that generates resistance and subaltern power (Foucault 2007).

For this reason, the main objective of this research was to reflect on how to generate intercultural dialogues for Indigenous women's access to justice. In Mexico, women in general, moreover Indigenous women in particular, when we denounce any kind of violence, we are discriminated against, we are racialized, and many of us are re-victimized by the justice system. From my point of view, this has to do with the encryption of justice(s), because although there are state mechanisms to protect our rights, they are not considered by the state legal system. On the contrary, they hinder access, generating more violence and human rights violations, a situation and perspective that I would like to develop here.

The women who participated in the research were or are members of the *Centro de Derechos de la Mujer de Chiapas A. C.* (CDMCH), an organization whose goal is to contribute to the advancement of gender, class, and ethnic equality in Chiapas, Mexico, especially in the Indigenous and *campesino*[3] regions. CDMCH acts through a creative process that promotes the knowledge and critical exercise of the different legal systems that exist in Chiapas: Indigenous, traditional, autonomous, state, national, and international, promoting timely changes in discriminatory customs and laws, as well as the forms of their application that violate women's rights from this legal pluralism.

To carry out the proposed analysis, I will take up some postulates from legal anthropology, Tseltal philosophy, and other Indigenous philosophies, as well as the theory of the encryption of power proposed for this book. It seems to me that this theoretical proposal can help unravel some of the knots of this research and explain from a different angle why the legal mechanisms of the state have been insufficient for women's access to justice and why then what I have called "heartfelt justice" is important as an alternative to decrypt justice(s).

As this research was inserted into the knowledge of the production of knowledge and meanings hidden by colonization and the universalization of concepts, the research was built through mutual collaboration with Tseltal women who contributed to different forms of research/collaboration/action to build more horizontal interactions and not reproduce exclusions and hegemonies in their own meanings. In this sense, in order to approach women's reality in a more horizontal way, I learned the Tseltal language in order to be able to share different experiences with them, trying to position myself in their different ways of being in the world and considering that these experiences are part of a historical process that shapes the concrete realities of women.

This helped me to know and learn about the different experiences that Indigenous women use as strategies to challenge their oppression, learning that there are different ways of understanding emancipation and resistance to patriarchal powers in concrete and situated contexts such as the one analyzed here. Thus, from the definition of their knowledge about justice, we build a process of co-theorization of concepts. Being able to "theorize about something is the product of asking questions and giving answers to some everyday problems" (Köhler 2015). This shows us that they are not finished concepts, but on the contrary, they demonstrate their theoretical potential (Köhler 2015).

These questions have made me wonder if the state is really a legitimate place to claim our rights and if it is possible to speak of a legitimate recognition of these rights in a state that revictimizes social movements and in particular women when they demand justice. I have asked myself if then, as the Tseltal women do, we can build from the collective other channels to access social justice outside a legalistic framework, and, if the answer is yes, what would they be?

Therefore, to argue the above, I have divided this chapter into four sections: The first is an introduction that has helped me situate and contextualize this research. In the second section, entitled "The encryption of power and Indigenous Justice in the Mexican context," I raise some questions about the constitutional reform of Indigenous rights, considering their encryption and how this has led to the invisibilization of other forms of knowledge. In the third section, "The justices of the o'tan: Other knowledge of justice," I analyze the meanings of justice in Tseltal law as other knowledges that open possibilities to decrypt state law and thus, to be able to access justice from knowledges born from the experiences of Tseltal women. Finally, I develop a final section as a conclusion, "Heart to decrypt justice (s) and generate intercultural dialogues," as a proposal for the generation of intercultural dialogues that allow us to access justice.

THE ENCRYPTION OF POWER AND INDIGENOUS JUSTICE IN THE MEXICAN CONTEXT

From the perspective of legal anthropology, we have shown how in Mexico, Indigenous law and its justice have paradoxically been subordinated to the power and verticality of the state. Since colonization, the Indigenous peoples have not been recognized as subjects of rights; on the contrary, they have been constructed as "the other" who had to be "domesticated" to gain access to the emerging Mexican society. Five centuries had to pass before Indigenous peoples were recognized as an active and living part of the Mexican state and before their individual and collective rights were recognized in the political constitution.

This legal recognition was the result of the struggle of the 1994 armed movement led by the Zapatista Army of National Liberation (EZLN), which was formed by various Indigenous peoples of the state of Chiapas and later joined by other peoples of Mexico and the world in their demands. The Indigenous peoples, who took up arms because they were tired of the permanent violence they experienced and the exclusion and discrimination they faced on a daily basis from society in general, demanded full recognition from the state and its institutions in order to be able to live in dignity and to exercise their rights based on their ethnic differences, without these differences becoming social exclusions.

Therefore, in the peace negotiations, it was agreed that constitutional reforms would be constructed for this full recognition, and their demands were set forth in the document "The Agreements on Indigenous Rights and Culture," better known as the "San Andres Agreements." In this document, the demands of the Indigenous peoples of Mexico were recognized, acknowledging the inequalities and historical exclusion that they have lived with since colonization, and therefore this said recognition would have to become reparation and remembrance that would allow the peoples to be part of the country's development and, finally, have justice (López 2016). Two years after intense discussions, these agreements were signed.

Consequently, for them to be discussed and approved within the branches of government, it was necessary for the Indigenous people to create a political movement to recover their historical memory. It was not until the year 2000 that discussions began among the three branches of government. For López (2016), the Zapatista struggle, the *accords,* and later the constitutional reform were a constitutive movement of the Indigenous peoples because, despite everything, from his point of view, there have been gradual changes that have politically and legally transformed the Mexican state regarding Indigenous matters (López 2016, 93). In 2001, after various debates in the Chamber of Deputies and the Senate, the reform to Article 2 of the Constitution was published in the Official Gazette of the Federation,[4] which recognized the multicultural composition of the country and through which it was supposed to have complied with these agreements.

Although this event can be seen as a historical milestone in the recognition of the rights of the Indigenous peoples, it is far from being so. This reform proved to be insufficient and was manipulated by the de facto powers of the state. According to the peoples, it does not contain the true sentiment and the real needs of the Indigenous political struggle; since the claims of autonomy and self-determination, although recognized, are subordinated to the constitutional and legal powers of the state, which ultimately becomes a deceptive language, in which, on the one hand, the Indigenous peoples are recognized with full rights, yet under the constitutional "tutelage" of the state, which shows that the colonized representations of the Indigenous continue to be the rule within political powers. This is an example of what Sanín-Restrepo calls the encryption of power, where, through supposed recognition, it achieves universalization and constructs prefigured human beings that limit epistemic imagination and colonializes knowledge, that is, it makes the legitimate voice of the people invisible. "The real problem with liberal universality is that it has never been an authentic universality, rights, freedom are minuscule concepts fraudulently elevated to the space of universal representation. In the face of this farce, the proposal must be a philosophy of the universality of the marginalized, the displaced, the poor; this is the goal of critical theory" (Sanín-Restrepo 2020, 3).

This question raises several paradoxes. I think this constitutional legal framework is the place where social struggles should be recognized, yet this is not the case. Therefore, is state recognition the legitimate place for social claims? Is it possible to speak of access to justice and recognition of rights within the legal framework of state power? Are there other channels of recognition and full access to collective rights outside the legal framework of the state? And, if the answer is yes, what are they?

What these reforms have shown us, in terms of the freedom to exercise one's rights and, therefore, one's concept of justice, is that far from being an impulse for democratization, they have served as a concept of additive legal pluralism (Sierra, 2005), which has become an obstacle to the genuine acceptance of the existence of other forms of government and justice, since a neo indigenist policy that does not allow for a fundamental change continues to prevail.

The reforms on the right to exercise one's own justice have only served to generate processes of mediation and alternative resolution of cases, lacking any autonomy to participate in civil or criminal proceedings. Since there is still a cultural representation and belief that legal autonomy is "dangerous," the prevailing idea is that, due to the mere fact of being Indigenous, the application of their justice will violate human rights, as if Indigenous people could not discern what a crime that violates dignity is. Henceforth, reducing Indigenous law to simple "uses and customs." This fear only reveals the hegemony of universalisms that prevent the recognition and respect of cultural differences and real alternatives for the full exercise of their justice (Sierra 2005).

On the contrary, as Zambrano mentions, Indigenous peoples, like any other people in the world, have the capacity to recognize the crimes committed in their communities. In this regard he mentions that,

> . . . unlawful acts (e.g., murder) are recognizable in every culture, regardless of their significance. Therefore, all cultures have legal systems to deal with such acts and to maintain collective order, with respect to what they know. All systems change and adapt according to their norms, according to their network of intercultural exchange. Therefore, it would not be a question of justifying homicides or crimes "culturally," but of demonstrating with satisfaction that Indigenous peoples have clear procedures to punish them, often with less severity, but with more justice than our systems. (Zambrano quoted by Bidaseca 2011, 82)

From my point of view, the demands of Indigenous peoples for constitutional and legal recognition are justified because, at least in Mexico, it has been shown that this seems to be the only way to be heard. Indigenous peoples have had to learn to dialogue within the language of the state and within the framework of recognized laws. However, I think that this question reinforces encryption because the meanings of their system of symbols are hidden away (Sanín-Restrepo 2020).

Notwithstanding, one could say that it is a misleading dialogue because this hierarchization of meanings inhibits the possibility of horizontal communication, as there is a hierarchical imbalance between the meanings of state justice and the diverse meanings of Indigenous justice. The result is that difference is denied and justice standardized. "The encryption of power is precisely the denial of difference as the order of the world" (Sanín-Restrepo, 2020).

Under this reform, it became clear over time that the state was building a position of power that denied difference. There was a clear exercise of encryption, since there is ". . . a primordial prohibition (political, legal, racial [I would add, patriarchal]) to access the use of language (as the first common of the difference)" (Sanín-Restrepo 2020).

In this sense, I agree with Bidaseca (2011) who mentions that justice, in this case in Mexico, has been built from a kind of *legal colonialism*; where "the other or the different other" is silenced and, therefore, cannot speak because it lacks spaces for enunciation, and the few spaces for it are within the language of the state. Therefore, the Indigenous rights encrypted in the constitution are intended to be the voice of the people, but according to the power of the state. That is to say, since the rights are set out in the frameworks and under the language of the state, what is outside of it is not valid.

Rosillo (2015) mentions that the language of the state is based on the hegemonic foundations of human rights that aim at encryption. According to the author, these hegemonic visions are due to three characteristics:

dogmatism, which has to do with an absolute foundation; reductionism, which leads to an ahistorical and decontextualized vision of the struggles for rights; and ethnocentrism, which states that human rights contain a Eurocentric vision of reality (Rosillo 2015, 2–3). To this discussion, I would add that there is also a patriarchal issue. From a feminist critique, we have established that the law has been built from a male point of view, which does not take into account women's problems, so historically, we have had to fight for the recognition of our human rights, which are also built with the same vision, where women's access to justice is always co-opted by the male meaning.[5]

Faced with this paradox, the meanings of justice for Tseltal women can be an alternative to decrypting justice, because they help make visible that another justice is possible, and through them, voices are diversified, making differences intelligible. Until now, law and justice, as conceptualized by the language of the state, have been concerned with the regulation of difference; they have become technologies of power and knowledge through their encryption. However, as I have proposed, justice constructed from situated experiences such as those practiced by Tseltal women from their own knowledge can be emancipatory proposals which, through decryption, contribute to the transformation of the patriarchal and colonized legal system.

THE O'TAN JUSTICES: OTHER KNOWLEDGE OF JUSTICE(S)

Although it has always been present and has developed over time alongside state law, Indigenous law in Mexico has been the shadow, the uncomfortable sibling of positive law, always reduced to customary law or "uses and customs"; it is seldom mentioned alongside other forms of law. From this point on, there is already a distinction in which the positive law of the state is hierarchically positioned above Indigenous law.

In this order of ideas, we can say that the same happens with the meaning of justice. It can only be given and defined by the state in its own terms and in its own language and meaning. Any definition that does not fall within the framework of the state cannot be considered justice. I do not intend here to enter into a philosophical discussion of what may or may not be justice based on the theories generated regarding it. Rather, what I want to do is focus the entire analysis on the characteristics that define Tseltal women's knowledge of justice, highlighting, at some moments, specific differences that help us to understand this meaning in a different way. However, I would like to mention that currently there is an excess to promote punitive justice, which tends much more toward individualization; this has broken the collective bonds and buttresses access to justice more as an individual revenge than a social goal. Hence the importance of looking at the knowledge of Tseltal women.

The Threads That Frame Tseltal Women's Knowledge of Justice(s)

Maya-Tzeltal justice in the Highlands of Chiapas cannot be understood without understanding the various points at which it is anchored. I will begin with the concept of the *we*. For the Tseltal and other Indigenous peoples of the Chiapas highlands, *"we" (nosotros) in their coexistence* has a different connotation from that of the Spanish of Western culture; it is not just a linguistic concept or conjugation of verbs, but of existence.

> *We* are a characteristic of the Tseltal language. It tends to be repeated constantly in everyday speech. And it does not only occur in the language, but we prevails in the speech as well as in the life, in the action, in the way of being of the people. It characterizes, so to speak the Tseltales. It represents a linguistic as well as an experiential element. (Lenkersdorf 2002, 26)

In Tseltal knowledge, there is no Western conception of reality where reason and feeling are separated, that is, the *I* as a subject or an individual corporality does not exist in the way the world is lived. Instead, this individual is integrated with the *We*, so we can speak of an *I/we (yo/nosotros)* from which the world is signified.

According to Le Goff and Truong (2005), there is evidence that in ancestral times, the body was connected to the world, to the agricultural cycle, and to other bodies. There was no signification of the human body as an autonomous, anthropocentric entity; therefore, it was not possible to think of the body or the human being outside of a communitarian framework and outside of the universe itself. That is to say, the fragmentation of the body and the mind occurs with modern thought, where we privilege reason over every form of existence. In the Tseltal sense of being in the world, this does not happen; everything is connected to everything; therefore, everything will have life and a reason for being. This integrity is what gives meaning to the world and is what allows for existence itself, is what builds the *us*.

Therefore, it can be argued that justice is also meant in the plural, hence the reference to justice(s). Justice in the singular does not make sense in the Tseltal language. In this sense, reparation through justice(s) will take care of the whole. Tseltal women do not seek justice for their individual well-being; they have always sought justice for the collective to live in peace and harmony, and this allows them to have individual well-being as well.

Now, this concept of the collective *I/we* is also linked to the philosophy of the Tseltal communities. Tseltal philosophy is centered on three elements: O'tan (heart), chu'lelal (soul), and chu'lel (spirit-consciousness). "From this conception of the world of life, other aspects are derived to build interpersonal relationships and the cosmos-earth with harmony, respect, dignity, justice and the exercise of all rights to the fullest as human beings, that is, a real and true Ich'el ta muk"[6] (López-Intzín 2013, 98).

The o' tan (heart) is seen not only as a biological part of the body but as a metaphor for the body and existence itself. In the words of Tseltal philosopher López-Intzín:

> The word *O'tan (Heart)* is present in our everyday language in different ways, that is why we can find expressions and concepts such as: *p'ijil O'tan* (wisdom of the heart), *smuk'ul O'tan* (greatness of the heart), *stse'elil O'tan* (the laughter of the heart, joy), *slekil o yutsil O'tan* (kindnees of the heart), *mel O'tan* (furrow of the heart, worry or sadness), *sujtesel O'tan* (to turn the heart around, to return to the road walked), *ich' O'tan* (to receive the heart but actually refers to learning or being educated through punishment such as forced labor, beatings, and imprisonment) *kux O'tan* (to rest the heart, to take a rest, to sleep), *ch'ay O'tan (to* lose the heart, to forget). We could go on listing other phrases, expressions and concepts that allude to the O'tan-heart and that have led us to believe that it is a central concept in our thought and culture as an example of a different rationality. (López-Intzín 2013, 74)

In this way, the O'tan (heart) is connected to the collective, with the *We*. It is not only the center of their cosmoexistence and corporeality; moreover, it is also a whole that makes collective life possible. In this sense, the narratives provided by López-Intzín show that the ways of meaning justice are indeed conceived from another place in a cosmogonic and subjective relationship with the other.

Another issue that constitutes the philosophy of the Tseltal justice(s) is the balance in their cosmoexistence. Paoli (1999) mentions that in Tseltal, the harmony of the community is important for the O'tan (heart). He mentions that "to achieve this dynamic of balance requires ts'ikel (tolerance), pek'elil (humility), ch'ujunel (believe-obey) ich'el ta muk' (respect) ch'abajel (pacification) and, when problems arise sujt'esel o'tanil (return to the heart)" (Paoli 1999, 143).

Therefore, Tseltal Indigenous law privileges "a good agreement," not only an agreement between two people, as is the case of the ones built by the state or transitional justice, where two people agree on what is best for them, always aiming at the individual; rather, it is a good community agreement that aims at the collective, because through this agreement balance is regained.

In this regard, López-Itzín tells us how time and space are conceived differently from our Westernized conception of life. He states that time is not conceived linearly, and space is not abstract; both are linked to an incarnated history that is transmitted through different issues, such as in the conception of nature, in rituals, and in life cycles. Everything finds meaning in a circular manner (Hernández 2022); that is, what one gives is repaid, what one damages is repaid in a negative way, therefore balance is an important matter of life. ". . . I asked the elders about these concepts, trying to understand them, and one of them replied that life itself is a circle, perhaps they are not referring to a cyclical life, but they do refer to the circular sense of becoming" (Hernández 2022).

Balance makes sense as a part of the whole because, in the cyclical dimension, what goes around comes around, so we have to ensure the common good.

However, in the research that I conducted, I met different women who were seeking justice for the multiple and different forms of violence that they faced in their families or in their communities. One theme that emerged in the different women's narratives was the importance of forgiveness, rather than denunciation within the framework of the state. This made me wonder if this way of understanding access to justice through forgiveness, that is, suj'tsel O'tan, was part of the knowledge of justice(s).

Of course, at first, I could not understand how, after living through the violence they had lived through, they would not want to access the state justice system. Over time, however, I realized that when the women talked about the importance of *healing their hearts or returning to the heart*, alluding to forgiveness, they were positioning themselves in their community's knowledge.

In general, in pluricultural contexts where there is a high presence of Indigenous peoples in Mexico, access to justice becomes a system through which the state exercises the power it has over Indigenous peoples; because, within the state justice system, they are racialized, discriminated against, revictimized, and violated by this bureaucratic structure that does not respond to the needs of the ways in which justice is understood. For example, I observed how Indigenous women in the state courts become just a file in which a coded text is written—encrypted language based on a Westernized vision of what law and justice are—where the lawyer becomes the interlocutor, making her and her way of understanding life and justice invisible.

The Tseltal women I accompanied in their search for justice knew this, so they decided to turn to the Indigenous law of their communities or to themselves *to heal their hearts through* an act of forgiveness. This issue made sense to me when I became aware of the three elements analyzed above: *the i/We, the philosophy of o' tan, and the balance of life*. I realized that the Tseltal women were not only disagreeing with the state's justice system, but they were reclaiming their own wisdom in this call to suj' tesel o' tanil (return to our hearts), which in a very simple translation into Spanish can mean forgiveness.

The Tseltal women taught me, through their experiences with violence, that not only did it hurt their bodies on this plane of life and from a vision of the individualized body, but that this violent act hurt their O'tan (heart), their ch'ulel (spirit); and because they are connected in this *I/We* to the collective, these acts of violence not only broke their hearts, but this breaking of the O'tan ended up breaking the community and the collectivity that unites them as a people. That's why the women talked to us about the importance of being able to *heal their hearts*, because it allowed them to repair what was broken and to regain what was lost.

This act of healing was not only an individual act, as restorative justice usually is, which is why I am moving away from that concept. On the contrary, by healing individually through forgiveness, by being part of a collective thought, the whole is also healed, and the broken fabric of the community is restructured. This is why I think that the Tseltal way of conceiving the world breaks with the dichotomous notions of the individual subject that encrypts the collective subject implanted by modernity and the coloniality of being.

Therefore, the justices of the Corazonar, as I have named them, are identified by the following characteristics,—and these are the strengths that can decrypt justice from the voice of what is called the people. First, they are collective and communitarian justices; that is, everyone in the community is responsible for both the complaint and the resolution of the conflict. Second, it is not a punitive justice; it is not isolated, but contextualized, that is, violence against women is a product of both the history of the community and the surrounding context; therefore, it can be repaired with the active participation of all. Insofar, it is not vengeful but seeks the common good.

> The *justice of the "we"* is neither idealized nor utopian but represents very demanding social relations. Every member of the community must recognize that he or she is jointly responsible for the other members of the social group of the "*we.*" The individualized people of the dominant society would hardly accept such co-responsibility with all that it implies. (Ceceña 1999)

When we pause to reflect on it, the reality emerges that encrypted justice, enshrined within the authority of the state, finds its framework in legal and political institutions. According to the prevailing narrative, it is believed that through these powers, we can strive to construct a more equitable society and facilitate access to justice. In a common judgment of state law, access to justice often ends with a penalty or punishment for the perpetrators. Nevertheless, no thought is given to repairing the damaged contexts in which the victims return to continue with their lives. In other words, from the point of view of the state, the demand for justice is satisfied by the conclusion of a trial and the imposition of a punishment as if the violence or the crime were individual problems between two parties. However, violence is also structural and is anchored in social and cultural dynamics that must also be changed and moved so as not to re-victimize people, in this case, women. The justice of the state does not change this fundamental problem, because in this encryption, through its power, it reduces both the offense and justice, leaving only the alternative of individual reparation, which is why violence always recurs.

When the Tseltal women spoke to me about the importance of forgiveness in their own knowledge of justice, they subverted the typical punitive vision encrypted in our laws and state norms; this knowledge points to other forms of social coexistence in which we privilege the common good and recognize that we are all responsible for the violence we experience, as well as for the justice we seek. The de-individualization of justice and its collectivization deciphers the voice not only of women, moreover also of the people.

> This morning I've been thinking a lot about who we are today, about the knowledge and practices that we've inherited . . . there's even a word in Tseltal that says *ya kak'bet ko'tan*: "I give you my heart" this expression is used when we transfer energy, knowledge, when someone inherits their history, what I received from my grandparents, from my grandmothers, that which makes me who I am, at the same time I am transferring it at this moment. For example, the same illnesses, many of the afflictions that I have, may have to do with my sister, my brother, my aunt, my uncle, my grandparents, my grandmothers, my great-great-grandmothers. These are aspects that continue to affect me, it has to do with things that they have already done, which makes me think a lot about how what I do now will affect the lives of my children, my grandchildren, granddaughters, and grandsons. Everything that happens in life comes back. (Hernández 2022)

Therefore, we have to inherit well-being, understanding, tolerance, and address issues that we have made invisible and lost through a punitive justice system.

BY WAY OF CONCLUSION: HEART TO DECRYPT JUSTICE(S) AND GENERATE INTERCULTURAL DIALOGUES.

When they organized an agroecological activity or a School of Human Rights event with the Center for Women's Rights of Chiapas, the Tseltal women performed a welcoming ritual in which they made a circle with flowers, placed candles, and an offering that each woman shared in the center of the circle.[7] Each time we opened the meetings or workshops, we gave thanks to the four directions and asked the universe to fill us with energy; we asked for Yutsil K'otantik (for the goodness of our heart).

Every time there was a ritual organized by the women and taught to the girls, I thought about the wisdom involved in those acts. That we should have serenity and kindness before we start a dialogue, in order to be able to think clearly about our dialogues and our proposals, always seemed to me to be a profound act of dialogue with the being/being. How much wisdom have we lost? I always asked myself, thinking about my concrete reality in a system that prevents us from seeing and searching in our deepest being, that drags us with the current and encloses us in a life of consumption and competition, in selfishness and violence. I thought about the need to make visible the wisdom of the heart of Tseltal women and how it has been devalued (fragments from the field diary, July 2014).

López-Itzín (2021) mentions that the original Maya Tseltal people, as well as the peoples who inhabited the south of what is now Mexico, suffered radical changes with the Spanish conquest and later with the establishment of colonies throughout the country. These peoples experienced a rupture in their daily lives and their way of being. This bifurcation created a rupture in all of their vital spaces: spiritual, political, legal, economic, linguistic, and epistemic. Through violence, bodies and spirits, minds and hearts were domesticated.

This situation was an important shock for the Tseltal people because, through various popular or academic analyses, some Indigenous people have realized that a large part of their institutions and forms of organization are a product of the hegemonic system that has been in place for centuries. A system that has racialized and excluded them from contemporary society and from access to their human rights, robbing them of their dignity and keeping their communities marginalized.

Therefore, I propose the concept of "Corazonar la justicia," which means generating a decolonizing proposal and a political positioning in the face of a Westernized-capitalist-neoliberal-heteropatriarchal-racist legal system that continues to exclude the wisdom of Indigenous peoples and women themselves when they seek to solve their problems of violence. It is a return to the collective notion of community welfare, to the common good. Yet, at the same time, it must also be an individual act that helps to *heal hearts.*

In this sense, forgiving violence for the Tseltal women in this research to access justice is an act for that "I" that helps them to heal the heart. Moreover, by finding themselves in the Tseltal cosmoexistence where that "I" is an "I/we," that forgiveness also connects the community and the collective. Therefore, to forgive justice is an act of reciprocity: *I heal my heart in order to continue being me, I forgive the community in order to continue being us.*

To heart justice from the knowledge of forgiveness helps women to put themselves at the center of a justice that seeks to restore the broken collectivity. It is a political act of resistance against a state legal system that is punitive, colonial, and patriarchal, as it excludes the voice of the people, in this case, Indigenous women. Tseltal women's knowledge subverts, through a notion of collective justice based on forgiveness, the power of the state that individualizes justice and privatizes it through the vertical power that defines which justice is valid and which is not. To heart justice in these terms helps to build the common benefit from the real needs of women without being revictimized and finding the justice they seek.

As community feminists have noted, being able to think of ourselves as women capable of breaking with the patriarchal system from different points, whether from the state or from the "heart," makes us subjects of rights and demonstrates that we can have political positions beyond the state. Perhaps it is time to "heart ourselves" and to "agree" as women, to think of ourselves from other places than just the establishment of laws and "gender alerts" that, far from changing the realities of women, seem to submerge them more in patriarchal domination.

Therefore, an exercise of heart-centered justice should include the generation of intercultural dialogues that allow both legal systems to enrich each other in order to transform themselves. Indigenous communities have the capacity to create their own frameworks for justice. These frameworks, however, do not impose rigid boundaries that lead to universalization. Instead, they recognize justice as a dynamic concept that evolves within its cultural context. Moreover, Indigenous communities can and should engage in permanent dialogue and negotiation with the established national government and international justice systems.

Continuing to co-rationalize justice only from the state framework closes the possibility of knowing other forms of justice that have brought better conditions to women. Seeking justice "at the heart," deconstructing it and not seeing it as a single way of accessing it, opens up infinite possibilities for us to position ourselves politically as women and to know beyond the law.

NOTES

1. Laura Saavedra, *Construyendo Justicia(s) más allá de la Ley: Las Experiencias de las Mujeres Indígenas que Participan con el Centro de Derechos de la Mujer de Chiapas A.C.* (PhD Anthropology, CIESAS, 2018).

2. Laura Saavedra, *Corazonar las Justicias: Los Saberes de las Mujeres Tzeltales Sobre Violencias, Justicias y Derechos Humanos*, 1st (Aguascalientes-San Luis Potosí, CENEJUS, UASLP, 2022).

3. The peasant regions in Mexico are specific places where the people who inhabit them are dedicated to the cultivation of different types of food, such as corn, for example. This precision is made because in Mexico the Indigenous and peasant regions experience multiple social and economic inequalities due to the neoliberal policies of the state. Hence, it is important to realize that despite this, many women and some collectives build strategies from their own knowledge for access to justice despite the deep inequalities they live under. It may seem that because they are impoverished women, they cannot build their own future; on the contrary, one of the findings of this research shows how Indigenous women from rural regions are building strategies against the violence and state domination that oppresses them through poverty and the dispossession of their rights.

4. Article 2, Constitution of the United Mexican States, Chamber of Deputies, last modified January 2024 https://www.diputados.gob.mx/LeyesBiblio/pdf/CPEUM.pdf.

5. Bibliography to delve deeper into the topic of gender, feminism, and law: Núñez, Lucía (coord.) Feminismos, Justicias y Derechos frente al Neoliberalismo. Aportes para la Reflexión Crítica (Mexico: UNAM, CIEG, 2023).

Núñez, Lucía. *El Género en la Ley Penal: Crítica Feminista de la Ilusión Punitiva* (Mexico: UNAM, CIEG, 2018).

Ruiz, Alicia. "La Construcción Jurídica de la Subjetividad no es Ajena a las Mujeres." In: *El derecho en el género y el género en el derecho* edited by, Haydee Birgin, 19–31. Buenos Aires: Biblios, 2000.

Smart, Carol. "La Teoría Feminista y el Discurso Jurídico." In: *El derecho en el género y el género en el derecho*, Edited by Haydee Birgin, 31–72, Buenos Aires: Biblios, 2000.

6. Ich'el ta muk' means, according to the Tseltal philosopher, taking up the knowledge of the Me'tik Rosa (mother Rosa), "foundation of the mere good or goodness maxime of life in life, of dignity to be in harmony" (López-Intzín 2013, 93).

7. According to Guerrero Arias (2010), "Corazonar" is born as an insurgent political response to the coloniality of power, knowledge, and being, as it displaces the hegemony of reason and shows that our humanity is constituted between the interrelation of affectivity and reason and that its horizon is existence. Hence, "Corazonar," from the insurgent wisdoms, in the sense of the dominant epistemologies, can contribute to the construction not only of a different academic and epistemic proposal but, above all, of other senses of existence (Guerrero 2010, 102).

BIBLIOGRAPHY

Bidaseca, Karina. 2011. "Mujeres Blancas Buscando Salvar a Mujeres Color Café: Desigualdad, Colonialismo Jurídico y Feminismo Postcolonial." In *Andamios. Revista de Investigación Social* 8, no. 17 (2011): 61–89.

Cámara de Diputados. 2024. "Constitución Política de los Estados Unidos Mexicanos." April 12, 2024. https://www.diputados.gob.mx/LeyesBiblio/pdf/CPEUM.pdf.

Ceceña, Ana Esther. 1999. "La Resistencia Como Espacio de Construcción del Nuevo Mundo." In *Chiapas*, no. 7 (1999). https://revistachiapas.org/No7/ch7.html.
Foucault, Michel. 2007. *Las Palabras y las Cosas*. Mexico City: Siglo XXI.
Gargallo, Francesca. 2010. "Una Metodología Para Detectar lo que de Hegemónico ha Recogido el Feminismo Académico Latinoamericano y Caribeño." In *Investigación Feminista. Epistemología, Metodología y Representaciones sociales*, edited by Norma Blázquez, Fátima Flores, and Maribel Ríos, 155–75. Mexico City: Centro de Investigaciones Interdisciplinarias en Ciencias y Humanidades, Universidad Nacional Autónoma de Mexico.
Guerrero, Patricio. 2010. "Corazonar Desde las Sabidurías Insurgentes el Sentido de las Epistemologías Dominantes, Para Construir Sentidos Otros de la Existencia." *Sophia, Colección de Filosofía de la Educación*, no. 8 (2010): 101–46.
Haraway, Donna. 1995. "Conocimientos Situados: La Cuestión Científica en el Feminismo y el Privilegio de la Perspectiva Parcial." In *Ciencia, Ciborgs y Mujeres. La Invención de la Naturaleza*, edited by Donna Haraway, 313–46. Madrid: Cátedra.
Hernández-Castillo, Aida. 2022. "Corazonar la Historia y la Memoria: Diálogos con el Intelectual Maya-Tseltal, Xuno López Intzin." *Disparidades. Revista de Antropología* 77, no. 1 (enero–junio 2022): 2–12. https://doi.org/10.3989/dra.2022.002.
Köhler, Axel. 2015. "Acerca de Nuestras Experiencias de Co-teorización." In *Prácticas Otras de Conocimiento(s). Entre Crisis, entre Guerras (Tomo 1),* edited by Xóchitl Leyva, Camila Pascal, Axel Köhler, et al., 401–28. Mexico City: Editorial Retos.
Le Goff, Jacques and Truong, Nicolas. 2005. *Una historia del cuerpo en la Edad Media*. Barcelona: Paidós.
Lenkersdorf, Carlos. 2002. *Filosofar en Clave Tojolabal*. Mexico City: Porrúa.
López, Francisco. 2016. "Los Acuerdos de San Andrés, Proceso Constituyente y Reconstitución de los Pueblos Indígenas." In *El Cotidiano*, no. 196 (2016): 87–94.
López-Intzín, Xuno. 2013. "Ich"el ta muk: La Trama en la Construcción del Lekil Kuxlejal (Vida Plena-digna-justa." In *Senti-pensar el Género. Perspectivas Desde los Pueblos Originarios*, edited by Georgina Méndez et al., 73–106. Jalisco: Red IINPIM, Red de Feminismo Descoloniales, La Casa del Lago.
López-Itzín, Xuno. 2021. Sp'ijilal O'tan: Saberes o Epistemologías del Corazón." Estrategias Resistentes, junio. https://resistantstrategies.hemi.press/spijilal-otan-saberes-o-epistemologias-del-corazon-es/?lang=es.
Núñez, Lucía. 2018. *El Género en la Ley Penal: Crítica Feminista de la Ilusión Punitiva*. Mexico City: UNAM, CIEG.
Núñez, Lucía (coord.). 2023. *Feminismos, Justicias y Derechos frente al Neoliberalismo. Aportes Para la Reflexión Crítica*. Mexico City: UNAM, CIEG.
Paoli, Antonio. 1999. "Comunidad tseltal y Socialización." *Revista Chiapas*, no. 7 (1999): 135–61.
Rosillo, Alejandro. 2015. "Fundamentar Derechos Humanos Para Desencriptar la Constitución." In *Revista de Estudos Jurídicos* 19, no. 29 (Enero–julio 2015): 1–21. http://seer.franca.unesp.br/index.php/estudosjuridicosunesp/index.
Ruiz, Alicia. 2000. "La Construcción Jurídica de la Subjetividad no es Ajena a las Mujeres." In *El Derecho en el Género y el Género en el Derecho,* edited by Haydee Birgin, 19–31. Buenos Aires: Biblios.

Saavedra, Laura. 2018. "Construyendo Justicia (s) más allá de la Ley: Las Experiencias de las Mujeres Indígenas que Participan con el Centro de Derechos de la Mujer de Chiapas A.C." PhD Anthropology, CIESAS-CDMX, Mexico City.

Sanín-Restrepo, Ricardo. 2020. "La Teoría de la Encriptación del Poder, Teorías Críticas y Migraciones Forzadas." Instituto de Investigaciones Jurídicas UNAM, April 12, 2020. https://ecdm.juridicas.unam.mx/sites/default/files/Migraci%C3%B3n%2C%20encriptaci%C3%B3n%20Sanin-Restrepo.pdf.

Sierra, María Teresa. 2005. "Derecho Indígena y Acceso a la Justicia en Mexico: Perspectivas Desde la Interlegalidad." *Revista IIDH*, no. 41 (2005): 287–314.

Smart, Carol. 2000. "La Teoría Feminista y el Discurso Jurídico." In *El Derecho en el Género y el Género en el Derecho*, edited by Haydee Birgin, 31–72. Buenos Aires: Biblios, 2000.

Chapter 6

Decryption of Liberal Transitional Justice

Critical Approaches from the Land as Central Problem in the Colombian Case

Michael Monclou-Chaparro, Julián Trujillo-Guerrero, María Daniela Delgado-Álvarez

ANYTHING BUT THE ECONOMIC SYSTEM

At the end of 2012, when peace dialogues began between the FARC-EP guerrilla and the national government, the then-incumbent president of Colombia, Juan Manuel Santos, drew the line between the negotiations and the framework of the transitional justice mechanisms that would be built in the country: "the political and economic model is not under discussion," he said.

This is not just any statement. It is an expression that summarizes the central problems and limitations of transitional justice in Colombia. Simultaneously, it sheds light on the objectives pursued by the majority of the country's traditional political elites who, after years of conflict and refusal to accept peace, have finally accepted the necessity of building it. Nevertheless, said peace is conditioned to a specific model of transitional justice limited to the consolidation of the rule of law in a democracy of formal procedures and in the process of capitalist modernization. Henceforth, it does not consist of the deepening of a radical democracy that addresses the material conditions of existence of the social majority, that is, that would seek to transform the structural causes (such as the land problem) that gave rise to the armed conflict in the first place. We call this way of conceiving and constructing justice in societies at war "liberal transitional justice (LTJ)."

This chapter aims to elaborate on a critique of LTJ in the context of land restitution in Colombia. To do so, we turn to the body of critical theory on the encryption and decryption of power as a useful tool for understanding how liberalism functions in societies at war and, above all, how it constructs forms of justice that are a simulacrum of democracy (Sanín-Restrepo and Méndez-Hincapié 2018; Sanín-Restrepo 2016). The question of the encryption of power is mainly ontological, for it asks, "what and who makes up the world, or how can the world be" (Sanín-Restrepo 2016, x). In a perspective similar to Mouffe (2000) and Badiou (2003), this is an understanding of the world that sees in the political the realm of immanence and of authentic democracy as the power of the people. It is the realm where difference flourishes. This perspective also points out that politics is a contingent order that is constructed in precise historical conditions of institutional coagulation of norms and procedures and is not a naturalized necessity. In this ontological scenario of democracy, difference is the character of the political: the space where all forms of life can be, where plebeian powers can rise.

The encryption of power lies in all acts, knowledge, technologies, languages, and laws that simulate democracy and evade difference through processes that obturate its immanence by means of transcendent models of being. They are models of identity that exclude the political and neutralize democratic power. They construct an essential and limited idea about what can be and what cannot be within a single possible framework, and even more, about "who counts" in the political space of the real (Sanín-Restrepo 2016, 2). To be recognized, difference must submit to an ideal boundary-creating principle that establishes what difference is and how it can be integrated within the machinery. This transcendent exercise, of both the power of encryption and the encrypted power, creates a government of difference that defines the official channels, allowing it to antagonize its deepest political demands, but in a neutralized way. Normative definitions, expert languages, authorized interpreters, and official procedures are established to grant a single order to the world. It is a domestication of democracy in the name of democracy.

Given this overview, the decryption of power operates as a counter-political intervention that remarks on the contingent character of all political coagulation and, therefore, the possibility of removing the transcendent model. At its political core, decryption is the authentic operation to "rehabilitate democracy" (Sanín-Restrepo 2016). It is at the same time a method, a theory, and a poetics, for it allows us to simultaneously expose the solidification of power, understand the political, and imagine and create new collective worlds from the now liberated democracy. But this democratic aperture is only possible if we first look closely at the operation of encryption. We must examine the way it works and actively intervene against it to recover what was taken from us.

Based on the encryption/decryption of power, our study on LTJ argues that it is a theory and practice of justice that assumes the capitalist development model as a formula for peace and, in doing so, risks promoting and deepening economic injustices. It establishes a limited and transcendent notion of justice rooted in mechanisms that construct a particular narrative about the past, a definition of victims, an inventory of what rights they can expect, and an idea about the future of society. These elements are connected inside a process of transition of societies toward an ideal scenario of peace understood as enclosed by the modernization equation of liberalism: peace = capitalism + liberal rule of law. This is why we argue that it is more appropriate to understand LTJ within the historical process of capitalism in peripheral societies. This would not only be a chapter in the history of transitions and their theories, as pointed out by Teitel (2003), Elster (2004), and Priemel (2023), but a moment in the global history of capitalism above all.

The text is organized into the following argumentative steps: First, we examine the discourse of LTJ as an encryption regime. Second, we highlight some of the political and legal instruments under which this discourse has been implemented in Colombia, particularly the Law of Victims and Land Restitution (Ley 1448 de 2011). Third, we use the critical tools offered by the Theory of Encryption of Power (TEP) to analyze said implementation, and we demonstrate that the land restitution program is embedded in an economic and transitional system that is not interested in land reform and thus focuses on the symptoms but leaves the causes of the armed conflict intact. Although the initial response to our critique may be that transitional models were not created to solve structural problems, our counterargument goes further. We assert that there is a problem with the justice model as a whole. This discussion is essentially a philosophical inquiry into the concept of justice underlying "temporary" and "transitional" justice, which have been encrypted and technified to avoid providing an in-depth response to a major democratic question: the means of production and the material conditions of existence of all forms of life. Fourth, our text proposes some final reflections marked by the fact that LTJ is anchored in the framework of a capitalist development model, the very model that gave rise to the conflict in the first place. This is why we propose to liberate transitional justice by deliberalizing to recover the possibility of building political and economic transitions linked to the radical and immanent character of democracy.

SOME TRAJECTORIES OF THE LIBERAL DISCOURSE OF TRANSNATIONAL JUSTICE

For liberals, transitional justice is like a roadmap that helps societies move past their armed conflicts and authoritarian regimes, paving the way for democracy after enduring serious human rights violations. In simple terms, it's a clear path toward peace. It's about transitioning from a state of war, often characterized by authoritarian structures, to the rule of law typical of modern liberal societies. Under this idea, the key mechanisms of transitional justice aim to establish an institutionalized understanding of the past—acknowledging what happened and what we now see as unjust—while also setting expectations for the future. It involves crafting a specific version of the past from the present, dealing with part of it, and using it to build a framework of temporary institutions for the emerging post-conflict society.

The most common mechanisms of transitional justice focus on holding people accountable through trials and truth commissions, restoring justice through comprehensive reparations, and securing peace through constitutional reforms, amnesties, and pardons (Olsen et al. 2010a; Revkin et al. 2024). This perspective on transitional justice is referred to as LTJ, which is essentially a political theory and practice dealing with transition and justice in societies affected by war.

How did LTJ come about, what does it involve, and how does it work? There are various theories about its origins. Some suggest it dates to Athenian democracy, arguing that it's not unique to modern democratic regimes (Elster 2004). Nevertheless, this depoliticizes its history and naturalizes what in reality is a fabrication, since it takes the elements of the liberal model and places them in a remote original past. This ignores the concrete process of its contemporary production and assumes as natural its current features and political objectives. Marx would not hesitate to call this operation a *robinsonade*. Others trace its roots to the late 1980s in Latin America (Arthur 2009; Revkin et al. 2024), crediting human rights movements in societies oppressed by military dictatorships and authoritarian rule for its emergence. In these contexts, the push for liberal democracy was driven by a desire for peace, which meant transitioning to a new system rather than simply ending conflict.

In any case, there seems to be a liberal consensus that transitional justice (liberal, of course) is a product of the post-World Wars (Teitel 2003). For such consensus, LTJ emerged as a response to efforts to build peace, as prompted by the European landscape of the time—physically and morally devastated by bombings, the atrocities of the concentration camps, and the use of atomic bombs. The necessity emerged, then, to adjudicate behaviors that, until 70 years ago, had not been categorized as unequivocally execrable crimes—genocide.[1] However, above all, LTJ was envisioned to be the cure for the evils that fascism and communism had brought to the world, characterized by the absence of a liberal state and economy, thereby necessitating their establishment (García Arboleda 2019). This approach to liberalism in the context of the emergence of LTJ can be traced, for example, in the analyses of both Popper (1945) and Arendt (1958), with all their differences. The liberal rule of law emerged as the most auspicious assurance of non-repetition. Viewing this process, even through the perspective of liberal apologists, reveals that the objective was not solely to extricate from war but to prevail in a distinctly specific conflict: that concerning the global order at stake. The amelioration of said evils lies in the advancement of the capitalist system, the ultimate victor in this contest and the primary beneficiary of liberal policies.

LTJ holds the promise of achieving a state of peace wherever its formula and principles are applied. Since the latter half of the twentieth century, what started as a vague field aimed at prosecuting war criminals has evolved into a sophisticated framework encompassing political, legal, and ideological institutions necessary for attaining capitalist peace. It became a blueprint, a template guided not just by the states and the capitalists' interests but by their new missionaries, such as the World Bank, the International Monetary Fund, and international aid. Here is how the model worked: there was a war, and the war ended. It is now time to rebuild the nation and society, advancing along the exponential function of progress. The truth about the conflict was reconstructed through various scenarios, while temporary courts facilitated swift judgments and condemnations of the actors involved. Transitory political powers were granted, and provisional budgets were allocated for reparations and reconstruction efforts. In that sense, the political economy of transitional justice legislation has only received tangential attention, as the Olsen, Payne, and Reiter (2010) study shows.

Liberal Transitional Justice seeks to provide truth, justice, and reparations, while guaranteeing non-repetition to the victims (Sánchez 2017; De Greiff 2020; Gissel 2022). To achieve these goals, standardized mechanisms are employed, including truth commissions, temporary courts, and administrative entities managing expenditures. In the Colombian context, these mechanisms have materialized in institutions like the Commission for the Clarification of Truth, Coexistence, and Non-Repetition (CEV), the Special Jurisdiction for Peace (JEP), and the Unit for the Search for Persons Disappeared in the Context and Due to the Armed Conflict (UBPD),[2] among others. These entities play a pivotal role in Colombia's post-conflict landscape, with some gaining global recognition. For instance, the JEP is setting international standards in transitional justice and serves as a model for national justice systems to investigate and prosecute war crimes and crimes against humanity within their territories, free from external court interventions.

Despite their progressive nature, these mechanisms are not immune to criticism, as exemplified by the Land Restitution Unit, whose shortcomings will be explored further in subsequent sections. For instance, Acosta and Sánchez (2021) critique the land restitution policy institutionalized in Law 1448 of 2011, highlighting its failure to effectively address restitution claims and act as a transformative transitional mechanism. Originally slated to operate for a decade, this policy's duration was extended until 2031 due to its underwhelming performance and the need to maintain its operation alongside the functioning of the new transitional justice mechanisms created after the peace agreements with the FARC-EP (studied by the Constitutional Court in ruling C-589 of 2019 and extended by Law 2078 of 2021).

Thus, operating under a presumed exceptionality, ostensibly justified by the greater good it promises, LTJ bestows extraordinary powers upon the state to reform itself and the society it manages. Nevertheless, this shows that liberal models of transitional justice appear not as anomalies or exceptions, but rather as the norm. They proliferate globally today and are presented as universal templates applicable to any society in conflict. This underscores the normalizing aspect of LTJ as a public policy for capitalist modernization.

Beyond its official objectives—or rather, through these—the primary objective of LTJ is to deepen capitalism, which is explicitly woven into the "official" narrative of transitional justice. LTJ, what we portray as the epitome of liberal consensus, as articulated by former UN Secretary-General Kofi Annan, emphasizes the restoration of the rule of law in conflict-ridden societies through the integration of justice, peace, and democracy (United Nations 2004). Annan outlines various processes and mechanisms aimed at addressing the legacies of widespread abuses, holding perpetrators accountable, delivering justice, and fostering reconciliation.

LTJ proposes to unequivocally advance the rule of law, specifying the context (societies transitioning from conflict to peace) and the approach (combining justice, peace, and democracy through prescribed processes and mechanisms of truth, justice, reparation, and non-repetition). However, the implications of these propositions, as well as the underlying concepts of justice, peace, democracy, and the operational mechanics of LTJ, are predetermined by a transcendent model that is applied here and there with some adjustments. Liberals assert their understanding of these concepts within the framework of the capitalist system. Thus, the proposal put forth by Annan only makes sense when viewed in relation to the socioeconomic dynamics of liberalism. This perspective disregards economic considerations precisely because the capitalist model inherent in LTJ encompasses them all. As a hegemonic force, it does not tolerate divergence; it either eliminates or assimilates it. *It is the encryption of power, stupid.*

The LTJ framework grapples with economic matters through reparations for victims. However, the interpretation and boundaries of this concept remain subject to ongoing debate. Louise Arbour, who served as UN High Commissioner for Human Rights from 2004 to 2008, is credited with spearheading a movement to broaden the scope of transitional justice by emphasizing violations of civil and political rights. In a 2006 speech, Arbour stressed the need for LTJ to also address discriminatory practices and violations of economic, social, and cultural rights occurring before and during conflicts to achieve more profound and substantive justice (Arbour 2007).

Since then, legal scholars and social scientists have sought to understand why transitional justice has often overlooked economic issues and inequality—a largely uncontested observation. It has not been a priority to address "economic, social, and cultural rights concerns, despite the indivisibility of these from civil and political rights as a long-accepted principle in international law" (Hoddy 2021, 93). Various explanations have been posited, including the legalistic origins of LTJ (McEvoy 2007; Urueña and Prada-Uribe 2018), its inherent promotion of a liberal peace and free-market model (Moyo 2014; Benavides, Mateos Martín, and Camps Febrer 2018; MacDonald 2017), its perception as a project of international professional elites disconnected from social demands (Gready and Robins 2014; Madlingozi 2010; Robins 2009), and the inherent challenges in addressing structural violence (Dancy and Wiebelhaus-Brahm 2015). As Miller (2008) points out, all this, consciously or not, has created an "invisibility effect of the economic" that entails significant costs for dealing with conflicts democratically: an incomplete understanding of the causes of the conflict, a focus on reparations that obstructs structural changes and the possibility of addressing inequality, and thus the risk of recurring or sustaining violence.

The existence of exclusion is acknowledged as a reality. However, the debate centers on how to address it. Two main camps emerge: those advocating for LTJ to confront structural inequalities and those opposing such efforts. The former argues that failing to address socioeconomic violence risks perpetuating conflict, hindering the fulfillment of LTJ objectives, and undermining its future viability (Muvingi 2009). They emphasize the interconnectedness between civil and political rights violations and economic, social, and cultural rights infringements (Laplante 2007; Arbour 2007). They also stress the importance of acknowledging economic and gender oppression in the construction of a society's past during transitional periods (Buckley-Zistel 2014; Miller 2008).

On the opposing side, detractors fear that incorporating structural inequality concerns into LTJ may dilute its primary objectives and strain its institutions (Robinson 2015). Instead, they propose addressing grievances related to structural inequality through broader political projects linked to state development efforts (Waldorf 2012). They also express concerns about potential legitimacy crises within the field (Waldorf 2012; McAuliffe 2014) and caution against reproducing technocratic biases through a convergence of LTJ and socioeconomic justice (Urueña and Prada-Uribe 2018).

Nevertheless, socioeconomic issues within LTJ have been increasingly scrutinized, resulting in the emergence of innovative proposals. Initially, the concept of "holistic transitional justice" gained traction, advocating for the acknowledgment of the multifaceted nature of victimization experiences and the application of various measures oriented toward both retributive and restorative justice (Sánchez 2017). However, this approach appears to fall short of the aspirations for transitional measures to evolve into comprehensive "measures of justice," rather than mere concessions in response to a complex reality (De Greiff 2014). This deficiency is particularly evident in the Colombian context, where the demands of victims often encompass broader socioeconomic issues such as access to healthcare, education, and employment. In this regard, Sánchez (2017) argues that the holistic perspective of LTJ fails to directly address inequalities and social exclusion.

A more groundbreaking proposal revolves around transformative reparations, which integrate distributive justice measures with corrective ones, reflecting the state's obligation to provide redress to victims (Uprimny-Yepes and Guzmán-Rodríguez 2010). This transformative approach aims to address the structural causes underlying violence while striving to restore victims to their pre-victimization state while rectifying the harm endured. This perspective is particularly pertinent considering Sánchez's critique of holistic LTJ (2017), suggesting that purely theoretical models, such as the one proposed, may not be practical to implement. Sánchez argues that any transitional proposal regarding land tenure or ownership must consider the structural inequities inherent in the system, necessitating a critique of the prevailing economic model (2017). This implies that cutting-edge proposals regarding LTJ's approach to socioeconomic structural issues are closely aligned with a re-evaluation of the economic paradigm, as proposed in this text.

Despite its obvious shortcomings, LTJ has worked because its "success" stories justify its being imported from one country to another, in the hope of comparing standards or results. The Colombian reparations program, while massive and unique, operates outside conventional standards and can be linked to post-World War II displacement efforts (Sikkink et al. 2014). However, despite its complexity, the Transitional Justice Research Collaborative (TJRC) undertook a comparative study of 120 reparations policies globally, spanning continents. This study on human rights norms, broad coverage of affected populations, and administrative reparations allowed for comparisons among vastly different transitional justice cases. Nevertheless, a persistent issue remains: the tendency to treat LTJ formulas as a manual for solving complex problems, often applying textbook-like rules.

Drawing upon the Nuremberg trials as a quintessential success story, conveying the necessity of LTJ and its effectiveness has not been overly challenging. However, its dissemination cannot be detached from the blockbuster narrative accompanying it, revealing its status as a "global enterprise" (Miller 2008, 268; Grewal 2023). Zinaida Miller (2008) notes that literature and descriptions of the processes of formation share a common language and terminology with which LTJ is practiced and discussed. In this sense, LTJ is portrayed as a paradigm for peacebuilding (García Arboleda 2019), aiming to ensure negative peace by instituting the mandates of liberal rule of law through a political, legal, and institutional formula with universal and expansionist aspirations, ultimately aiming to deepen capitalism.

LAND RESTITUTION AS PART OF TRANSITIONAL JUSTICE. TECHNIQUE, EXPERTISE, AND LIMITATIONS FOR THE VICTIMS OF THE COLOMBIAN ARMED CONFLICT

In Colombia, the discourse and formulas of transitional justice emerged at the beginning of this century, especially with the paramilitary demobilization process. This process is particularly interesting because Colombia was quickly inserted into the international debates on truth, justice, and reparations, and has become an international reference and even a transitional laboratory (Sikkink et al. 2014).

Authors such as Rodríguez (2017) and Vidal (2007) reconstructed how the policy of care for those affected by natural disasters moved to a policy of humanitarian emergency care for forced displacement and, finally, to reparations as a fundamental measure of transition. Some of the main formulas of transitional justice were Law 387 of 1997 on forced displacement, the Justice and Peace Law (Law 975 of 2005), which was born in the context of the demobilization of paramilitary groups, the Law on Victims and Land Restitution (Law 1448 of 2011, which we will explain in the following sections), and the system of Truth, Justice, Reparation and Non-Repetition. The latter is the result of the peace agreements between the government of Colombia and the Revolutionary Armed Forces of Colombia (FARC).

After several attempts and discussions, the Colombian Congress in 2011 enacted Law 1448, known as the Victims and Land Restitution Law.[3] This statute stems from a radical change within the state, one that we welcome: the frontal and official recognition of the armed conflict in Colombia. It is important to underline that during the two governments of Álvaro Uribe (2002–2006 and 2006–2010), there was an absolute denial of both the armed conflict and the massive forced displacement of peoples. Furthermore, a governmental discourse labeled "State of Opinion" was instituted, wherein political dissent and leftist ideologies were framed as alliances with armed guerrilla movements or characterized as terrorist rhetoric (Delgado Marulanda 2013). Now, the question that arises is: What does the armed conflict consist of, and how is this conflict dealt with?

Law 1448 contains a series of typologies, procedures, symbols, methods, and formulas aimed at enabling those who lost land as a result of the armed conflict to recover it. For example, although the law does not exactly define what internal armed conflict means, it appeals to international humanitarian and human rights law. It does, however, define who a victim of the conflict is.[4] For this purpose, it delimits its scope in time, since only those who have suffered harm due to events that occurred after January 1, 1985, are deemed victims. This first limit already tells us that those who suffered violations due to the armed conflict before this date are not victims.

Victims Law also delimits who is entitled to claim a land restitution process. Only those who possess legal entitlements to the land, whether through property rights or analogous forms recognized by Colombian law, are eligible to petition for land restitution. Additionally, this entitlement must be substantiated by events occurring since January 1, 1991. This legal relationship is mediated by property rights and the so-called rights (or facts) of possession and occupation.[5] In other words, the connection with the dispossessed land is limited by law, technicalities, and politics. Thus, we can perceive how a set of requirements is being built. Other impactful elements of the Victims Law are gradualness and sustainability. According to the first, policies must be developed gradually, respecting the public budget. The second, closely related to the former, privileges the fiscal sustainability of the law. In the name of gradualness, there is a definition of space, what the Victims Law calls "security conditions." To operationalize the policy, rural areas were geographically divided, with priority given to regions unaffected by conflict and conducive to safe return. So, if the land a victim claimed did not fit within said spatial definition of security, there would be no restitution.[6] The absence of security is nothing other than the fact that the war continues. And that could be understood under the alert made by Miller (2008) about ongoing cycles of violence as a consequence of ignoring economic matters. "By ignoring the deeper roots of conflict, the relationship of inequality to reconciliation and the injustice of maldistribution, transitional justice mechanisms may actively contribute to new outbreaks of violence" (Miller 2008, 288). The Victims Law began with a ten-year term starting in 2011. However, in 2021, given that restitution was moving in slow motion, the Colombian Congress extended the law for an additional ten years, until 2031.

This law also creates registries, censuses, and government institutions that involve an entire state bureaucracy. For example, the Land Restitution Unit, the Victims Unit, and the Historical Memory Center.[7] These institutions are later developed by other norms and regulated processes that build a complex apparatus that victims have to learn to navigate. It all produces a precise conception of transitional justice and imposes the conditions under which it occurs.

DECRYPTION

The liberal encryption of transitional justice hinders imagination and thus the possibility of creating an alternate world that is not a product of the existing capitalist system, which still is the only realistic possibility for liberals. Like any discourse, LTJ is an articulation that constructs a field of objectivity. Herein lies its ontological character. It is a system of relations, domains of knowledge (disciplines, subjects, and objects of knowledge), juridical devices, and technologies of power where our subjectivities and our social reality are produced at every moment. Anything excluded from the discourse of LTJ lacks objectivity and, consequently, is rendered nonexistent within the realm of official transitional justice discourse.

This has profound implications for history, as it does something with history. Following Walter Benjamin (1968), LTJ can be a form of collective forgetting imposed by the victorious powers. It constructs a very particular relationship with the past that results in a story about conflict and peacebuilding that marginalizes narratives, events, and subjects that do not gain official recognition. Various institutions, such as transitional courts and truth commissions, explicitly or implicitly undertake this task. Through their proceedings, narratives concerning the conflict, its victims, perpetrators, and potential resolutions (whether legally binding or not) are constructed. Democratizing this history from the perspective of the victims and the territories has been, precisely, the main political task of the Colombian Truth Commission (2017–2022), caught at the crossroads of being a liberal institution that offers an official yet non-legally binding story, but which faces the challenge of democratically including the victims in the production of its truth.

The narrative of conflict fabricated in LTJ sets the discourse for potential pathways for any resolution. Solutions primarily hinge upon how the issues are framed. As Miller sharply points out about the South African Truth Commission, apartheid "can become a story about racism or about specific, individual rights violations rather than about long-term, systemic abuses born of a colonial project with economic objectives" (2008, 280). If we follow this gesture, we can ask: What stories are at stake in Colombian transitional justice? What is the narrative of our conflict? Is it a tale framed within the confines of LTJ, portraying a struggle between the state and illegal armed groups, resulting in severe crimes against civilians? Or is it a broader narrative encompassing the formation of the state, the expansion of capitalism through land accumulation, the colonial struggle against drugs, and the pervasive deprivation of material conditions for most of society within their respective territories?

Experts

Today, LTJ discourse is a hyper-specialized domain of law. It is an authentic experience of encryption that could even be named an Encryptopedia. The rules, processes, and stages are standardized and have an academic, expert, and professional discourse on their definition and scope (Stan and Nedelsky 2023). This is a specific way of researching, producing, and disseminating knowledge. It has led to the construction of an expert canon and, as a political effect, to a proper way of putting transitional justice into practice that leaves out alternative theoretical and practical approaches that question the core assumptions of the field (Davidović and Turner 2023).

The liberal guild also has institutes funded by international cooperation, non-governmental organizations, academic journals, and conferences. This expansive domain spans university education and international diplomacy, extending its influence far beyond the confines of the legal profession. There are as many liberal transitional justice experts as there are armed conflict experts in the world.

The LTJ's discourse is encrypted in a technical jargon that seems decipherable only decipherable for experts or those who have access to such qualifications. These are the spokespersons of power, well-versed in their intricacies and rituals. They are the technicians who know how to interpret the law and can speak to the state through solemn official forms. The political effect is that matters of the common space are removed to a higher sphere only accessible to those who have the keys to enter. Justice and social conflict, two issues that concern us all, are misrepresented as the exclusive domain of experts.

The role of these figures in the encryption of power is fundamental because they elaborate reality and make it immune to difference, far from the public contagion of the layman, such as the victims of the armed conflict.[8] As the authors of the encryption theory of power have asserted, "what is altered eventually is reality itself" and, in that sense, there is a paradox that "lies in the fact that the construction of what we perceive as complex or traumatic realities is created precisely by the encryption of language" (Sanín-Restrepo and Méndez-Hincapié 2018, 16).

This theory points out that "the mission of the expert is to transform a political problem into a technical problem and from there into a rigid statute of meanings that are self-referential and isolated from common language" (Sanín-Restrepo 2018, xix). It is through this technification of life that experts conquer the privileged place to diagnose the problem, its solution, and the criteria of its success. As we have already said, LTJ tends to define the problem as an uncivilized and authoritarian situation where armed actors violate the order of international human rights law and, consequently, the authorized solution is to implement a rule of law regime where capitalism and its market are both the form and the guarantee of peace. In this context, experts serve as the ultimate evaluators of the *efficacy* or *effectiveness* of each transitional process. They base their judgment on transcendent criteria established in advance by the liberal recipe and subsequently studied by comparativists (Olsen, Payne, and Reiter 2010). Finally, in the face of each failure or need for adjustment, it is once again the experts who are called upon to restore order and prescribe LTJ as the solution. Paradoxically, this prescription functions as an inexhaustible and self-justifying remedy, ostensibly saving us from the very failures it perpetuates.

Simulacrum

In its form, encrypted by liberalism, transitional justice is a closed model wherein both the problem and its solution are prescribed. This is a framework that closes off the possibility of constructing a complex and rebellious narrative about our past that is linked to the construction of alternative worlds. Within the encryption machinery of LTJ, the product of a historical arrangement, that is, the contingent, is subsumed into a single natural and necessary order. As a result, the divergent viewpoints and debates within a political community regarding the causes of its wars and their potential solutions become assimilated and tamed by the transcendent model that rules over the sacred domain of the experts.

As noted by Sanín-Restrepo (2014), this is a false dialectic trapped in the idea of identity. It is a controlled and decaffeinated scene that simulates conflict and difference. Antagonism is illegitimately staged in liberal procedures and is embedded within the permanent crisis of capitalism as the engine of its reproduction. "What appears to be in commotion and agonizing crossings is in reality suppressed from the start and what remains is an image, a specter of antagonism" (Sanín-Restrepo 2014, 275). It is a limitation of the understanding of the world and the democratic imagination that fraudulently prescribes a story about conflict and a definition of what is just and what is unjust in a society, and how to resolve it. It seals off the possibility of constructing our own narratives about conflict and its solutions from the radical terrain of democratic difference.

For this encrypted order, the injustice that its mechanisms deal with is not the real violence that occurs in the territories: the pervasive inequality, land accumulation, and political exclusion that underpin the capitalist order. Victims in Colombia persistently highlight and denounce this form of violence.

In this construct, injustice is narrowly defined within temporal, spatial, and technical confines, focusing solely on specific acts against specific victims with access to specific reparations. Justice is encrypted, captured, and governed within the normative and procedural machinery of the liberal politics of capitalism. "The radical point is that encryption cements power and knowledge, state and capital, and politics and economy as impenetrable progenies, where the key to all rests in the simple fact that democracy must not be" (Sanín-Restrepo 2018, xxvi).

In short, a depoliticized model of justice is produced that deprives the people of their democratic power. Difference loses its capacity to name justice and to elaborate what its deepest problems consist of, for example, those linked to land as a means of livelihood. Although in Colombia the victims of the armed conflict and their demands for justice have a central place in transitional politics, LTJ constructs an essentialized image of them that ends up neutralizing the most powerful aspects of their demands. There is a definition of victim and of victimizing events that limits the possibility to include certain economic violences in the transitional arrangement.

The *Las Pavas* case is an example of this situation. Even though the way of life specific to *campesinos* in *Hacienda Las Pavas* in Bolívar, Colombia, was almost exterminated due to "legal" undertakings of economic development that involved radical intervention and transformation of their territory, their demands cannot be processed within the channels of transitional justice, even though they *are* part of the armed conflict (García Arboleda 2019). Moreover, based on said static definitions, there is a risk that victims are reduced from politically imaginative agents to passive recipients of the state's goods and services. In the inscription of power, their plebeian power is neutralized as they become beneficiaries of the state.

The effect of economic invisibility pointed out by Miller (2008) entails an invisibilization of certain political subjects that have been traditionally excluded from both transitional justice studies and its actual mechanisms. As an example, Hoddy's studies on the *campesinado* (peasants) have shown that the growing sensitivity to the formal recognition of their rights contrasts with the inability of the transitional justice field to understand and address the structural causes that have led to their violation. In fact, "the field has not considered why redressing (or failing to redress) structural and systemic violence experienced by peasants might matter to building future peace and stability" (Hoddy 2021, 92).

In a typical encryption operation, a paradoxical disempowerment of power is carried out in the name of victims. It is true that LTJ pursues the restitution of the lands that victims lost in the armed conflict, and, in that sense, it would not be appropriate to speak of dispossession. It's essential to recognize a deeper issue at play. We argue that through this encrypted and controlled form of justice, land restitution inadvertently impedes the profound social transformations demanded by victims. The radical nature of the political power of victims in Colombia is not only to seek restitution to the situation before the victimizing event but, crucially, in forging a new reality altogether. Rather than returning us to a past situation in which the causes of conflict and inequality are still in force, it is a question of imagining and building another possible world in the future, where the conditions that allowed violence to emerge, injustice and inequality do not exist. Thus, shifting from a conception of justice that accepts the world as it is and merely manages it, we propose another that aims to construct a new one—an aspiration that marks a substantial divergence between the two.

Given these limitations, some scholars in Colombia have introduced the concept of "transformative reparation." This approach seeks to provide comprehensive reparation to victims in such a way that it is not only a formula of corrective justice that restores the past, but also a formula of distributive justice that addresses the contexts of inequality and poverty of the victims (Uprimny-Yepes and Guzmán-Rodríguez 2010). This notion of reparation has been adopted by the official discourse of the LJT, for example, in the official notion of reparation in Article 25 of Law 1448 of 2011 and in the Colombian Constitutional Court. Although we believe the notion is headed in the right direction, that of responding to the demands of the victims and their economic needs, we consider that it ends up encrypted in a contradiction that simulates social transformation: it pretends to modify economic situations while paradoxically accepting the gearing of capitalism and the liberal order as an unalterable assumption.

ELEMENTS ON THE AGRARIAN QUESTION AS A CAUSE OF THE COLOMBIAN ARMED CONFLICT

The absence of economic issues in the current framework of LTJ does not necessarily lead to the conclusion that it is inherently impossible to construct an alternative model of transitional justice that explicitly considers them. What would happen if, unlike the current functioning of LTJ, we were to build a theory and practice of transitional justice that addresses economic issues, and moreover, that responds to the problem of inequality and economic injustice as one of the causes of war? Perhaps an alternative is to consider the agrarian problem as a central issue in the origin and therefore in the way out of the armed conflict.

Land in Colombia is hyper-concentrated. Although imperfect, the Gini index calculates how concentrated rural property is. The Gini index ranges from 0 to 1, with 0 being an equitable distribution and 1 an inequitable distribution. In other words, the closer the coefficient is to 1, the more concentrated the land ownership is among a select few. In Colombia, the Gini index is 0.891 (Ibáñez Londoño and Muñoz, 2011). In clearer words, almost 78% of the land in the country is in the hands of 13.7% of landowners. Furthermore, farms larger than 500 hectares represent only 0.4% of the total number of farms and occupy 67.7% of the productive land. This means that land is in the hands of very few people and that these few people control large amounts of productive land (Ward and Baldinelli 2020).

As recognized by the Truth Commission in its final report on the armed conflict (2022), the power struggle over land has been one of the primary causes of the Colombian armed conflict. We could even go briefly further back to the colony and trace how the desire to grab land was a constant in the Spanish empire. For example, it is worth recalling that one of the earliest Papal bulls concerning American colonization was the division of the planet between Spain and Portugal. This mentality regarding spatiality, resource extraction, and the need to control the destiny of entire generations is part of a colonial project (Herrera 2014). When independence occurred, the tensions between projects of independence and the Colombian nation-state were unable to resolve the land issue, and the balance was tilted toward the Colombian elites through the model of *Haciendas*. By the late nineteenth century, *Haciendas* had such autonomy that they could be seen as microstates. They had their own currency, policing and surveillance regime, prisons, punishments, and coercive mechanisms against subalternized peoples (Vega 2004).

Latifundism was the rule in Colombia, and during the first decades of the twentieth century, the liberals came to power with reformist intentions. However, between 1850 and 1920, thousands of *colonos* (squatters) opened new agricultural lands only to be dispossessed of them and turned into tenants by landowners. The continuous formation of latifundia practically limited the economic possibilities of *colonos* in frontier regions. This did not seem to be a problem for the traditional political class governing from the country's center. Even in Colombia, the land problem and its magnitude were not clear before 1920 (LeGrand 1986).

The years between 1946 and 1966 are known in Colombia as *La Violencia*. This was a period of civil war, massacres, land dispossession, and armed struggles between members of the liberal and conservative parties that left a toll of 300,000 dead (Hobsbawm 2016). *La Violencia* reshaped the countryside and forced internal displacement toward municipal centers. The countryside bore the brunt of the war's onslaught.

In "La reforma agraria," an article originally published in 1969 and compiled along with "Campesinos de los Andes" (2017), the Colombian sociologist Orlando Fals Borda acknowledges that an agrarian reform cannot exist solely by legal mandate. There is a necessity for provisions that allow reaching the goal of agrarian reform with the least possible disruptions (Fals Borda 2017). The author recognizes that land invasions and the parceling of large estates alone do not guarantee the well-being of *campesinos*. The solution does not lie in merely handing over a piece of land, even though the government initiated colonization and parceling processes in 1960 through Law 20 (Fals Borda 2017). According to Fals' data, by that time, 5% of landowners in Colombia occupied 45% of the declared land, while 95% of *campesinos* had only 55% of the land. These data are not only more favorable than the current data but, from a present-day perspective, could well be a bold target for land reform.

The works of the Historical Memory Center (CNMH 2010; CNMH 2013; CNMH 2018) are a fundamental resource for understanding how agrarian reform initiatives, such as land policies in Colombia, have almost invariably failed despite numerous attempts. In response to any reform effort, there has been a counter-reform shaped by violence and dispossession, which compounded the state's ineffectiveness, often in collusion with paramilitary groups.

The main political pact in Colombia, the 1991 Constitution, emphasized the social and ecological function of land and property as fundamental to the Republic. However, the material conditions of the rural world and the *campesinado* have not substantially improved since then.[9] On the contrary, the *campesinado* has been the primary victim of the Colombian armed conflict, and the urban-rural disconnect is so pronounced that the daily wage earned by a *campesino* for a day's work could barely cover a couple's expenses for two Starbucks coffees in front of Bogotá's most emblematic upper-class park. Today, after a reform in 2023, the constitution extolled *campesinos* as subjects deserving special protection. Although they are different historical processes, the struggles of black and Indigenous peoples share similarities. They all revolve around the recognition of their territorial rights, grounded in the understanding that territory is essential for the reproduction of their livelihoods and cultural systems.

La tierra es para quien la trabaja, "the land is for those who work it" goes a famous adage in Colombia. However, as demonstrated, land in Colombia increasingly belongs to a privileged few. Colombia may not be a nation of owners, but when discussions turn to agrarian reform, which implies the need for the distribution of property, fear grips existing landowners. Traditionally, the idea of property distribution has been associated with communism. This is paradoxical, considering that the reforms have never sought to abolish property.

This brief review of some elements of the agrarian question denotes a central idea: whether it is private property or not, the main point is the material feasibility of guaranteeing the life of all ways of being. The Colombian armed conflict arose in the face of the failure of agrarian reforms and the enclosure of political space in an oligarchic republic in which land ownership is unequal.[10]

TRANSITIONAL JUSTICE OUTSIDE OF LIBERAL SIMULACRUM

Decryption reveals that we have the capacity to dismantle the existing model and approach our conflicts outside the confines of expert-defined problems and solutions. By adopting a perspective that views armed conflict through the lens of land issues within the context of capitalist development, we open the possibility of constructing an alternative form of transitional justice. If this is the problem, and if we make clear the contingent character of LTJ, our transitional justice narratives, concepts, and mechanisms could be constructed to address the core problems that gave rise to the armed conflict in the first place. Only then can our transitional solutions match our structural problems.

Decryption is also an act of politicization and desecration of law and public issues that concern us all, not just experts (Trujillo-Guerrero 2019). It empowers us to create alternative notions of justice, about the history of the armed conflict and about the object of a transition. Therefore, we believe that it is not a matter of renouncing transitional justice as a whole but rather of revising it and shaking it off its worst demons, namely liberalism. The political endeavor of decryption consists of linking transitional justice to the radical experience of democracy and the hidden people. This enables a concept of justice that addresses the material conditions of existence of the victims and intervenes in the social production of existence. By exposing the operation of encrypted power and the twisted and contingent character of LJT, we can point to other horizons. This, indeed, embodies the poetic and creative essence of decryption.

NOTES

1. Nevertheless, considering the course of history and the double standards of the liberal Western order in judging this crime, genocide does not in itself appear to be outrageous.

2. *Comisión para el Esclarecimiento de la Verdad, la Convivencia y la No Repetición* (CEV), *Jurisdicción Especial para la Paz* (JEP), and the *Unidad de Búsqueda de Personas dadas por Desaparecidas en el contexto y en razón del conflicto armado* (UBPD).

3. For a more detailed understanding of the regulations, process, and action of the land restitution route, we suggest consulting Sánchez 2017.

4. Article 3, Law 1448 of 2011.

5. Colombian civil law defines possession as a fact according to which a person behaves as the owner of a property and thus reflects it before other people for a determined period. Occupation, in Colombian agrarian law, implies the work, habitation, and vital connection of the *campesinado* on lands called *baldíos* and belonging to the state.

6. The scope of the "security conditions" slowed down the restitution process so much that the Colombian Constitutional Court ruled to push the Land Restitution Unit to move forward with the processes. See: Ruling T-679-2015.

7. *Unidad de Restitución de Tierras*, *Unidad para la Atención y Reparación Integral a las Víctimas* and *Centro Nacional de Memoria Histórica.*

8. An example of this is the "obstacle course" that the victims had to go through for the Congress of the Republic to approve the Special Transitory Peace Constituencies (*Circunscripciones Transitorias Especiales de Paz*), a measure contemplated in the 2016 Peace Accord to guarantee their political participation, which had been denied for decades (Monclou 2021).

9. The meaning we give to the concept *campesinado,* which derives from the word *campesino,* follows the Colombian historian Marco Palacios (2012). In his taxonomic definition, *campesinos* are small agrarian producers who work the land. They grow and harvest food both for themselves and for trade. They have a family farm, a system of agriculture and traditional production with little technification and a cultural and moral environment, as well as a physical space called *vereda.* In the Colombian social class system, according to Palacios, they belong to the lowest class. This definition is complemented by that of the *sujeto campesino*, which encompasses "a historical and intercultural dimension, its relationship with the land and nature, and emphasizes family and community work" (Güiza Gómez et al. 2020, 50). To further explore this concept, we recommend referring to "La Constitución del Campesinado" (Güiza Gómez et al. 2020).

10. For a deeper understanding of the agrarian issue as a fundamental factor contributing to the armed conflict in Colombia, we recommend consulting the following: Le Grand 1986; Reyes Posada 2016, Sánchez and Meertens 1983; Machado 2009.

BIBLIOGRAPHY

Acosta, Aarón Alfredo, and Nelson Camilo Sánchez. 2021. *¿Barreras Insuperables? Un Análisis de la Etapa Administrativa del Proceso de Restitución de Tierras.* Bogotá: Editorial Dejusticia. https://www.dejusticia.org/wp-content/uploads/2021/12/Doc75_Web-1.pdf.

Arbour, Louise. 2007. "Economic and Social Justice for Societies in Transition." *New York University Journal of International Law and Politics* 40(1): 1–28. https://heinonline.org/HOL/Page?handle=hein.journals/nyuilp40&div=8.

Arendt, Hannah. 1958. *The Origins of Totalitarianism.* Cleveland, OH: The World Publishing Company. https://cheirif.wordpress.com/wp-content/uploads/2014/08/hannah-arendt-the-origins-of-totalitarianism-meridian-1962.pdf.

Arthur, Paige. 2009. "How 'Transitions' Reshaped Human Rights: A Conceptual History of Transitional Justice." *Human Rights Quarterly* 31(2): 321–67. http://www.jstor.org/stable/20486755.

Badiou, Alain. 2003. *Infinite Thought: Truth and the Return to Philosophy.* London: Continuum. http://www.elimeyerhoff.com/books/Badiou/Badiou-Infinite_Thought.pdf.

Benavides, Farid, Oscar Mateos Martin, and Blanca Camps Febrer. 2018. "Límites y Desafíos de la Justicia Transicional en las Nuevas Transiciones: Un Análisis Crítico a Partir de los Casos de Sierra Leona, Marruecos y Colombia." *Relaciones Internacionales*, no. 38: 121–45. https://doi.org/10.15366/relacionesinternacionales2018.38.006.

Benjamin, Walter. 1968. *Illuminations.* New York: Schocken Books. https://voidnetwork.gr/wp-content/uploads/2016/08/Illuminations-Essays-and-Reflections-Walter-Benjamin-edit-by-Hannah-Arendt-Harry-Zohn.pdf.

Buckley-Zistel, Susanne. 2014. "Truth Commissions, Human Rights and Gender. Normative Changes in Transitional Moments." http://dx.doi.org/10.2139/ssrn.2432164.

CNMH, Centro Nacional de Memoria Histórica. 2013. *La Política de Reforma Agraria y Tierras en Colombia. Esbozo de una Memoria Institucional.* Bogotá: Imprenta Nacional. https://www.centrodememoriahistorica.gov.co/descargas/informes2013/agraria/politica-agraria-tierras.pdf.

CNMH, Centro Nacional de Memoria Histórica, and Gonzalo Sánchez, eds. 2010. *La Tierra en Disputa. Memorias del Despojo en la Costa Caribe 1960–2010.* Informe de La Comisión Nacional de Reparación y Reconciliación. Bogotá: Grupo de Memoria Histórica y Ediciones Semana. https://www.centrodememoriahistorica.gov.co/descargas/informes2010/tierra_conflicto/la_tierra_en_%20disputa.pdf.

Comisión de la Verdad. 2022. *No Matarás. Relato Histórico del Conflicto Armado Interno en Colombia.* Bogotá: Comisión de la Verdad. https://www.comisiondelaverdad.co/sites/default/files/descargables/2022-08/CEV_NARRATIVA%20HISTORICA_DIGITAL_2022.pdf.

Constitutional Court of Colombia. Judge: Luis Ernesto Vargas Silva. Ruling C-715, 2012.

Constitutional Court of Colombia. Judge: Antonio José Lizarazo Ocampo. Ruling C-589, 2019.

Dancy, Geoff, and Eric Wiebelhaus-Brahm. 2015. "Bridge to Human Development or Vehicle of Inequality? Transitional Justice and Economic Structures." *International Journal of Transitional Justice* 9(1). https://ssrn.com/abstract=2584586.

Davidović, Maja and Catherine Turner. 2023. "What Counts as Transitional Justice Scholarship? Citational Recognition and Disciplinary Hierarchies in Theory and Practice." *International Studies Quarterly* 67(4). https://doi.org/10.1093/isq/sqad091.

De Greiff, Pablo. 2014. "Transitional Justice and Development." In Bruce Currie-Alder, Ravi Kanbur, David M. Malone, and Rohinton Medhora (eds.) *International*

Development: Ideas, Experience, and Prospects, 412–27. Oxford: Oxford Academic. https://doi.org/10.1093/acprof:oso/9780199671656.003.0025.

De Greiff, Pablo. 2020. "The Future of the Past: Reflections on the Present State and Prospects of Transitional Justice." *The International Journal of Transitional Justice* 14(2): 251–59. https://doi.org/10.1093/ijtj/ijaa013.

Delgado Marulanda, Alba Lucía. 2013. "La Polémica en el Discurso del Expresidente Colombiano Álvaro Uribe Vélez: Los Argumentos Ad Hominem y Su Función Como Configuradores Del Enemigo Político, El «terrorismo»." *Cuadernos de Lingüística Hispánica*, no. 22: 91–108. https://doi.org/10.19053/0121053x.2157.

Elster, Jon. 2004. *Closing the Books. Transitional Justice in Historical Perspective.* Cambridge: Cambridge University Press. https://search.ebscohost.com/login.aspx?direct=true&AuthType=sso&db=nlebk&AN=174143&lang=es&site=eds-live&scope=site.

Fals Borda, Orlando. 2017. *Campesinos de Los Andes y Otros Escritos Antológicos.* Bogotá: Editorial Universidad Nacional.

García Arboleda, Juan Felipe. 2019. *El Exterminio de la Isla de Papayal: Etnografías Sobre el Estado y la Construcción de Paz*. Bogotá: Editorial Pontificia Universidad Javeriana.

Gissel, Line Engbo. 2022. "The Standardisation of Transitional Justice." *European Journal of International Relations* 28(4): 859–84. https://doi.org/10.1177/13540661221120980.

Gready, Paul, and Simon Robins. 2014. "From Transitional to Transformative Justice: A New Agenda for Practice." *International Journal of Transitional Justice* 8(3): 339–61. https://doi.org/10.1093/ijtj/iju013.

Grewal, Kiran Kaur. 2023. "The Epistemic Violence of Transitional Justice: A View from Sri Lanka." *International Journal of Transitional Justice* 17(2): 322–38. https://doi.org/10.1093/ijtj/ijad016.

Güiza Gómez, Diana Isabel, Ana Jimena Bautista Revelo, Ana María Malagón Pérez, and Rodrigo Uprimny Yepes. 2020. *La Constitución del Campesinado: Luchas por Reconocimiento y Redistribución en el Campo Jurídico*. Bogotá: Editorial Dejusticia. https://www.dejusticia.org/wp-content/uploads/2020/10/La-constitucion-del-campesinado.pdf.

Herrera, Marta. 2007. *Ordenar para Controlar*. Bogotá: Ediciones Uniandes.

Hobsbawm, Eric. 2016. *Viva la Revolución. Hobsbawm on Latin America*. London: Little Brown Book Group.

Hoddy, Eric T. 2021. "Peasants' Rights and Agrarian Violence in Transitional Settings: From Transitional Justice to Transformative Agrarian Justice." *Journal of Human Rights* 20(1): 91–109. https://doi.org/10.1080/14754835.2020.1850242.

Ibáñez Londoño, Ana, and Juan Carlos Muñoz. 2011. "La Persistencia de la Concentración de la Tierra en Colombia: ¿Qué pasó entre 2000 y 2010?" *Notas de Política*, no. 9: 1–4. Bogotá: Escuela de Gobierno Alberto Lleras Camargo and CEDE.

Laplante, Lisa J. 2008. "Transitional Justice and Peace Building: Diagnosing and Addressing the Socioeconomic Roots of Violence Through a Human Rights Framework." *The International Journal of Transitional Justice* 2(3): 331–55. http://dx.doi.org/ijn031.

Le Grand, Catherine. 1986. *Frontier Expansion and Peasant Protest in Colombia, 1830–1936*. Albuquerque, NM: University of New Mexico Press.

MacDonald, Anna. 2017. "Transitional Justice and Political Economies of Survival in Post-conflict Northern Uganda." *Development and Change* 48(2): 286–311. https://doi.org/10.1111/dech.12298.

Machado, Absalón. 2009. *Ensayos Para la historia de la Política de Tierras en Colombia: de la Colonia a la Creación del Frente Nacional*. Bogotá: Universidad Nacional de Colombia. https://fce.unal.edu.co/media/files/CentroEditorial/catalogo/Libros_Digitalizados/O_ensayos-politica-tierras.pdf.

Madlingozi, Tshepo. 2010. "On Transitional Justice Entrepreneurs and the Production of Victims." *Journal of Human Rights Practice* 2(2): 208–28. https://doi.org/10.1093/jhuman/huq005.

McAuliffe, Padraig. 2014. "The Prospects for Transitional Justice in Catalyzing Socioeconomic Justice in Postconflict States: A Critical Assessment in Light of Somalia's Transition." *Northeast African Studies* 14(2): 77–110. https://doi.org/10.14321/nortafristud.14.2.0077.

McEvoy, Kieran. 2007. "Beyond Legalism: Towards a Thicker Understanding of Transitional Justice." *Journal of Law and Society* 34(4): 411–40. http://www.jstor.org/stable/20109761.

Miller, Zinaida. 2008. "Effects of Invisibility: In Search of the 'Economic' in Transitional Justice." *International Journal of Transitional Justice* 2(3): 266–91. https://doi.org/10.1093/ijtj/ijn022.

Monclou-Chaparro, Michael. 2021. "Las Circunscripciones de Paz: Una Carrera de Obstáculos a Contrarreloj" *El Espectador,* November 3, 2021. https://www.elespectador.com/colombia-20/analistas/las-circunscripciones-de-paz-una-carrera-de-obstaculos-a-contrarreloj/

Mouffe, Chantal. 2000. *The Democratic Paradox*. London: Verso Books.

Moyo, Khanyisela. 2015. "Mimicry, Transitional Justice and the Land Question in Racially Divided Former Settler Colonies." *International Journal of Transitional Justice* 9(1): 70–89. https://doi.org/10.1093/ijtj/iju026.

Muvingi, Ismael. 2009. "Sitting on Powder Kegs: Socioeconomic Rights in Transitional Societies." *International Journal of Transitional Justice* 3(2): 163–82. https://doi.org/10.1093/ijtj/ijp010.

Olsen, Tricia D., Leigh A. Payne, and Andrew G. Reiter. 2010. "At What Cost? the Political Economy of Transitional Justice." *Taiwan Journal of Democracy* 6(1): 165–84.

Olsen, Tricia D., Leigh A. Payne, and Andrew G. Reiter. 2010a. *Transitional Justice in Balance: Comparing Processes, Weighting Efficacy*. Washington, DC: United States Institute of Peace Press.

Palacios, Marco. 2012. *¿De Quién Es La Tierra? Propiedad, Politización y Protesta Campesina En La Década De 1930*. Bogotá: Universidad De Los Andes.

Popper, Karl. 1945. *The Open Society and its Enemies*. London: Routledge.

Priemel, Kim Christian. 2023. "Genealogies of Transitional Justice." In J. Meierhenrich, A. L. Hinton, and L. Douglas (eds.) *The Oxford Handbook of Transitional Justice*. Oxford Academic. https://doi.org/10.1093/oxfordhb/9780198704355.013.8.

Revkin, Mara, Ala Alrababah, and Rachel Myrick. 2024. "Evidence-Based Transitional Justice: Incorporating Public Opinion into the Field, with New Data from Iraq and Ukraine." *Yale Law Journal* 133(5): 1582–1675. https://search.ebscohost.com/login.aspx?direct=true&AuthType=sso&db=eoh&AN=2109681&lang=es&site=eds-live&scope=site.

Reyes Posada, Alejandro. 2016. *Guerreros y Campesinos. Despojo y Restitución de Tierras En Colombia*. Bogotá: Ariel.

Robins, Simon. 2009. "Whose Voices? Understanding Victims' Needs in Transition: Nepali Voices: Perceptions of Truth, Justice, Reconciliation, Reparations and the Transition in Nepal By the International Centre for Transitional Justice and the Advocacy Forum, March 2008." *Journal of Human Rights Practice* 1(2): 320–31. https://doi.org/10.1093/jhuman/hup006.

Robinson, Isabel. 2015. "Truth Commissions and Anti-Corruption: Towards a Complementary Framework?" *International Journal of Transitional Justice* 9(1): 33–50. https://doi.org/10.1093/ijtj/iju022.

Rodríguez, Nicolás. 2017. "La naturalización de la violencia: damnificados, víctimas y desarrollo en la segunda mitad del siglo XX colombiano". PhD dissertation, Université de Montréal . https://hdl.handle.net/1866/20470.

Sánchez, Gonzalo, and Donny Meertens. 1983. *Bandoleros, Gamonales y Campesinos: El Caso de La Violencia En Colombia*. Bogotá: El Áncora Editores.

Sánchez, Nelson Camilo. 2017. *Tierra en Transición. Justicia Transicional, Restitución de Tierras y Política Agraria en Colombia*. Bogotá: Editorial Dejusticia. https://www.dejusticia.org/wp-content/uploads/2017/10/Tierra-en-transicio%CC%81n-Versio%CC%81n PDF-para-WEB.pdf.

Sanín Restrepo, Ricardo. 2014. *Teoría Crítica Constitucional. La Democracia a la Enésima Potencia*. Valencia: Tirant lo Blanch.

Sanín-Restrepo, Ricardo. 2016. *Decolonizing Democracy: Power in a Solid State*. London: Rowman & Littlefield International.

Sanín-Restrepo, Ricardo (Ed.). 2018. *Decrypting Power*. London: Rowman & Littlefield International.

Sanín-Restrepo, Ricardo and Gabriel Méndez-Hincapie. 2018. "The Encrypted Constitution." In Ricardo Sanín-Restrepo (ed.) *Decrypting Power*, 1–27. London: Rowman & Littlefield International.

Sikkink, Kathryn, Bridget Marchesi, Peter Dixon, and Federica D'Alessandra. 2014. "Reparaciones Integrales en Colombia: Logros y Desafíos. Evaluación Comparativa y Global (Borrador)." Harvard Kennedy School Carr Center for Human Rights Policy. https://docplayer.es/36698027-Reparaciones-integrales-en-colombia-logros-y-desafios-evaluacion-comparativa-y-global.html#google_vignette.

Stan, Lavinia, and Nadya Nedelsky, eds. 2023. *Encyclopedia of Transitional Justice* (2nd ed.). Cambridge: Cambridge University Press.

Teitel, Ruti. 2003. "Transitional Justice Genealogy (Symposium: Human Rights in Transition)." *Harvard Human Rights Journal* 16. https://ssrn.com/abstract=4041414.

Trujillo-Guerrero, Julián. 2019. "Politización y Profanación de los Dispositivos Jurídicos Neoliberales. El Caso del Derecho a la Consulta Previa en Colombia." *Estudios de Derecho* 76(168): 167–95. https://orcid.org/0000-0002-9484-4874.

United Nations, Security Council. 2004. Report of the Secretary-General: The Rule of Law and Transitional Justice in Conflict and Post-Conflict Societies (S/2004/616). New York: United Nations.

Uprimny-Yepes, Rodrigo, and Diana Esther Guzmán-Rodríguez. 2010. "En Búsqueda de un Concepto Transformador y Participativo Para las Reparaciones en Contextos Transicionales." *International Law, Revista Colombiana de Derecho Internacional* 17: 231–86.

Urueña, René, and María Angélica Prada. 2018. "Transitional Justice and Economic Policy." *Annual Review of Law and Social Science* 141(1): 397–410. https://doi.org/10.1146/annurev-lawsocsci-101317-031259.

Vega, Renán. 2004. *Gente Muy Rebelde. Indígenas, Campesinos y Protestas Agrarias*. Bogotá: Ediciones Pensamiento Crítico.

Vidal, Roberto. 2007. *Derecho Global y Desplazamiento Interno. La Creación, Uso y Desaparición Del Desplazamiento Forzado Por La Violencia En Colombia.* Bogotá: Pontificia Universidad Javeriana.

Waldorf, Lars. 2012. "Anticipating the Past: Transitional Justice and Socio-Economic Wrongs." *Social and Legal Studies* 21(2): 171–86. https://doi.org/10.1177/0964663911435827.

Ward, Anseeuw, and Giulia Maria Baldinelli. 2020. "Uneven Ground. Land Inequality at the Heart of Unequal Societies." *International Land Coalition, OXFAM.* https://oi-files-d8-prod.s3.eu-west-2.amazonaws.com/s3fs-public/2020-11/uneven-ground-land-inequality-unequal-societies.pdf.

Chapter 7

Decrypting Power in the Territory

The Case of the Union of Cooperatives Tosepan, Titataniske

María Elena Rojas and Jaime Ortega

Inspired by the theory of decryption of power, we propose to develop the paradigm of Social Solidarity Economy (SSE) anchored to a concrete form in the territory. The theory of decryption contributes to unraveling the networks of economic power, money, and market. In this case, a portion of Mexican territory, which is the focus of our attention, shows the concrete way of decrypting the power of the conventional economy. The current civilizational crisis—or very probably already, a real collapse—has driven important portions of societies to seek alternatives of social organization and reproduction. The order and form of reproduction of life, commanded by mercantile forms and the expansion of capital, represents for many a dead end, an incomplete format, and a life based on the continuous disorder of the communitarian. Disorder that extends from the material to the symbolic and is characterized by a strong presence of uncertainty and helplessness. It is for this reason that, in recent decades, a trend has strongly emerged that, under the generic name of *social solidarity economy*, brings together the most varied efforts that propose the need to organize life of the "here and now" in a different way. It has often been spoken of as "another economy," but in the context of this book, it may well be considered that the alternative "decrypts" in Sanín-Restrepo's and Machado-Araujo's sense, the prevailing economic form (Sanín-Restrepo and Machado-Araujo 2020).

In the following pages, we will develop a set of arguments that will allow us to understand both the major trajectories of the formation of the social solidarity economy, its sources for the Latin American case, and the growing importance of grounding the analysis of the different experiences in the notion of territory and territoriality, in the vein of researcher Carlos Walter

Porto Goncalves (Porto-Goncalves 2009). Finally, we will exemplify the case of the Tosepan cooperative, one of the most deeply rooted cooperative experiences in the history of Mexico.

We will emphasize the forms of the construction of another economy based on a specific experience with the notion of territory as a form of social construction that involves collective action, symbolic elements, and politicization processes. In a similar line to the paradigm of *de-encryption*, we argue that the "other economy" presupposed in these scales contributes to unveiling the power of the market, money, and capital. This spatial scale, as well as the temporal ones, allows us to precisely locate the elements that configure the social conflict of our time, as well as the construction of concrete alternatives beyond traditional paradigms.

SOCIAL AND SOLIDARITY ECONOMY: DECOMMODIFICATION AND COMMONS

The twentieth century witnessed social experiments that started with top (the state) down (peoples and societies) exercises in the search for the transformation of the conditions for the reproduction of life. Of course, we are referring to the experiences known as *real socialism*, which began with the Russian Revolution of 1917 and were followed by others, such as China's in 1949, Cuba's in 1959, and countless other examples scattered throughout the rest of Asia and Africa. Although those experiences were based on the diagnosis that capitalist society was doomed to failure, they nevertheless opposed a model with (some) similar anchors, by concentrating their efforts on strengthening the state as the main, and sometimes the only, driving force behind industrial modernization. Although they controlled and contained market expansion, they aspired to a broad process of urbanization, accelerated industrialization and, in general, productive progress. Nuts and bolts, machines, and asphalt configured the horizon of sovereignty of the most important political revolutions during the last century.

Faced with this economic and geopolitical panorama, typical of the twentieth century, the social classes were confronted with the need to seek alternatives beyond the state, the revolutionary events, and the modernizations promoted by them. In this sense, de-encryption makes it possible to overcome Marxist paradigms, since it is not attributed to a single social group but is part of the broad perspectives of the diversity of actors. Thus, in the middle of the century, the work of Karl Polanyi emerged as one of the theoretical pillars of what we now call the social and solidarity economy. His approach privileges the criticism of what he called "the obsolete market mentality," typical of nineteenth-century liberalism, which articulated social relations in most countries. It was through his most famous work *The Great Transformation* that Polanyi (2016) established the historical understanding that led to labor, land, and money being considered interchangeable objects, giving way to the concept of commodification. Polanyi's work allows us to understand the origin of the welfare state as a mechanism to contain the process of commodification. It is an exercise that, in fact, contributed to the de-encryption of the power of money and the market. Nancy Fraser has pointed out that Polanyi's work allows us to understand why it is not possible to think of a market extended to the totality of society (Fraser 2022).

Polanyi's work became a contiguous path to that of the Marxist critique of political economy, which focused on the mechanisms of exploitation, particularly centered on the factory world. However, Polanyi's emphasis was more on the idea of protection than on the mechanisms driving commodification. He made the problem of commodification the fundamental element in the exercise of a different vision of the economy. The growing commodification of the "living worlds"—the principle found in labor, land, and money—was the object of criticism, later continued by his daughter, Kari Polanyi, in a tone much more inclined to converge with socialism. We can point out that Polanyi laid a cornerstone by not only looking at exploitation, but by placing the emphasis on the market and the commodifying dynamics it implied, allowing us to imagine distribution mechanisms outside the market.

The arguments in favor of "another economy" are at the basis of the social and solidarity economy. However, it is an exercise in de-encrypting power because it helps to strip the autonomized mechanism of money and the market of its foundation. There is another aspect, still present today, worth mentioning, not only as a theoretical argument but also as a very elaborate empirical research exercise: the "governance of the commons" (Ostrom 1990).

Elinor Ostrom was at the forefront of one of the strongest attempts to transform the view of the management of the commons and the possibilities of "self-governance." Her argument, initially conceived as a countersense to the so-called "tragedy of the commons," went from being a wake-up call on the possibilities of managing the commons to the construction of a scaffolding of broad proportions in the different fields of the social sciences. All of this would later result in the awarding of the Nobel Prize in economic sciences. Ostrom's argument starts by demonstrating that Garrett Hardin's (2005) assessment of the impossibility of adequate collective management of the "commons" cannot be universalized. From a complex web of data and methodologies, Ostrom registers possibilities for collective action to manage the commons effectively, summarizing this idea as "let's work together." Her work included empirical elements and elaborate processes that demonstrated, both in the laboratory and in the field, that collective action allows for self-governance over the commons, without the need to fall into the dichotomy between state and market.

Although the works of Polanyi and Ostrom are now commonplace in all bibliographies dealing with issues related to the construction of the social and solidarity economy, the notion of territory is not found in them. In the case of Polanyi, it is clear that his argument belongs more to historical sociology and less to empirical analysis. With Ostrom, on the other hand, an empirical construction, typical of the crossroads between political science and economic science, so common in the Anglo-Saxon world, is present. However, her work is a reference because it allows us to build scaffolding to think about both decommodification and the government of the commons.

Nevertheless, the problem of territory is incorporated as an axis within the Latin American tradition of critical reflection on the forms of reproduction of life commanded by capital. In the following section, we will present some basic ideas, which we will later develop into a construction in which the territory gains a privileged place.

THE LATIN AMERICAN TRADITION

It is not only in Europe and the United States where we find inputs for thinking about the paths along which the social and solidarity economy is moving. We can find numerous passages, around the different social theories produced in Latin America, that enable this perspective. In Latin America, a more militant vision of the social and solidarity economy has been built, as stated by the Ecuadorian researcher Giuseppina Sara da Ros (2007). This can be explained by the formulation of social traditions that have wrested spaces of control from both markets and states, as well as much more violent modernization processes than those that occurred, at least during the twentieth century, in Europe and the United States. There have been several sources of social thought, some of which are listed below.

The first has to do with the rehabilitation of a certain *peasant* tradition in the mid-twentieth century, as a result of the intense mobilizations that shook Latin American societies. Peasants were also present in El Salvador, Peru, Colombia, Bolivia, and even in northern Argentina, a society traditionally associated with industrial dynamics. Confronted with the failure of existing agrarian reforms, such as those in Mexico, the challenge of initiating new ones, like in Brazil, or the need for radicalization of the ones where only initial steps had been taken, as in Chile or Peru, a significant portion of the intelligentsia and political organizations endeavored to construct alternative solutions rooted in the peasant world. There were also examples of the study of traditional forms that went beyond mercantile exchange.

At a crossroads between politics and anthropology, works such as those of Dominique Temple (1983) in the Andean area rehabilitated the discussion on the "gift." Establishing a link with other traditions that in the past, such as Marcel Mauss, or in a contemporary form, problematized the existence of a wealth not exclusively traversed by the mercantile dimension of exchange. Thus, anthropology, from Pierre Clastres (1996) to Michael Taussing (1993), as well as the contributions of Jacques Godelier (1998) or Jacques Derrida (1995), were part of the discussions that some anthropologists were having in the region. As these discussions were rehabilitated, they showed not only that other paths could exist, but also that, in fact, other forms of economy had taken place, conceptualizing wealth in a different way from the currently dominant one.

The Marxist perspective has made significant contributions, especially through its critical analysis of the prevailing economic system. Gradually, this has led to the development of tangible alternatives, moving beyond merely theoretical frameworks. This is the case of Anibal Quijano's work on the popular economy and the construction of categories such as "social private" and "non-state public" (Quijano 1988), which he developed in the 1980s. We could also add Franz Hinkelammert's last work, co-authored with Henry Mora, which establishes the basis for proposing "an economy for life" (Hinkelammert and Mora 2006). Recent interpretations of Quijano's work have emphasized its value in fostering a deeper understanding of reciprocity (López 2018), while Hinkelammert's approach has been included in contemporary discussions on social and solidarity economy.

A Marxist who contributed significantly to the construction of this paradigm in a clear and direct way was Paul Singer (2013). Of German origin but based in Brazil, the economist developed numerous works in a Marxist key during the 1970s and 1980s. Toward the first decade of the twenty-first century, he became a reference for solidarity economy, defining it as a mode of production and a mode of distribution: "The solidarity mode of production and distribution seems, at first glance, a hybrid between capitalism and small commodity production. But, in reality, it constitutes a synthesis that surpasses both," in addition to defining it as a "creation in continuous process" (Singer 2000).

In contemporary times, other contemporary authors, such as José Luis Coraggio or Mario Saúl Schujman from Argentina, have raised perspectives from the experiences of their country, where the cooperative and solidarity movement has been accompanied, at times, by the impulse of state action. The state of the question in Latin America is very diverse and contemplates practical experiences—as in the case of Quijano—trajectories of high theoretical level—such as Hinkelammert—or the search for a conceptual construction that accompanies concrete political experiences.

TERRITORY AND SOCIAL SOLIDARITY ECONOMY

SSE is the name given to multiple associative and collaborative experiences, which place at the center the reproduction of life in opposition to the reproduction of capital. It is a multidimensional field of social interaction and organization (Altschuler and Muñoz 2015) of a new way of doing economy, among which we find ejidos, agrarian communities, cooperative societies, solidarity collectives, enterprises that belong mostly or exclusively to workers, community enterprises, savings and credit banks, and even forms of exchange such as barter or fair market, and so on. Despite their differences, all these practices are based on the assumption of the need to immediately overcome the scenario of wage labor and the domination of capital.

As has been pointed out in numerous Latin American experiences, their existence has been mediated by intense processes of mobilization and collective action. In the case of Mexico, the experiences of the Pascual and the Tradoc cooperatives based in Jalisco are famous. Both of them, located in urban areas and linked to industrial work, were the result of conflict processes won through collective organization based on self-management and mutual aid.

There is, however, a set of experiences directly associated with territory as space and livelihood. In this section, we seek to follow up on the differentiated ways in which the problem of territory and territoriality (in general, space) has been conceptualized. Among the most significant contributions to think about spatiality linked to the issue of political mobilization is the work of Porto-Goncalves.

The theorist and geographer has set guidelines to think about the multiple dimensions called on behalf of the territory:

> Territory is appropriated space, space made its own thing, in short, territory is instituted by subjects and social groups that affirm themselves through it. Thus, there is always territory and territoriality, that is, social processes of territorialization. In the same territory there are always multiple territorialities. However, territory tends to naturalize social and power relations, since it becomes a refuge, a place where everyone feels at home, even in a divided society. (Porto-Goncalves 2009)

In addition to the category of territory, it is necessary to understand that collective action expresses concrete forms of decryption of the abstract power of money, which can be captured from the notion of territoriality. Territory corresponds to unity, while territoriality corresponds to differentiation, the product of that process of decryption to which the critique of the capitalist form of organizing the economy refers. Each of these is a product of social construction, encapsulating the intricate relationships among humans as well as their essential connection to the environment.

Several approaches from social economy have problematized the relationship between organizational experiences and the territory. Pérez González, for example, points out that if the social economy calls for the sustenance of life, the territory plays a "par excellence" role (Pérez 2011) to the extent that solidarity practices are intertwined with "history, tradition" (Pérez 2011). Laura Rincón Gamba, for her part, resorts to the multiple territorialities and assumes that these are always overlapping and in dispute, and to that extent the territory and its actors "cannot be considered, in general terms and as a natural fact by the mere location of people in a territorial context" (Rincón Gamba 2012).

Specifically, José Luis Coraggio (2011) pointed out that the territory must encompass natural and social processes in interaction and mutual dependence, that is, it comprises a natural complex whole, in which various living beings cohabit, including human beings in community or society. Thus, "given a settled population with its own forms of sociability, its "living space," its historical environment—natural and built—is determined. And the development of human life (always in community or society) comprises them both in that unit we call territory." The Argentine emphasized that: "territories" would thus be socio-historical regions resulting from the development of the metabolism and the spiritual world of communities or societies (Coraggio 2011).

Therefore, the territory joins the natural and the social in constant interrelations of multiple variables that shape the environments, as well as the various forms of life and their reproduction. In the social order of capital, it has been the state that orders and rationalizes (through border regionalization) the control and legislation around private property of the territory. This makes it possible for the interactions that take place in this space to be considered as market relations. Coraggio points out that the SSE seeks communal ownership of territory as a solid basis for emancipation from wage labor and the reproduction of capital, by ensuring an alternative way of reproducing life outside the mechanisms of control, such as the subjection of wage labor. A new consensual, democratic regionalization, reflecting the will of the community or networks of communities, their culture and interculturality, and facilitating the management of *another* economy whose purpose is to achieve "good living" through the practice of solidarity and mutual aid.

For their part, Ana María Torres, Leonardo Cardona, and Leonardo Monroy have pointed out the need to think of the concept of "the local" as a motive for development in terms of "productive and marketing resources [but] also of human, institutional and cultural relations" (Torres, Cardona, and Monroy 2019). In a similar sense, Guillermo Díaz has argued that if "territoriality is also fundamental in the construction of *another* economy" (Díaz

2015), it is precisely due to proximity relations. Meanwhile, Altschuler and Muñoz (2015) point out that contemporary perspectives of critical geography bring three interrelationships to address the concept of territory:

(a) a close relationship between territory and power, conceiving the latter in a relational mode and present in all social relations; (b) the idea of territory no longer normally evokes the "national territory" and the nation-state as its sole manager, but deconstructs the nation and the regions as historical-social and political constructions; and (c) the territory is denaturalized as something fixed or immutable, giving rise to flexible conceptions of territories and their historical forms. It is thus proposed that there are not only exclusive, juxtaposed, and continuous territories, but also overlapping, discontinuous, and networked territories, crossed by various forces and power relations (Altschuler and Muñoz 2015).

For the different organizations and collectives that make up the SSE, the struggle for territory is essential in the search for emancipation from the control and reproduction of capital. They understand that one way out of the capital-wage labor relationship is to achieve collective appropriation of the means of production, so that collective ownership of the territory is the basis for the construction of communities that practice autonomy to produce and reproduce the lives of their associates, as well as their context of action and interrelation. For this reason: "SSE experiences usually have significant territorial links, both in the way they emerge and develop, and in the objectives and collectives they are oriented towards or that drive them" (Altschuler and Muñoz 2015).

In this sense, SSE organizations and collectives establish solidarity-based territorial dynamics by building networks of collaboration and reciprocity, practicing solidarity, mutual aid, and direct democratic forms, that is, they act as "agents of change and socioeconomic transformation in the territories" (Mozas and Bernal 2006), in a process of interrelationships ranging from local networks to other regional, national, and international networks. On all these scales, there is a shared spirit for this perspective: "It is there where the social economy becomes important as an alternative and dynamic model in the territories. The form of production is related to the space insofar as it is locally based, from which it is also nourished, not only in terms of productive and marketing resources, but also in terms of human, institutional and cultural relations" (Torres, Cardona, and Monroy 2019).

In this way, the SSE works to establish another form of economic development focused on the welfare of people and the environment, so that: "an effective option to enhance the capabilities of popular economy entrepreneurship is to promote socioeconomic and organizational strategies in the key to SSE in the framework of territorial development strategies" (Altschuler and Muñoz 2015). This potential of the SSE to create *another* economy centered on people and away from the reproduction of capital, in search of a development based on the reproduction of life and care for the environment, is emphasized by Aracena (2019) when he states that: "The merit of cooperativism lies in being an institution that annuls the separation between workers and the means of production, and makes possible the decommodification of the workforce" (Aracena, 2019). In this way, the associates and co-owners of the means of production can carry out an alternative production to the capitalist system by having the concrete bases to free themselves from the capital-salaried labor exploitation relationship. To illustrate this possibility of SSE organizations, the following section presents the emblematic case of the Union of Cooperatives Tosepan Titataniske located in the Northeastern Sierra of Puebla, Mexico.

TOSEPAN: FROM PRODUCTIVE APPROPRIATION TO TERRITORIAL DEFENSE

The Union of Tosepan Cooperatives (UCT) "Titataniske," which in Náhuatl means "United We Shall Overcome," began in 1977. It is an example of a broad trajectory that involved the transformation of the peasant movement, which crossed the entire history of the twentieth century. Toward the 1970s, as the official corporate bodies were worn out, a current emerged within the peasant movement that went from the demand for "independence" from the state—a fundamental slogan since the 1940s—to that of "autonomy," the latter resting, above all, on the idea of productive appropriation.

The history of the Tosepan has enabled the study of a set of experiences, becoming, perhaps, the most addressed experience in the academic world. Today we can explore its history from different perspectives. From environmental education (Moguel 2010), corporate social responsibility (Sema de la Garza and Martínez 2009), or specific problems such as coffee production (Tosepan Titataniske 2021), cultural-identity dilemmas (Bernkopfová 2014), or educational issues (Rojas and Rojas 2020). In this chapter, we will focus on showing the advances around the defense of identity and territory through the implementation of collective programs and projects focused on the reproduction of the community life of its members with the aim of achieving the Yeknemelis, that is, the "good life."[1]

Thus, following the articulated conception of this experience:

> The Yeknemilis is a lineage transferred from a memory that encompasses cultural codes loaded with values that correspond to a teaching-learning instrument and transmitted generationally as a set of knowledge, beliefs, wisdom, uses and customs that cause a harmonious interrelationship between humanity and

> nature. Therefore, language, agriculture, milpa, art, textiles, edible plants, good food and habitat are the active articulation of a territorial organization whose legacy is the defense of the land from a collective organization of work and common property. (González 2020)

As shown by its cultural and philosophical foundations, the UCT has undergone an organizational process that has allowed its associates to progressively advance in priority levels, going from achieving subsistence as a collective to the point of projecting to achieve human development collectively, ensuring a community living space—territory—that makes it possible to achieve a good life or Yeknemelis. In order to obtain these elements, collective action is based on 12 fundamental principles that all members are encouraged to adhere to in their daily lives: "autonomy, kindness, dialogue of knowledge, transparency, equity, mutual help, taking into account the other, community work, respect, trust, generosity, and belonging" (González 2020). Such elements can contribute to concrete and specific forms of decryption of the power of money and the market, by displacing the abstract character of these elements and returning sovereignty to the producing subjects.

Most of Tosepan's associates belong to the Náhuatl and Totonaca ethnic groups, whose culture conceives nature as Mother Earth; hence, they have a particular way of feeling, walking, and looking at the territory. Thus, their relationship with nature is one of respect and care for biodiversity since it is the space in which the community can develop collective life projects based on organic production, accompanied by educational and training processes in various areas including agriculture, agroforestry, savings, handicrafts, coffee, ecotourism, forestry, and the production of native bee honey. Their productive activities have the common and collective as their axis: "to achieve human and ecological wellbeing, the interconnections, and interdependencies of the whole 'socio-natural metabolism' at different levels must be prioritized and, therefore, give greater visibility to relationships than to delocalized economic and political systems" (González 2020).

In their territory, says González, citing Toledo, Moguel, Durán Albores, Rodríguez, and Ayón, the cooperative families of the Tosepan have an average of one hectare of land: "In these plots we find that, out of a universe of 150 species of cultivated plants, 92% are native or local and only 8% are introduced. On the other hand, the biodiversity of the plots is classified as follows: 57% of the plants are food and medicine, 18% energy, 10% wood and 6% are ornamental plants" (González 2020). Land tenure of the members of the Tosepan has changed over time due to legislative modifications; initially, it was communal property, which was affected by the Lerdo Law in 1856, where: "they opted to deed the plots and in those years the small property arises, which to date is the type of tenure that prevails in most of the Sierra" (González 2020).

Under the governments that applied neoliberal economic policies in Mexico, another important legislative modification occurred in 1992, in Article 27 of the Constitution of the United Mexican States, which allows the privatization and sale of communal and ejido lands in order to facilitate the development of extractive projects in the national territory: "This is how the Mexican territory is being handed over to large fractionators, under the development model that exalts an idea of nation, and in turn marks privileges for extractive economies, over other identities and other solidarity and cooperative economies" (González 2020). The result of this neoliberal policy to facilitate extractivism within the territories has caused heavy damage to biodiversity, deforestation, soil erosion, contamination of water resources, accumulation of waste, and environmental pollution. This affectation of the territory hinders the life of living beings and endangers human life, which is why the UCT initiated actions in defense of the territory, becoming an important actor in the region, as stated by González: "In recent years and as a result of the defense of life and territory that we have had to face, we have been reflecting on the importance of recovering the forms of governance in a collective manner, from that community thinking; where the good living or Yeknemilis should be sought" (González 2020).

It was in 2009 when the actions against the territory of the Northeastern Sierra of Puebla began in a more forceful way through the concession and federal authorization of extractive megaprojects for mining, hydroelectric, tourism, and trade, mostly to large transnationals seeking to benefit from the natural resources of the country and that usually destroy the way of living, organizing, and the rights of the inhabitants of the region. For this reason, the UCT considers them as "projects of death that clash with the projects of life that we are proposing" (González 2020). They clearly expose the damage they cause as follows: "It is theirs a mad race in which they kill the soils, pollute the waters, cut down the forests, enclose the rivers, besides displacing and destroying the communities and mercilessly exploiting the work of the people" (Cobo, Paz and Bartra 2018)

The following is a brief historical overview of the projects against the territory and the actions taken by the UCT to defend the territory, its natural resources, and the rights of the region's inhabitants:

> In 2008 we became aware that powerful tourism entrepreneurs were targeting landscapes, forests, and waters of the Sierra Nororiental in order to create here a "School for high quality tourism," managed by the Universidad Anáhuac, and then a large hotel complex in the springs area that, among other damages, would leave the inhabitants of the lowlands without water. (Cobo, Paz and Bartra 2018)

In 2009, an attempt was made to impose the "Bosques de niebla" project to install tourist infrastructure in an area of springs that supply water to approximately 18,000 inhabitants of the municipality of Cuetzalan, which resulted in the signing of an agreement between the municipality and the Benémerita Universidad Autónoma de Puebla to carry out the ecological planning of the municipality. A broad popular consultation was carried out through the methodology of dialogue of knowledge, achieving that on October 15, 2010, the municipal council unanimously approved the Ecological Land Management Program of Cuetzalan. Complementing the actions to defend the territory, in December 2010, the Sustainable Urban Development Scheme of Cuetzalan was approved, thus achieving the first Integrated Land Management (OTI) in Mexico. To ensure compliance with the guidelines of this ordinance, the Integral Territorial Ecological Ordinance Committee (COTIC) was formed.

In November 2010, the COTIC, at the request of the municipality of Cuetzalan, analyzed the project to authorize the opening of a Walmart store. After reviewing and evaluating the case and determining the impact on employment of the population and the impact on cultural affectation, it ruled to deny the opening of the store. The agreement was ratified in a public assembly and by the municipal council: "This is followed by the intention of the then governor, Rafael Moreno Valle, to create what they call Rural Cities, artificial towns where they want to concentrate the population for purposes that only later we understood. The first one, developed by Grupo Azteca, was to be established in Zautla, but fortunately in 2011 we stopped it" (Cobo, Paz, and Bartra 2018, 16).

In 2012, the Tiyat Tlali Council was formed, of which the UCT is a member, against megaprojects estimated at 105 mining concessions, the hydraulic affectation of 35 municipalities and the establishment of 9 hydroelectric plants. In the same year, in the Ajajalpan River area, there was a struggle against Grupo Mexico, which intended to use the water to generate electricity for the consumption of its companies. Faced with this threat, approximately 70 residents of the municipality of Olintla prevented the passage of a backhoe loader that would start the works and then organized a camp that was nourished by the solidarity of more residents. This action began in December 2012 and continued until October 2013, when Grupo Mexico issued a statement in which it reported that it was withdrawing from the municipality.

On the other hand, it is important to note the following sequence:

At the end of 2012, in a forum that the Tiyat Tlali Council convened in Ixtacamaxtitlán, it was reported the existence of a gigantic regional plan that includes 22 mining projects served by 6 hydroelectric works designed to provide them with water and energy. Additionally, the plan included the construction of several rural cities where the displaced population would be concentrated. The beneficiaries were Chinese companies such as JDC

Minerals, Canadian companies such as Almaden Minerals, and Mexican companies such as Carlos Slim's Frisco and Grupo Ferrominero (Cobo, Paz, and Bartra 2018).

Faced with this strong threat, it was necessary to strengthen the organization and unity for the defense of the territory, having to face constant battles against megaprojects, as was the case in 2012 in Tlamanca, Maseual municipality of Zautla, where the Chinese company JDC Minerals intended to reopen La Lupe, an old mine holding a concession. The community met and analyzed the threat of this project. As a result they organized and undertook actions in defense of their territory, as follows: "in October of that year seven hundred people participated in an informative assembly and in November the villagers, and those in solidarity with us, held a three-kilometer march and a municipal assembly attended by seven thousand people. There the mayor gave the mining company twenty-four hours to leave the community. And the Chinese left" (Cobo, Paz and Bartra 2018).

In addition, in 2013, three concessions were granted to mining companies for the exploitation of gold, silver, copper, and other minerals, which would affect part of the municipality of Cuetzalan del Progreso and the municipality of Tlatlauquitepec. These concessions would affect part of the municipality of Cuetzalan del Progreso and the municipality of Tlatlauquitepec, covering high areas where the aquifers are recharged and where the springs that supply water to most of the communities of Cuetzalan are located. Therefore, the COTIC, at the request of the inhabitants, held 30 informative assemblies from May 2014 to September 2019.

In the lower zone, the threat comes mainly from the extraction of oil and gas through what is known as hydraulic fracturing. This method uses pressurized water mixed with toxic substances to break rocks at great depths and release the hydrocarbons they contain. The so-called fracking pollutes the soil, water, and air . . . and is even more destructive than ordinary oil wells (Cobo, Paz, and Bartra 2018).

In the fourth assembly held on September 7, 2014, in the community of Zacatipan, 32 representatives from the municipalities of Tlatlauquitepec, Yaonahuac, and Cuetzalan formed the *Masewal Altepetajpianij Council,* or the guardians of the territory, and agreed to take legal action by filing an injunction against those who authorized the concessions for the exploitation of minerals in the three municipalities. By means of this action, the following resolution was obtained: "flat suspension, this means that, until this situation is legally resolved, the more than 7 thousand hectares granted for mining under the open-pit exploitation modality cannot be carried out within the ancestral territory of the Masewal people" (González 2020).

In the fifth assembly held on October 8, 2014, in the municipality of Yaonahuac, the intention to affect the water resource in the Apulco River was reported, because the Ministry of Environment and Natural Resources (Semarnat) authorized a private company to dam the river at four points. The assembly agreed to hold a public citizen consultation on the Environmental Impact Statement (MIA) that this project would cause. Many steps were taken, and finally in May 2015, Semarnat denied the authorization of the environmental impact statements.

Adding to the situation of territorial affectation, the Federal Electricity Commission (CFE) intended to lay 20 kilometers of high voltage lines called Cuetzalan Entronque Teziutlán II-Tajín (LAT project) toward an electrical substation owned by the CFE, which generated many tensions within the municipality of Cuetzalan and constant attacks on the COTIC. In the sixteenth assembly in the municipality of Hueytamalco, the municipal president of Cuetzalan was demanded to close this work because it had not been approved by the technical body of COTIC. However, the president refused to comply with the agreement of the assembly, so the assembly decided to make a symbolic seizure of the place where the electrical substation would be located.

Faced with various maneuvers executed by the municipal president to try to approve the work, violating the rights of the inhabitants by not consulting them in a free, prior, and informed manner, it was agreed to demand that he respect the agreement of the people, and so the work was shut down and a camp was set up on nearby private land, with alternating guards of approximately 40 people. The camp had the particularity of being active in constant reflection through the execution of several workshops, in addition to the accompaniment and solidarity of various organizations, students, and academics from different universities. This activity began on November 19, 2016, and ended on October 2, 2017, when the city council delivered a letter to the *Masewal Altepetajpianij Council*, in which the council stated that it would not renew the change of land use of the LAT project of the CFE.

In response to this resolution, the CFE counterattacked by filing a criminal lawsuit against four members of COTIC and four participants from another organization, accusing them of obstructing the construction of a public work, that is, the CFE's LAT project. As can be seen in reviewing this historical process of territorial defense, the UCT has had to face constant battles with transnational corporations and municipal, state, and federal governments, which in many different ways have taken action to dispossess them of their territories and natural resources. In this process, in the opinion of the UCT members, there have been important lessons learned, especially the understanding that only with organization, unity, and perseverance they be able to defend their territory and resources, expressing it as follows:

The good use we make of legal resources, but above all the fact that in addition to our strong community life we have regional organizations, we are united, and we have learned to mobilize ourselves, is what has allowed us to stop the megaprojects of death in our municipality. The maseualmej of Zautla and Ixtacamaxtitlán and the tutunakus of Olintla have stopped the mining companies, and in other municipalities, such as Tuzamapan de Galeana, Zoquiapan, and Jonotla, the town council assemblies have followed suit by rejecting hydroelectric or mining projects. On balance, we can say that our actions are producing results. However, the threat is regional, and it is not enough to stop it in one place if it prospers in others. So, resistance must also be regional (Cobo, Paz, and Bartra 2018).

This call for the unity of regional organizations and to undertake joint actions in defense of the territory is the basis of the work that the UCT is promoting and which will effectively provide them with the best opportunities to defend themselves from attacks on their territory. The balance they make of this process is positive, and they explain it as follows: "The threats that worry everyone have united us as never before despite the fact that we shared history and territory. Because of the need to resist, today we are united maseualmej, tutunakus and mestizos; poor and not so poor; communities and ejidos; poblanos and veracruzanos. And we are also united among organizations that used to look at each other from afar with suspicion and now we march together" (Cobo, Paz, and Bartra 2018).

The UCT exemplifies how a cooperative organization serves as a dynamic arena where members, united by shared principles and values, can collectively defend their cultural heritage and exercise their autonomy. As joint proprietors of the means of production, they are empowered to pursue the collective good, free from the dictates of capital. The defense of territory, we argue, is the key to decrypting the power of money and the market. For, through collective action, territory is the linchpin for fostering the organization of a non-capitalist economy. In the specific case of the UCT, the cultural and identity rescue of the Mazehual people, the cooperative organization, and the defense of the territory, together with constant processes of education and training to achieve the Yeknemelis or good life, have made it an example for other organizations in the country and are a hope for the development and consolidation of the Social Solidarity Economy movement. They have shown the importance of the cooperative organization as the space that allows them to act united in defense of their territory, their Indigenous identity, their culture, and constant education.

We would like many territories in Mexico to work in this way, where the people are the ones who put forward their proposals, who manage the resources we have, but in many places, this is not what is happening. "We are being dispossessed of our territories and we are just waiting in the wings. So, I see that within the Tosepan cooperative movement, is where we have the greatest possibilities to develop, as part of education, the very part of politics" (Interview of Adelgundo González, 2015).

SOCIAL ECONOMY AND TERRITORY

The case of Tosepan is a good example of the overlapping between the forms of SSE and the defense of the territory. The notions of common goods or decommodification, put forward by figures such as Polanyi or Ostrom in the global arena of discussion, are part of a web of socio-political disputes. As we described in the first part, the notion of territory gains weight in the discussions on the construction of another economy, intersecting with socio-political disputes from below. It is this notion that anchors, in a practical way, the notion of decryption that summons us here, in the manner of a "practical critique," situated.

The construction of another economy takes place in a context of growing social conflict, where different dynamics intersect. One comes from large transnational companies in search of raw materials, another from sectors of the neoliberal state that contribute to access, without consultation, or above the interests of peoples and communities, and finally, the resistance of social groups, who use a variety of repertoires. In this case, in the action itself, they build and rebuild the territory. The defense of their vital space is the construction of multiple territorialities, linked to solidarity, the defense of vital territory, and the construction of alternatives. Tosepan is a sample of the vitality of a territory in solidarity even in times of increased violence and dispossession (Rúa and Monroy 2018).

NOTE

1. "The etymology of the word yek whose meaning is 'pure, true, good,' and of nemilis which means 'Life' *that is* why the word is translated into Spanish as 'Vida Buena' (Good Life)." (González 2020, 152).

BIBLIOGRAPHY

Altschuler, Bruce. and Cecilia. Muñoz Cancela. 2015. "From Extension to Training and Incubation. The Development of Academic-Territorial Practices in Social Solidarity Economy at the National University of Quilmes." *Revista +E digital version*, no. 5 (2015): 128–35.

Aracena Pérez, Freddy. 2019. "Esbozo de una Economía Política del Trabajo Asociado. La Teoría Crítica de Karl Marx como Fundamento de la Doctrina Cooperativista" *Revista Idelcoop*, no. 27 (2019): 13–31.

Bernkopfová, Michala. 2014. *The Cultural Identity of the Nahua of the Northeastern Sierra of Puebla and the Influence of the Union of Tosepan Cooperatives*. Prague: Charles University of Prague.

Clastres, Pierre. 1996. *Research in Political Anthropology*. Barcelona: Gedisa.
Cobo, Rosario, Lorena Paz et al. 2018. *We are Tosepan!* México City: Circo Maya.
Coraggio, José Luis. 2011. *Economía Social y Solidaria: el Trabajo Antes que el Capital*. Quito: AbyaYala.
Derrida, Jacques. 1995. *Giving (the) Time: The Counterfeit Currency*. Barcelona: Paidos.
Díaz Guillermo. 2015. "Economías Solidarias y Territorio: Hacia una Construcción Compleja o un Análisis Desde la Complejidad." *Otra economía,* no. 17: 123–35.
Fraser, Nancy. 2022. *Cannibal Capitalism: How Our System is Devouring Democracy, Care, and the Planet – and What We Can Do About It*. New York: Verso Books.
González, Álvarez Adelgundo. 2020. *Kaltaixpetaniloyan Casa Donde Se Abre el Espítitu Soñado El Despertar del Pueblo Pasewal*. Master's thesis, Universidad Autónoma Metropolitana-Unidad Xochimilco, Mexico City.
Hardin, Garret. 2005. "The Tragedy of the Commons." *Polis* 4, no. 10 (2005): 1–11.
Hinkelammert, Franz and Henry Mora. 2006. *Towards an Economy for Life*. Costa Risa: UCR.
Interview of Adelgundo González Álvarez. November 5, 2011.
López, Dania. 2018. "The Place of Reciprocity in the Thought of Aníbal Quijano." In *Breaking the Cage of Domination. Essays Around the Work of Aníbal Quijano*, comp. Victor Hugo Pacheco. Santiago: Doble Ciencia, 163–204.
Moguel, Patricia. 2010. "Seis Desafíos Para la Educación Ambiental: La Experiencia de la Cooperativa Tosepan Titataniske en la Sierra Norte de Puebla." In *Educación ambiental y manejo de ecosistemas en México,* coords. Alicia Castillo and Édgar González. México City: Instituto Nacional de Ecología, 179–201.
Mozas Moral, Adoración and Enrique Bernal Jurado. 2006. "Territorial Development and Social Economy." *Revista de Economía Pública, Social y Cooperativa,* no. 55 (2006): 125–40.
Ostrom, Elionor. 2009. *El Gobierno de los Comunes*. México City: FCE.
Pérez González, María del Carmen. 2009. "Economía Social y Desarrollo Territorial." In *Los Pueblos: Entre un Crecimiento Económico y un Desarrollo Sostenible,* 13–26. Zaragoza: University of Zaragoza, 13–26.
Polanyi, Karl. 2016. *La Gran Transformación*. México City. FCE.
Porto Goncalves, Gonzalo. 2009. "De Saberes y Territorios: Diversidad y Emancipación a Partir de la Experiencia Latinoamericana." *Polis* 4, no. 22 (2009): 121–36.
Quijano, Aníbal. 1988. "Otra Noción de lo Privado, Otra Noción de lo Público: Notas Para un Debate Latinoamericano." *CEPAL Review*, no. 35 (1988): 101–15.
Rincón Gamba, Laura. 2012. "Territories and Subjects of the Social and Solidarity Economy." *Otra economía,* no. 10 (2012): 24–36.
Rojas Herrera, María Elena and Diana Rojas Méndez. 2020. "Educating for Solidarity: The Experience of the Union of Cooperatives Tosepan Titataniske." *Textual,* no. 76 (2020): 45–73.
Rúa, Sohely and Verel Monroy. 2018. "Territorio Solidario para la Paz un Modelo de Integración Económica Solidaria en Colombia." In *Economía social en contextos*

de violencia: México y Colombia, coord. Nadie Castillo. México City: Universidad Iberoamericana, 1828.

Sanín-Restrepo, Ricardo and Marinella Machado-Araujo. 2020. "A Teoria da Encriptação do Poder: Itinerário de uma ideia." *Revista da Faculdade Mineira de Direito Puc Minas*, no. 45 (2020): 2.

Sara da Ros, Giuseppina. 2007. "Solidarity Economy: Theoretical Aspects and Experiences." *UNiRCOOP* 5, no. 1 (2007): 10–27.

Sema de la Garza, Elena and Dora Martínez Garcés. 2009. "Integridad en la Responsabilidad Social Empresarial: Caso de la Cooperativa TOSEPAN TITATANISKE." *Otra economía*, no. 4 (2009): 122–39.

Singer, Paul. 2013. *Ensaios Sobre Economia Solidária*. Sao Paulo: Almamedina.

Taussing, Michael. 1993. *The Devil and the Fetishim of Merchadinse in South America*. México City: Nueva Imagen.

Temple, Domenique. 1983. *La Dialéctica del Don: Ensayo Sobre la Economía de las Comunidades Indígenas*. Bolivia: Difusión Inti.

Torres Hernández Ana María, et al. 2019. "Economía Solidaria: Una Dinámica del Territorio Social." *Universidad y Sociedad* 11, no. 4 (2019): 493–97.

Tosepan Titataniske. 2021. "Problems in the Coffee Production of the Tosepan Titataniske Cooperative." *Revista Vinculando*, January 12, 2021. http://vinculando.org/documentos/cuetzalan/proyectos_tosepan.html.

Chapter 8

Multiple Layers of Asylum Access in Mexico

An Example of the Encryption of Administrative Justice

Luisa Gabriela Morales-Vega

In the last five years, the number of asylum applications received by the Mexican government has grown exponentially to the point of being considered in third place in the world of states with the highest number of asylum applications. In general terms, the vast majority of people who request asylum are of Central American and Caribbean origin (mainly from Haiti and Honduras), although they also come from South America and some from Africa and other world regions. The Mexican government agency whose function is to process these requests is the Mexican Refugee Aid Commission (COMAR by its acronym in Spanish).

This agency has a minimal and insufficient budget and staff, demonstrating its inability to process the number of requests. For example, it has resolved only approximately 17% of the requests received in the first half of 2023. Although almost half of these have been positive, the small number of resolutions accounts for the inaccessibility of asylum in Mexico (COMAR, 2023).[1] However, in the same period over the last five years, the Federal Court of Administrative Justice (TFJA) has resolved hundreds of lawsuits filed by those who consider they have been wronged by the decision they obtained from COMAR.

Based on the preceding, it can be seen how, unlike previous years in which asylum (even under the refugee regime) belonged exclusively to the sphere of political decision, considering it as a state prerogative, the development of inter-American and domestic criteria in the region has awarded it the aspect of human rights. This could, in the first instance, be considered a process that decrypts the broad power of the Federal Executive; however, the fact that complaints are submitted to the courts does not guarantee the obtention of refuge, and perhaps it only represents another level in its inaccessibility or concealment.

The theory of the encryption of power is a part of Latin American decolonial thought. It proposes a reexamination of the political in Western modernity, suggesting that politics creates distinct models of existence and eliminates any entity that does not fit into these models. According to the theory, law as normativity has been the means by which such models are established and enforced.

In this article, we will examine three main components of this theory: the intertwined legal and judicial language, the role of interpreters of this language, and the concept of the "Hidden People" as a challenging notion of the people as a sovereign subject.

Resorting to these concepts will allow us to argue that seeking asylum is considered a threat to national security in Mexico. As a result, the government uses various resources to combat it, including the actions of the courts. The courts, seemingly ruling in favor of the people and acting in accordance with the law, form a subtle and complex way of repelling those who enter the country irregularly seeking asylum and representing the Hidden People.

In this sense, the article intends to analyze the reasoning contained in the rulings issued by the TFJA that revoke COMAR's decisions in favor of the people as well as their effects, to identify useful discourses to demonstrate the hypothesis that I have previously supported: *Migration* (now under the figure of asylum seeking) *as a risk to National Security is frontally attacked by the State as long as "the hidden people" conform it; Which is constituted as such under the raciality logic that has served as the basis of the Doctrine of National Security in the Hemisphere* (Morales 2021)

To achieve the proposed objective, a first point will describe the dynamics of asylum applications issued to the Mexican government in the last five years, as well as their trajectory when they are challenged in court; then the TFJA rulings issued will be studied and their arguments will be contrasted, classifying them by the region where they are issued and by the reasons for their annulation to identify if there are elements that allow us to appreciate a process of decryption of ordinary administrative justice in this type of process based on the influx of requests and the different discourses built around asylum.

Finally, the argument will focus on how the federal court's administrative justice in Mexico contributes to the rejection of migration. This strengthens the barriers to asylum seekers by making it difficult for them to access their rights under the guise of recognition. This nullifies any possibility of challenge and fulfills the function of the law by making it difficult for asylum seekers to claim their rights, reducing their claim to a technical discussion between government offices.

DYNAMICS OF ASYLUM APPLICATIONS IN MEXICO

The purpose of this chapter is to discuss how administrative justice is implemented in Mexico and the way it remains encrypted. Specifically, we will focus on the government's management of asylums, analyzing it at two levels. First, we will briefly look at how the Mexican Refugee Aid Commission (COMAR) has handled asylum requests in Mexico in recent years. Second, we will examine the exercise of administrative justice itself, which is carried out by the Federal Court of Administrative Justice, when resolving lawsuits that people present to challenge COMAR's decisions.

First, let's clarify what is meant by administrative justice in Mexico. As in states with a rule of law, control mechanisms must exist to ensure that public administration is subject to legality. Therefore, administrative justice refers to the set of legal and procedural instruments that protect individuals against the public administration by providing people with tools to challenge government decisions or actions that impact their rights and interests.

The concept of jurisdictional bodies is important when it comes to protecting rights and interests. These institutions refer to courts that are administrative in nature and don't belong to the judicial branch but rather fall under the executive branch. In Mexico, there are two types of the aforementioned jurisdictional bodies—state-level courts and the federal court. This work specifically focuses on the federal court (TFJA, as it stands for Federal Court of Administrative Justice in Spanish), as it has the power to resolve matters related to immigration and asylum. Therefore, the TFJA is competent to decide on the legality of the actions taken by the government regarding immigration and asylum based on federal attributions to rule about these matters.

COMAR is a relatively new institution that was established by presidential decree on July 22, 1980.[2] Its purpose was to study and address the needs of foreign refugees in the national territory. The name COMAR is derived from the word "aid," which reflects the institution's mission. According to the second article of the decree, COMAR was originally tasked with specific functions:

"Second. The Commission will be responsible for the following tasks:

I. Conducting studies on the needs of foreign refugees within the National Territory.
II. Proposing relations and exchanges with international organizations created to aid refugees.
III. Approving aid projects for refugees in the country.
IV. Seeking permanent solutions to refugee problems.
V. Issuing its Internal Regulations.
VI. Carrying out any other necessary functions to fulfill its purposes."

Back in 1980, when COMAR was constituted, refugees were considered *non-immigrants* in Mexico according to the General Population Law, and the National Migration Institute was responsible for granting refugee status. In 2011, two laws were issued to exclusively regulate asylum and migration and separate them from the population policy that still governs the General Population Law.

The *Law on Refugees, Complementary Protection*, and *Political Asylum* provides for refugees in Mexico and outlines the procedure for their recognition. According to this law, the Ministry of the Interior is responsible for carrying out this procedure. It was not until March 7, 2011,[3] that, through another decree, this time signed by the head of the Ministry of the Interior, these powers were delegated to the head of COMAR. Finally, on April 2, 2013, the "Internal Regulations of the Ministry of the Interior"[4] were issued. Unlike laws that are issued by Congress, these regulations were issued by the President of the Republic. The regulation establishes that COMAR has the authority to exercise the powers granted to the Ministry of the Interior by the legislation on refugees and complementary protection.

As seen, a law issued by Congress did not formally establish this commission but was created by the president of the Republic as a consultative body without decision-making powers. Later, through another decree, COMAR was given the responsibility of deciding on asylum applications submitted in Mexico, and this is the essential task that COMAR performs today. Despite the legal measures, the act of granting asylum remains an exclusive power of the President of the Republic. Although COMAR is responsible for handling and deciding on asylum requests, in fact, it is the presidential power that makes the final decision without any constitutional or parliamentary oversight. This means that the president can modify the asylum process at his discretion.

Through the Law on Refugees, Mexican law recognizes and regulates the right to seek and be granted asylum, which from an inter-American perspective is considered the right to seek and enjoy protection in a foreign country from persecution. It is enshrined in the regional human rights instruments, "as well as the jus cogens character of the principle of nonrefoulement, including non-rejection at borders and indirect refoulment, and the integration of process guarantees in refugee status determination procedures, so that they are fair and efficient."[5]

Article 11 of the Mexican Constitution guarantees this right at the national level, and Article 13 of the Law on Refugees outlines the conditions that must be met for a foreign person to request recognition of refugee status from the Mexican State. These conditions are based on the guidelines established in the Convention on the Status of Refugees and the Cartagena Declaration.

According to the aforementioned Article 13 of the law, any foreigner present in the national territory can be granted refugee status, given that they have valid reasons for being outside their country and are unable or unwilling to return to it. These valid reasons could include fears of persecution based on factors such as race, religion, nationality, gender, membership in a certain social group or political opinions. Additionally, refugee status may be granted if their life, security, or freedom is at risk due to generalized violence, foreign aggressions, internal conflicts, massive violations of human rights, or other circumstances that have severely disrupted public order.[6]

As per the Law on Refugees (Articles 18 to 25), the administrative procedure for seeking recognition as a refugee is subject to certain rules, as follows:

a. A foreigner who is in the national territory must submit a written request for recognition within 30 business days of entering the country. However, if it is not possible for the foreigner to submit the application within this time, they may do so as soon as they are able.
b. Upon receiving a request, the authority will issue a certificate of processing.
c. The request must include the foreigner's complete and accurate identification information, the reasons for seeking recognition, and any supporting evidence. Evidence may be provided at any time during the procedure.
d. The authority must interview the applicant, considering their age, nationality, cultural context, and gender.
e. The foreigner may be supported by a translator or interpreter and specialists to facilitate understanding during the procedures and interviews.
f. The authority must issue a written resolution within 45 business days of receiving the request. To properly justify the resolution, the authority may request information from the Foreign Ministry about the applicant's place of origin. The Foreign Ministry has 15 days to provide this information, or it will be assumed that no information is available.
g. The 45-day period for issuing the resolution may be extended for a maximum of 45 additional business days in certain exceptional circumstances, such as a lack of information, lack of intervention by a translator or specialist during interviews, health reasons of the applicant, or when the applicant requests more time to provide additional evidence.
h. If a refugee's case is resolved positively and they are recognized as refugees, they will be granted permanent resident status and issued a respective card. However, if the resolution is negative, they may challenge it before the same authority or through a nullity trial before the TFJA.

It's important to highlight some of the legal rules regarding the issuance of resolutions. These rules mandate that COMAR's resolutions be properly founded and justified, requiring interviews and the involvement of third parties. It's also noteworthy that if foreigners are granted refugee status, they will be able to obtain permanent residence in the country.

In regard to statistics, this government agency has observed a consistent increase in the number of individuals seeking recognition as refugees. This suggests that more and more people are seeking asylum, as demonstrated by official statistics that show a rise in the number of applications for recognition of refugee status.

COMAR publishes the number of applications received per year,[7] and the Migration Policy Unit of the National Migration Institute announces the number of people who have received a permanent resident card annually[8] for being recognized as a refugee. Both data are presented in table 7.1.

Over the last five years, there has been a notable increase in the number of applications received. Despite this trend, the number of individuals recognized as refugees and subsequently documented as permanent residents remains low.[9] In fact, last year's statistics indicate that just over 10% of those recognized as refugees were granted permanent residency.

According to the 2023 report of the United Nations High Commissioner for Refugees, Mexico is one of the top three countries in the world that received the highest number of asylum applications.[10] This data is interesting, especially given the contrast between the number of applications and the number of refugees with permanent authorization to stay in Mexico, because despite discouraging numbers, people continue to arrive and request asylum. This can be explained by Mexico's proximity to the United States and the restrictive asylum policies of the U.S. government, which have forced people to remain in Mexico.

Finally, according to the procedural legal rules, in the event of a refusal from the authority, dissatisfied applicants may seek administrative justice by filing a nullity trial against the resolution before the TFJA. This work studies the

Table 8.1 Comparison of Asylum Applications and Granted Refugee Status

Year	*Asylum Seeking Applications*	*Refugee Status Granted and Properly Documented as Permanent Residents in Mexico*	*Percentage*
2019	70,351	5,626	7.99
2020	40,996	16,845	41
2021	131,448	19,474	14.81
2022	119,273	20,464	17.15
2023	140,982	15,743	11.16

current jurisdictional control of the right to seek and obtain asylum in Mexico. To achieve this, in the next section, the study analyzes 92 verdicts, which declare null or invalid the refusals of COMAR to provide asylum to people.

JURISDICTIONAL CONTROL OF THE RIGHT TO SEEK ASYLUM IN MEXICO

To begin this section, I would like to provide some clarification on the methodology used. My objective is to contribute to the demonstration of the working hypothesis that has guided my research in recent years. To achieve this, I examined rulings issued by the TFJA that declared the nullity of the resolutions issued by COMAR that denied recognition of refugee status to asylum seekers.

Initially, I planned to analyze both the rulings that annuled and those that validated the COMAR resolutions. However, during my analysis, I realized that the rulings that annuled the denial of asylum, and therefore could be considered, at first sight, beneficial for asylum seekers were much more illustrative of the encryption of the right to seek and receive asylum and thereby safeguard life, liberty, and personal integrity.

The interest in this type of rulings does not end in their ability to illustrate the encryption of the power of the state to provide refuge to foreigners. The real interest lies in the strength they have to keep this right hidden and inaccessible, so the rulings were chosen based on an in-depth analysis of the case approach and resolution that exhibits a discernible pattern.

As we will see, the encryption in administrative justice operates consistently against the "hidden people," since it affects almost all of the people who have requested and have been denied asylum in Mexico in the last five years. These individuals come from Central and South American countries, specifically Honduras, Haiti, Cuba, and Venezuela, and the situation of acute vulnerability and legal and economic fragility in which they find themselves has been widely documented.

In order to understand who the hidden people are, it is important to note that, according to Ricardo Sanín-Restrepo, in our region, politics and democracy are not closely linked. Democracy is seen as more of a simulation, made possible by the artificial constructs of the law. The concept of "the people" as outlined in modern constitutions is a legal construct that excludes most individuals who do not fit into this category.

Power is encrypted when politics and democracy are detached from each other, and democracy is simulated through the construction of false totalities in the meaning of "the people" (Sanín-Restrepo 2017).

This exclusion is necessary for the concept to exist as a whole, as it relies on the existence of an outside group that is not part of the totality. Without this excluded group, the legal and political systems would be meaningless (Sanín-Restrepo 2012).

The aforementioned confirms the thesis that there is a strategic model of legal exclusion that has been in place since the processes of independence in Latin America. This model uses the concept of the nation as a universalizing force, which has allowed certain elites to define who can be included or excluded from society. This privileged position held by these elites has been maintained for centuries (Sanín-Restrepo 2017, 2018).

Following the previous paragraphs, the total number of rulings was reduced to 92, all of them issued between 2018 and 2023; the documents examined are the public versions[11] of the rulings systematically published on the TFJA official website[12] and they were classified based on the following criteria:

1. The region of the country where they were issued.
2. The reasons that led to the annulment of the COMAR resolutions that denied asylum to the applicants, as well as the effects of said annulments.

I discovered 33 resolutions were released by TFJA chambers located along the Gulf of Mexico. These chambers cover the states of Chiapas, Tabasco, Veracruz, and Tamaulipas—which form the main migratory corridor in the country. Thousands of people travel through this corridor on their way to the United States.

Nine rulings were issued by chambers located on the border with the United States. These chambers are located in the cities of Tijuana, Chihuahua, Torreón, and Monterrey. Meanwhile, 34 rulings were issued by chambers located in Mexico City, including nine by the Superior Chamber of the Court. The remaining rulings were issued by regional chambers located in the central and western parts of the country: the Regional Room of the Center I in Aguascalientes, the Western Regional Room in Guadalajara, the Eastern Regional Room in Puebla, and the Northeast Regional Room in the State of Mexico.

The court divides its chambers based on territorial jurisdiction, and this shows how jurisdictional control is concentrated in the regions with the most significant presence of migrants and asylum seekers: the Gulf of Mexico and Mexico City, including those issued by the Superior Chamber that attracted cases that seemed relevant due to their importance or novelty.

Regarding the reasons why the COMAR resolutions were declared null and void, we can divide the rulings into six groups.

1. Due to the lack of any of the formalities of the procedure, 37 rulings.[13]

These rulings highlight the formal omission and return the matter to the COMAR for the correction of the formal violations and the issuance of a new resolution. This will indefinitely extend the decision on people's rights.

These types of rulings, which make up the majority, may appear favorable because they overturn a decision by COMAR. However, what they actually do is point out a formal defect, meaning aspects that are not relevant to the substantive resolution of the matter. In other words, they do not overturn decisions because they are based on incorrect or unfair reasoning, nor do they challenge the legal basis used by COMAR or provide instructions on how the final decision on the asylum request should be made. Instead, after a quick review by the court, it is determined that in some instances, a notification was made, or a certain procedure was carried out without meeting all the necessary formal requirements. This means that it only acknowledges the formal oversight but does not address the substance of the decision and its foundations.

The result is that the decision is returned to COMAR so that it can be improved, but this implies that the procedure must be taken back to the point where the formal requirements were violated and redone to comply with the legal standards. In short, people are sent back to the beginning of the process, citing a formal violation as the reason, but without a guarantee that the outcome will be different. In fact, since the "legality" of the actions of the authority has been reinforced, the outcome will likely be even more robust in every case.

2. Because it was issued by an authority considered nonexistent due to its incompetence, 16 rulings.[14]

This means that the authority that issued the resolution denying asylum to the applicant is not located within COMAR's organizational charts or official documents.

Or, if localized, the regulations need to expressly empower them to carry out these procedures and decide whether to recognize a foreigner's refugee status.

The effect of these rulings is to return the matter to COMAR so that the procedure can be reinstated, and this time, the official whose powers are provided for in the regulations can act.

3. Because the asylum application was submitted after the deadline (30 business days) which means that it was considered out of time. This resulted in ten rulings.[15]

The chambers of the TFJA have found that, in these cases, COMAR failed to take into account the factual circumstances that made it impossible for the applicants to submit their application within the 30-day period specified by the law. As a result, the petition was dismissed.

The rulings have the effect of returning the matters to COMAR and requiring it to accept the request and initiate the process as soon as possible.

4. Lack of motivation and justification of the rulings, five rulings.[16]

According to the political constitution, every act of authority must be well-founded and motivated. This implies that the authority must not only specify the legal precepts on which its decision is based but also explain the reasons why they are applicable and how they justify the outcome obtained. If the authority fails to do so, it is considered a severe vice.

In case of non-compliance with the aforementioned requirements, the files will be returned to COMAR with a request to issue a new resolution that is properly based and reasoned. However, this does not guarantee a favorable decision.

5. Because the COMAR resolution was a fictitious refusal, four rulings.[17]

The fictive refusal is a type of administrative silence that is established by law. It is used when there is no timely resolution of administrative procedures. This technique allows petitions addressed to the administrative authority to be understood as rejected.

In the case of the asylum seeker, the fictitious refusal is updated when the COMAR fails to issue a resolution. This omission is considered a negative effect. In other words, since there is no resolution, it will be regarded as a denial by some legal provision.

The purpose of this type of resolution is to send the matter back to COMAR. It allows them to issue a duly founded and motivated resolution.

6. Rulings that declare nullity of the resolution that denied refuge and that resolve the matter in substance and order COMAR to grant asylum, 17 rulings.[18]

These are the rulings that found that the COMAR resolutions were issued in accordance with the law by a competent authority, were well-founded and motivated, and that they respected all the formalities of the procedure. However, their reasoning and the conclusions they reached were contrary to the rights of people or ignored criteria already established on the matter.

Within this group, two rulings annuled COMAR resolutions that denied asylum, arguing that the applicants had two nationalities and that they should avail themselves of the protection of their other nationality before requesting it from a third state. The chambers found that this imposed a disproportionate burden on people who were at risk and therefore imposed an unjustified restriction on their rights.

Eight rulings annuled resolutions that considered the threshold of persecution or the state of widespread violations of human rights were not proven; that is, the assessment that the COMAR made of the evidence aired in the procedure was incorrect or unjustified, according to the TFJA. Three of these cases concerned the threat of the applicant being recruited by gangs in his place of residence, and one more concerned the threat of being recruited by the guerrilla group known as the Armed Revolutionary Forces of Colombia (FARC in its Spanish acronym).

Three rulings handed down by the Tabasco Court ordered the procedure to be reinstated because it involved the rights of children who did not appear at the procedure, and, therefore, their concerns or requests were not heard. Thus, COMAR did not observe the *principle of the best interest of children.* In the opinion of the Chamber, two other rulings did not correctly weigh the child's rights to family unity, which was also considered a violation of the principle mentioned above. COMAR was compelled to issue a new resolution prioritizing the child's interest in this case.

In another ruling, it was noted that the administrative authority failed to consider the applicant's vulnerable state. The applicant identified as gay and lived in a society where discrimination against people with this sexual orientation was prevalent.

A final ruling by this group annuled the COMAR resolution through which it ordered the cessation of the asylum enjoyed by the applicant, considering that the legal provision of having "taken refuge in his country of origin" was updated because he traveled to his country due to the death of his father.

After summarizing the meaning of the rulings, it is important to note that annuling the decisions of COMAR (the Mexican refugee agency) does not necessarily mean that the applicants have won their case. Instead, it puts them in a position where they must go through the application process again with the same authority that initially denied their asylum request.

The administrative authority is not only authorized but also the sole interpreter responsible for deciphering the content of the asylum. Encryption serves to disguise purely ideological decisions as purely technical, making them appear to be the result of the meticulous application of scientific methods—which in this case are presented as legally regulated procedures—and therefore not open to challenge (Méndez-Hincapíe and Sanín-Restrepo 2012).

These decisions become unassailable for the following reasons: as mentioned above, the authority gained its powers through a unilateral decision of the executive branch, and the procedures were standardized over time. When these provisions were established, the current number of people trying to access asylum in Mexico was unimaginable, creating a material inability to cope with the workload. Furthermore, the restrictive immigration policies of the United States have significant repercussions on Mexico's political decisions, such as asylum granting. Despite the social and political complexity, the courts have jurisdiction only to point out technical deficiencies.

In essence, Mexico's rejection of irregular migrants seeking asylum is effectively disguised by the interpreters' actions, presenting it as a purely technical issue that can be addressed through legal channels rather than a political decision influenced by a variety of extra-legal factors.

RIGHT TO ASYLUM IS ENCRYPTED BY COMAR AND TFJA

As mentioned earlier, the decision-making power of COMAR is not established by law, neither formally nor materially. Its authority is based on an internal regulation and a few loose decrees issued by the executive branch. In simpler words, the origins of their power stem from state authority rather than from a democratic decision made by Congress through the enactment of a law. The organization lacks democratic legitimacy, as reflected in its constitution. This is due to its weak and limited institutional design, which was initially designed as a mere consulting agency and later focused on simple procedures, without considering the significant impact of its decisions on the complex phenomenon of contemporary forced migration.

It can be stated that the Ministry of the Interior originally holds the power to grant asylum. This power has been delegated to officials within the same ministry, which is common for administrative functions that require a high level of discretion. However, in this case, the power holds significant importance due to the large number of migrants in the region and the consensus that granting asylum under the refugee regime is a fundamental human right.

Given the current circumstances and from a formal perspective based on what is established in the political constitution with regards to human rights, it is unreasonable to entrust the enormous responsibility of managing the Mexican state's asylum requests to a small and resource-limited agency, especially when such an agency was created with a consultative vocation and is facing a significant increase in requests.

Based on the above reasoning, the question arises as to why there are significant inconsistencies and errors in international protection procedures, which is an essential humanitarian institution worldwide. For instance, the procedures may omit basic formalities and allow unauthorized individuals to govern them, which could result in the procedures being declared null. In some cases, the public official who signed the decision may even be deemed nonexistent in the sense of issuing resolutions for which they are not authorized. This cannot be seen as a simple oversight but rather as an authentic artifice to vent the procedures with total disarray, regardless of whether human life or safety depends on them.

Up to this point, the state, through COMAR, attempts to turn the political issue of forced migration into a technical one by encrypting asylum. The language used is so technical that it is isolated from the common language and uses a rigid statute of inaccessible and self-referential meanings that make up a highly specialized procedure (Morales 2021). However, this procedure frequently fails to meet the many normative requirements established for its substantiation.

Indeed, the theory of encryption of power suggests that when individuals who create specialized languages become spokespeople of power as domination, they develop power-oriented liturgies with the aim of subduing those who may claim to be interpreters of power. By doing so, they render their language as a fixed and impenetrable reality, thereby monopolizing reality in a hegemonic group (Sanín-Restrepo 2018).

This particular group is extremely exclusive and tends to exclude others. Unlike most other positions and assignments, the coordination of COMAR, as well as the directorates that have decision-making authority delegated by presidential decrees, does not have a set of requirements and qualifications established by law. This is because the interpreters in this group explicitly choose other interpreters directly and arbitrarily. Ensuring the impenetrability of the group, and therefore maintaining cohesion of criteria and prioritizing technical discussions over completely political or ideological issues, strengthens asylum encryption in Mexico through legal procedures.

Encryption is also evident by forcing asylum seekers to face highly sophisticated and, paradoxically, weakly regulated procedures, making them more unassailable than the already authoritative decisions presented under the presumption of legality.

Regarding the administrative justice imparted by the TFJA, encryption arises from the moment it becomes a court of annulment, also known as a court of legality. Its function is limited to reviewing whether the decisions of COMAR have complied with what is stated. After carrying out this review, the law mandates that if it is found that COMAR decisions have not met the requirements, they must be returned to the same authority. However, this authority enjoys broad discretion and a weak legal framework.

From a theoretical perspective, out of the 92 rulings through which this federal court exercises control of legality, less than 20% of them have the effect of modifying the decision. The vast majority of the rulings warn of illegal actions. However, by returning the study of the case to COMAR, applicants are condemned to yet another long period of uncertainty. This, in turn, maintains the applicant's deep degree of vulnerability. Those seeking to be recognized as refugees in Mexico lack protection options by definition.

In that sense, the political constitution, together with the Law on Refugees, hides the way to access asylum since they formulate it through a language expressed in terms of universality and non-discrimination that suddenly becomes a reserved and narrow set of rules whose purpose is to maintain the sovereign will to retain the situation as it is and thereby preserve intact the possibility of the existence of the things that have been previously established: the formidable restriction on asylum in Mexico.

In other words, when the extensive and inclusive conventional, constitutional, and legal formulas come to fruition in the actions of the officials/interpreters provided for in the regulatory norms, they are diluted and left to the discretion of the interpreters against whose assessment there is no means of defense because, as has been demonstrated, the "nullity trial" before the TFJA only exacerbates the inaccessibility of the right to asylum.

Based on the above, despite the grandiose speeches about the rights of migrants, migration is considered a risk to national security and is fought by the state. The state employs not only a bellicose and obvious strategy by entrusting migrant containment to the armed forces but also subtle and complex forms, such as the one analyzed here, by ensuring that asylum is inaccessible while still appearing to follow the rules, the political power of rejected applicants is neutralized, and they are portrayed as lacking the merit to be considered refugees in Mexico.

Ordinary administrative justice is developed on a daily basis according to legal and procedural guidelines, turning administrative justice into another slab that is placed on the already hidden and inaccessible languages that cover the right to asylum. It all translates into a deep inaccessibility of the right to asylum, thereby depriving thousands and thousands of people of the possibility of obtaining international protection in Mexico, regardless of whether or not it annuls the actions of COMAR.

In conclusion, how administrative justice deals with asylum cases is a clear example of the way in which this institution and the rights it is supposed to protect—such as life, security, liberty, and integrity—lose their meaning, because they cannot be reliably identified through the actions of the administrative authority, nor through the mechanism of administrative justice. As a result, the rulings passed by the administrative justice system do not support the meaning of these rights.

NOTES

1. "The COMAR in numbers," Mexican Refugge Aid Commission, last modified December 2023, https://www.gob.mx/comar/articulos/la-comar-en-numeros-327441?idiom=es.

2. "Agreement by which an Intersecretarial Commission is created on a permanent basis to study the needs of foreign refugees in the National Territory, which will be called the Mexican Refugee Aid Commission," Official Journal of the Federation accessed November 2, 2023, https://www.dof.gob.mx/nota_detalle.php?codigo=4857130&fecha=22/07/1980#gsc.tab=0.

3. "Agreement by which faculties to exercise the powers regarding Refugees and Complementary Protection provided in the Law on Refugees and Complementary Protection are delegated in favor of the Undersecretary of Population, Migration and Religious Affairs; of the Head of the General Coordination of the Mexican Refugee Aid Commission and the Head of the National Migration Institute," accessed November 2, 2023 https://dof.gob.mx/nota_detalle.php?codigo=5180784&fecha=07/03/2011#gsc.tab=0.

4. "Internal Regulations of the Ministry of the Interior." Official Journal of the Federation, accessed November 2, 2023, https://www.diputados.gob.mx/LeyesBiblio/regla/n197.pdf.

5. "Advisory Opinion OC 25/18." Interamerican Court on Human Rights, accessed August 22, 2023, https://www.corteidh.or.cr/docs/opiniones/seriea_25_ing.pdf.

6. "Law on Refugees, Complementary Protection and Political Asylum," Official Journal of the Federation, last modified October 30, 2014, https://www.dof.gob.mx/nota_detalle.php?codigo=5175823&fecha=27/01/2011#gsc.tab=0.

7. The COMAR in numbers," Mexican Refugge Aid Commission, last modified December 2023, https://www.gob.mx/comar/articulos/la-comar-en-numeros-327441?idiom=es.

8. "Statistical Bulletin," Immigration Policy Unit, last modified December 21, 2023, https://portales.segob.gob.mx/es/PoliticaMigratoria/Direccion_de_Estadistica#est.

9. 2020 was an unusual year for migration due to the pandemic, but by 2021, trends had returned to normal.

10. "Principales resultados de ACNUR en México," last modified October 2023, https://www.acnur.org/media/principales-resultados-de-acnur-en-mexico-en-2021-proteccion-y-soluciones-en-pandemia.

11. The Public Version of Judgments is the official rulings issued by courts, from which any parts or sections containing confidential or reserved information have been removed. The preparation, registration, and publication of the public versions comply

with the agreements published on July 14, 2015, and June 13, 2023, in the Official Gazette of the Federation.

12. "Review of Public Sentences," Federal Court of Administrative Justice, accessed September, 2023, http://sentencias.tfjfa.gob.mx:8080/SICSEJLDOC/faces/content/public/consultasentencia.xhtml.

13. File numbers: 400/20-13-01-2, 4403/18-13-01-9, 1950/19-13-01-8, 4405/18-13-01-3, 1512/20-13-01-7, 4404/18-13-01-7, 1342/19-18-01-6, 1950/19-13-01-8, 930/22-19-01-1, 925/22-19-01-6, 2936/15-19-01-3, 24/21-26-01-1, 829/20-26-01-2, 250/20-26-01-2, 848/20-26-01-4, 96/21-26-01-4, 13097/22-17-11-2, 253/21-01-01-7, 1053/18-12-01-7, 3605/18-11-01-2, 5928/22-07-01-3, 10094/18-07-02-3, 7760/18-07-02-9, 8622/18-07-03-5, 8624/18-07-03-9, 7683/18-07-03-9, 6084/22-17-07-8, 20907/20-17-08-6, 28080/21-17-10-4, 203/22-26-01-4, 60/22-26-01-4, 278/22-26-01-5, 260/22-26-01-5, 1368/21-26-01-5, 61/22-26-01-5, 11/22-26-01-5, 20306/19-17-05-8.

14. File numbers: 1076/19-15-01-4, 5928/22-07-01-3, 3218/21-17-07-4, 5333/21-17-07-2, 5334/21-17-07-2, 4564/22-17-08-7, 15261/21-17-09-9, 24281/21-17-03-3/647/22-PL-08-04, 2980/15-13-01-1/1975/16-PL-06-04, 2903/15-17-08-2/1677/16-PL-03-04, 27884/14-17-07-1/528/15-PL-09-04, 13026/16-17-08-3/574/17-PL-09-04, 2984/15-13-01-4/1468/16-PL-07-04, 715/17-17-02-6/2224/17/PL-03-04, 24700/16-17-13-1/1617/17-PL-03-04, 247/17-19-01-7- OT/3434/17-PL-03-04.

15. File numbers: 600/22-08-01-7, 523/22-18-01-3, 11982/20-17-01-4, 2658/21-17-03-6, 1737/19-17-08-3, 6729/20-17-08-9, 2916/20-17-09-6, 5925/20-17-11-8, 5513/22-17-11-2, 5342/20-17-05-8.

16. File numbers: 607/18-19-01-5, 7263/17-06-01-5, 26893/19-17-02-2, 2602/19-07-03-5, 21626/20-17-05-5.

17. File numbers: 931/19-18-01-7, 8620/18-07-01-3, 555/18-01-02-1, 5012/19-07-02-6.

18. File numbers: 1031/20-08-01-3, 3259/17-13-01-4, 416/22-19-01-6, 320/17-26-01-5, 639/18-26-01-2, 569/17-26-01-6, 223/17-26-01-6, 2450/21-01-01-4, 1520/19-01-01-4, 4377/22-07-02-7, 16586/17-17-09-8, 22044/16-17-09-2, 17997/20-17-12-4, 10831/18-17-12-1, 4627/17-05-01-3, 2702/22-06-02-5, 2450/21-01-01-4.

BIBLIOGRAPHY

Agreement by which an Intersecretarial Commission is created on a permanent basis to study the needs of foreign refugees in the National Territory, which will be called the Mexican Refugee Aid Commission. 1980. Official Journal of the Federation. https://www.dof.gob.mx/nota_detalle.php?codigo=4857130&fecha=22/07/1980#gsc.tab=0.

Agreement by which faculties to exercise the powers regarding Refugees and Complementary Protection provided in the Law on Refugees and Complementary Protection are delegated in favor of the Undersecretary of Population, Migration and Religious Affairs; of the Head of the General Coordination of the Mexican Refugee

Aid Commission and the Head of the National Migration Institute. 2011. https://dof.gob.mx/nota_detalle.php?codigo=5180784&fecha=07/03/2011#gsc.tab=0.

COMAR (Mexican Commission of Refugee Aid) La COMAR en números. 2023 gob.mx. https://www.gob.mx/Comar/articulos/la-Comar-en-numeros-327441?idiom=es.

Federal Court of Administrative Justice. 2023. *Review of Public Sentences*. Accessed September 2023. http://sentencias.tfjfa.gob.mx:8080/SICSEJLDOC/faces/content/public/consultasentencia.xhtml.

Immigration Policy Unit. "Monthly Migration Statistics Bulletin." Accessed January 30, 2023 http://www.politicamigratoria.gob.mx/work/models/PoliticaMigratoria/CEM/Estadisticas/Boletines_Estadisticos/2023/Boletin_2023.pdf

Interamerican Court on Human Rights. 2018. Advisory Opinion OC-25/18 The Institution of Asylum and its Recognition as a Human Right in the Inter-AmericanProtection System, May 30, https://www.corteidh.or.cr/docs/opiniones/seriea_25_ing.pdf.

Internal Regulations of the Ministry of the Interior. Official Journal of the Federation. https://www.diputados.gob.mx/LeyesBiblio/pdf/LRPCAP.pdf. https://www.diputados.gob.mx/LeyesBiblio/regla/n197.pdf.

Law on Refugees, Complementary Protection and Political Asylum. 2014 Official Journal of the Federation. October 30. https://www.diputados.gob.mx/LeyesBiblio/pdf/LRPCAP.pdf

Méndez-Hincapíe, Gabriel and Ricardo Sanín-Restrepo. 2012. "La Constitución Encriptada. Nuevas Formas de Emancipación del Poder Global." In *REDHES*, vol. IV, pp. 97–120.

Mexican Law Dictionary. 2017. *Administrative Silence*. Mexico City: Universidad Nacional Autónoma de México

Morales, Luisa. 2021. "Asylum as an Encrypted Legal Category in Contemporary Law." In *Nómadas,* vol. 34, pp. 31–47.

Sanín-Restrepo, Ricardo. 2012. "Cinco tesis desde el Pueblo Oculto." In *Oxímora,* vol. 1, pp. 10–39.

Sanín-Restrepo, Ricardo. 2017. "The Razor's Edge of Politics: Notes on the Meaning of the Encryption of Power." In *Critical Legal Theory*, https://criticallegalthinking.com/2017/08/03/razors-edge-politics-notes-meaning-encryption-power/.

Sanín-Restrepo, Ricardo. 2018. "Aclaraciones fundamentales sobre la encriptación del poder y el pueblo oculto como categorías fundamentales de una nueva democracia." In: *La disputa por el derecho: la globalización hegemónica vs la defensa de los pueblos y grupos sociales Mexico. Edited by A. Hernández and M. Burgos. Universidad Nacional Autónoma de México*, pp. 151–74.

United Nations High Commissioner on Refugees. 2021. "Principales resultados de ACNUR en México." Last modified October 2023. https://www.acnur.org/mx/sites/es-mx/files/2023-05/Informe%202022%20Espa%C3%B1ol.pdf.

Conclusions

Ricardo Sanín-Restrepo and
Marinella Machado-Araujo

As mentioned in the presentation, we will draw conclusions from the book by examining it thematically. We will delve into and reveal the main conceptual frameworks of the theory, demonstrating how each chapter, as well as the book as a whole, transforms and enriches the theory by capturing and renewing these frameworks.[1]

As we asserted previously, and this is paramount,[2] the prevailing reality of the world we live in has become impossible; it is a negation of itself. It produces massive suffering in the name of untouchable principles that are simply the gearbox for greed and brutal accumulation. Democracy is constricted by the rule of necessity, while difference is neutralized, criminalized, or excluded in the name of a simulated and barren model of humanity.

Is there a path toward another world? This book tries to prove that there is; nevertheless, it not only proves that another world is possible but, more importantly, that such a world already exists. It has been marginalized and lies below the clutter of hegemony, but it breathes and produces the truth of difference. We simply need another arrangement of the sensible to register it, another perception to allow its sway to show us the way. This is perhaps the golden thread that binds the whole book together, and we can formulate it with simplicity: The world we live in is a world of difference and immanent becoming; it is occluded and negated by the simulacrum of power as potestas that systematically imposes its fallacious model of man (through constitutions, the market, the rule of law) onto the world.

Nonetheless, even though the path to seeing and partaking in this world might be steered by a change of perspective, the thrive to turn it into "the" world, to truly make it come to fruition for all, ending the horror of hegemonic Western potestas, is not an easy one. It entails bravery, joy, struggle, and an openness of heart when facing monumental hurdles imposed on change by an ever-encroaching power as potestas. The latter grows and spreads in the air, anesthetizing thought, paralyzing action, destroying links of solidarity, turning joy into deep sadness and desperation, and making "good people" content with the crumbs of ideology they are fed. And where its dictum, shrieked by a cacophony of corporations and the brutality of sovereignty, is "be content with misery, do not demand change, things could get worse."

What is the path, then? There is no one single path, there are many, and they entail partaking with body and soul in the works of resistance of the hidden people: works of intensifying paradoxes and grounding power ontologically (chapter 1), works of poetry (chapter 2), of decrypting epistemology (chapter 3), of building decrypted communalities (chapters 4 and 5), of recovering alternative systems of justice (chapters 5, 6, and 8), of reconfiguring new territories (chapters 4 and 7). The book pretends to be nothing more than a discrete call toward those paths, as only the hidden people hold the keys of transformation—a discrete call that, however, is powerfully coated in theoretical rigor and sincerity and the far-reaching results of very thorough case studies.

Let us announce these particular advances, highlighting how each chapter, individually and within an ample and integrated dialogue with the rest of the book, contributes to doing so.

TURNING THE TABLES ON SIMULACRA

One of the main features of encryption is to consolidate a form, a display, a sensibility, and the tools through which we may register and compose reality. In this sense, it is a complex machine of selection of what acts count, which acts are criminalized, and worse, which acts should remain invisible (nonexistent).

The articles of the book, especially its longest section, devoted to case studies, are highly successful in overturning simulacra. They turn the tables on power as domination (potestas), through an extensive network of cases that intertwine and surface new possibilities of contact, friction, and creating new spaces of justice and equality. Here, we begin to see another, brighter reality unfolding before our eyes. Through the struggles and fresh lines of solidarity amongst peoples in resistance, we begin to understand that everything that hides power and neutralizes or denies agency as difference is a simulation, while everything that produces difference is the only possibility of being *in* and *of* the world, that is, the only possibility toward justice.

For most chapters (see 3–8), traditional systems of justice are responsible for hiding diverse forms of beingness and denying agency. Conversely, alternative forms of justice, aligned with new political organizations that integrate seamlessly with the environment and reject the separation from nature, establish an inherent connection between power and beingness (including posthuman beingness). This demonstrates that difference is the only way to exist within and as part of the world, and that, as long as this is not so, any discussion regarding justice is destined to justify and impose a hidden transcendent model that denies justice and democracy.

All of the chapters in the book took it into heart that decryption is an invitation to test the limits of our imagination and reincorporate the invisible, to look toward the improbable, to truly follow the *event* of the people in their becoming, in our becoming. Only through daring can we begin to see and feel that the people, always in resistance to transcendent models of oppression, are permanently exercising difference, practicing democracy, creating a world of inclusion pitted against uniformity, identity, and the violence of the model. The daring of migrants crossing invisible powder keg lines, of the ancient Afro-Brazilian practice of quilombismo, the Tseltal women, and the Tosepan cooperative in Mexico, peasant organizations standing against the war in Colombia. They all exercise permanent popular power and reignite territories of justice, they are the people in resistance, the true bearers of solidarity and inclusiveness. They oppose the formidable power of potestas that needs to create a unanimous, homogeneous, flat-out world where only the gray-dull of the debtor, sugarcoated in the technicolor of the spectacle, barely survives.

As this book proves, as long as democracy as the possibility of the world is not deemed the radical condition of possibility of justice or justice itself, other spurious mediators (race, nation, state, money, profit) will impose their thirdness as a transcendent model and will define justice and injustice to their liking.

ALTERITY AND CONFLICT

The book is a network of ideas grouped around the theory of encryption of power and extended as a decrypting endeavor. Among other things, this network of living ideas shows that encryption obstructs even the act of naming injustice and envisioning change from within formal institutions and discourses (law, press, social networks, justice tribunals). It erases the potential for declaring, "Here I am, this is me, this is my pain."

A key takeaway of the book is showing how the encrypted world, more than anything else, is the impossibility of the other, of structuring the world through otherness. The other is qualified, set apart, distanced, and enclosed in semiotic prejudice.[3] Beyond the languages of law, symbols, social shibboleths, and images, encryption conceals the possibility of being, while it denies immanent difference as the ungrounded ground of the world.

Nevertheless, in this nullification of the other, encryption is also a form of fashioning reality (as we can see, not simply as a given social fact of the type "every power is constructed," but in a very particular and precise historical way). Encryption guarantees absolute control over areas of conflict. Normative and empirical bases become subject to manipulation by those in power. Thus, the encryptor—the expert—shapes reality by dictating what is real and how to deal with it (ultimately promising to save us from the reality they have created; it is the encryptor who launches the poisoned dart of "everything is a construction").

The totality of their authority rests on the idea that a predefined model (such as capital, in tandem with the nation-state or the constitution) supersedes and fully orders any emergent interactions. Accordingly, encryption doesn't necessarily prevent language itself, but rather it restricts its transmission, norms, and distribution. Most importantly, it limits the ability to discuss the underlying reality that language refers to.

This is perhaps the trap of encryption that all the articles of this book overcome as a cluster of ideas and actions. Chapter 1 supersedes the impossibility of alterity by focusing its lens on what the hidden people do. Chapter 2 does it by reinvigorating poetry, dance, and movement, as forms of meeting and creating a time-space of communality. Chapter 3 strips coloniality to the bare bones of a power without legitimacy. Chapters 4–8 enliven forms of communalities that prove that only in alterity is the world possible.

DECRYPTING TRANSCENDENT MODELS

As we described before,

> The apparent perfect circularity (of transcendent models) collapses when we acknowledge that the model that serves as a frontier for existence is arranged from within by those who already belong to the body politic. Henceforth, the model is not an absolute and universal principle but simply the rules of the necessity of power that the mighty fix through violence to garner a criterion of certainty for inclusion and exclusion. (Sanín-Restrepo 2018)

The latter is given flesh and a body by the chapters in the book, as they prove it thoroughly and without a margin of doubt.

As several chapters prove, when confronting war as an abyss of the human condition, pure violence, as an element of contrast, makes encryption painfully crisp. There is no justification, no amount of human suffering, no amount of ecological destruction, to question the holy place of capitalism as the bedrock of a transcendent legal, political, and economic model. This allows us to see that transcendent models behave as theologically infallible figures, as Aquinas' unmovable mover, the uncaused cause of causes. As the authors of the sixth chapter conclude, transcendent models are "a domestication of democracy in the name of democracy."

In chapter 3, Sabelo J. Ndlovu-Gatsheni decrypts epistemic violence and has many capillary endings leading to and from chapter 4. The latter, in a highly sophisticated manner, decrypts the capacity of transcendent models to collapse "time, history, and events into one single point, a monolith called the state" (from our introduction). Chapter 6 speaks directly to chapter 7, devoted to Social Solidarity Economy (SSE), as a particular manifestation of territoriality as opposed to the Western construction of territory—building communities and building new alternative models emphasizes constructing an economy based on an utterly new notion of space. To that degree, it proves that classical Western territory, as a reigning transcendent model, corresponds to unity, hierarchy, and flatness, while *territoriality* corresponds to differentiation and multiplicity. In between decryption and territoriality, Rojas and Ortega not only fashion a profound critique of capitalism and its organizing of the economy, but, more importantly, they free new forms to construct and share in spaces stemming from the decolonial practices of the Tosepan cooperative. As the authors recognize, it is "one of the most deeply rooted cooperative experiences in the history of Mexico."

What is vital in their work is the knowledge that the act of following social movements, stepping away from traditional Western forms of communities and social links, requires a profound shift in vision, theoretical structure, and methodology that always leads to a frontal challenge to transcendent models.

As both chapters tear down transcendent models, it helps them to unravel how hegemonic economic power networks, money dynamics, and market structures act and pervade societies. Additionally, all of this is accomplished under the auspices of traditional disciplines and legal practices, but specifically, the preponderant role the state plays to create the situation.

If we add the results of the other case studies, we can conclude something very sharp: transcendent models are permanently defeated at their game by the hidden people. The problem is then how to connect these changes on a global scale. One of the ways in which transcendent models inhibit these types of connections is by creating perpetual crises that force new social and political movements to attend to the crisis, to the urgent, before looking for thicker and wider lines of solidarity. Not to mention the high capacity that neoliberalism has had since the 1980s to pit other time allies (working class against migrants, just as an example) against each other.

DECRYPTING JUSTICE SYSTEMS

The marrow of the decrypting endeavor is justice, or rather what stands in its stead: the intertwined pairing of a judicial system and law.

Chapter 6 decrypts what Monclou-Chaparro, Trujillo-Guerrero, and Delgado-Álvarez call "liberal transitional justice" (LTJ). The authors are not content to highlight certain technical shortcomings of the system that could be adjusted or improved upon; more importantly, they demonstrate with great precision that the system constitutes a primordial encryption of power. Its veiled purpose is to maintain capitalism, as a transcendent model, intact. Systems of justice, as a cog in the machine of neoliberalism and coloniality, are built in to appease conflict without solving it, simply transforming it into the codes of the hegemonic system. A fundamental kind of simulacrum that preserves the transcendent models intact.

We must connect the aforementioned with chapter 8 to get a full spectrum of the encryption of judicial systems. In the latter, Morales-Vega deals with how high-intensity conflicts, such as forced displacement, global drug wars, gentrification of whole nations, and the loss of subjective rights, are constantly turned into highly sophisticated and opaque technical judicial problems. The author gives us hard evidence as to how, through a sophisticated interchange of processes, defunding, and the muddling of the language of the law, the full political intensity of the refugee as hidden people is absorbed into the state's anatomy, where it is regurgitated as a tamed totality. It describes how forced migrants painstakingly have to tread inside dark passages between administrative and judicial courts and legal proceedings where, individually, their existence is reduced to a simple judicial footnote and collectively, the problem, at heart political, is neutralized and hidden as a technical legal issue.

COLONIALITY AND EPISTEMOLOGICAL HEGEMONY

Chapter 3 puts epistemic injustice front and center of the problem, and therefore, of the solution, meticulously establishing the tools to do so. Here, the means as well as the aim is a critical shift from the dominant Eurocentric way of thinking to the restorative knowledge systems stemming from the Global South. From the Global North's hierarchical rigidity of models to "insurgent universalities" begot by alternative epistemologies emerging from the rich narratives of resistance that are always producing new forms of justice vis-à-vis oppression. Insofar, the author provides us with a vivid example of how the hidden people in resistance create new meanings and new realms of possibilities for the contingency of politics.

This shift also requires recognizing a manifold of contemporary crises (ecological, racial, patriarchal), conjunctures, and other global challenges as opportunities to recover the epistemologies of the Global South. Among other things, the author calls for a critical examination of emancipation projects that neglect these perspectives and advocates for a justice paradigm that is built on the decryption of colonial legacies and the articulation of resistance and liberation.

Henceforth, one top criterion used by the book editors was how promising were the proposals of chapters in engaging with the core of epistemic justice within the enunciation of the theory of encryption of power. The result could not have been better. Each case study takes these challenges to their limit, demonstrating each hypothesis thereof.

As chapter 3 gives the theoretical foundation for decrypting epistemological injustice, the other chapters will carry it further and drive it deeper, giving it flesh and turning its decryption into a living experience. Chapter 4 gives us Quilombismo—a new praxis, a new language—the lived experience and cosmology of marginal groups that dismembers epistemological hegemony and its impetus to sit atop any model of knowledge. Chapter 6 connects traditional systems of justice as forms of epistemological hegemony, opposing the idea of plebeian imagination. Chapters 5 and 8 warn us of the huge capacity of transcendent models to absorb, filter, and transform demands into soft laws that produce soft identities, and specifically how, through constitutional maneuvers, liberal progressists deactivate hardline political questions and offer a kind of diluted recognition through simulation, achieving a false universalization in the construction of prefigured human beings. The bottom line is that a limit to epistemic imagination is harshly imposed and, through it, knowledge is colonized, making the legitimate voice of the people invisible. Nevertheless, all the case studies intensify the political imagination of the marginalized, of the hidden people, to decrypt epistemic injustice, showing once more, that exuberance of ideas and abundance of reality is on the side of the hidden people, while narrowness and scarceness are on the side of encryption.

In chapter 2, Oscar Guardiola-Rivera illuminates a similar path under a new light. On one side, the chapter describes old ways of encryption that are at heart mythical, dealing with the need for an original origin beyond origins (transcendent models), and how these old ways conceal, propagate, and obfuscate power are resurfacing through the refinement and empowerment of encryption via new technologies that make the occultation subtler and mightier. On the other hand, the reinvigoration of the capacity of old forms of resistance and creation, which the author calls "fantastic critique," paradox, the magical, and the unexpected, serve as forms to slice through the magic of oppression dressed in new clothes, creating new meanings while decrypting what seemed to be formidable, unchangeable constructions or even static eras written in the stone of history. Bringing the latter to a new light means that, like with the emperor, we not only know he is nude, but now we can share that knowledge with others.

TEP AS A THERAPEUTIC THEORY

The book tackles, head-on, the acutest forms of injustice, of acts that are so unjust they sicken and throw every ounce of our humanity into dismay. These acts take us to an abyss where one seems not to be able to deal with the world, where we must believe that such atrocities cannot happen. Nevertheless, as the book proves, they not only happen, but they also happen under the auspices of Sacrosanct principles such as the rule of law and the free determination of peoples and so on. As chapters 1, 3, 4, and 8 excel in showing us, when injustice is so abhorrent it leaves no place for words, language fails in describing the atrocity. But it is not a failure of our feelings nor of language, it is a failure of the possibilities of inscribing a situation within a language that has been confiscated and encrypted. So, every time we try to inscribe one thing in the other, that is, our feelings and true knowledge of injustice within the availability of a symbolic world, we are met with a solid wall of impossibility, a mediator that oddly explains, twisting and bending our feelings and knowledge of injustice into cold, caustic, technical terms (law, rule of law, nation-state sovereignty) that only deepen our feeling of injustice while intensifying the injustice itself. Hence, we need to decrypt simply to see and feel, and most importantly, partake in the true resistance exercised by the hidden people.

To decrypt is to render being possible. It involves recognizing that power as domination hinges on blocking access to politics. In this framework, politics, as unqualified difference, and the concept of justice, are immanent to each other. Decryption, at its core, seeks to reverse exclusion—the primordial form of power that qualifies and conditions being and belonging.

THE HIDDEN PEOPLE AND RESISTANCE AS NEW COMMUNITIES

Chapter 1 formulates a strong thesis of power, sovereignty, resistance, and democracy that was only latent in previous writings. As the authors put it, "if the transcendent model creates itself through the exclusion of difference and is ontologically founded in the necessary uniformity of being, then it follows that the hidden people logically define politics as the truth of the being of difference in permanent resistance." This means, "the resistance of the hidden people is not co-relative to any mind, it does not need the included and its institutions to bring it to fruition by laws, philosophical theses or any other institution." Difference, in this precise ontological grounding, can indeed be simulated (as almost anything else) by transcendent models, but it can never be appropriated by them (unless as a precondition of their own dissolution).

When we engross this reading with what the chapters on case studies uphold, the fundamental outcome is that if we follow the rigid designs of encrypted power (constitutions, the state, the market, etc.), justice remains an obtrusive and contradictory idea and discourse. Nevertheless, if we begin to see, feel, and especially partake in what the hidden people in resistance do (Quilombos, Social Solidarity Economy, Tseltal women, forced migrants), then justice as an action, an idea, and a discourse will shine its own light, transforming the ways we understand and live in the world.

As chapter 2 proves, the child, the trickster, the Chaman, the emergence of the absent exemplify to perfection what the hidden people are and do. The spiritual, as that which is absent and whose appearance would destroy the world as we know it, is unleashed through these powers. This chapter curves the decayed straight line of time in history; it corrodes the walls of perfection of the law, but more importantly, it shows us another mode of sharing in the world. The child and the trickster are unbound, unbridled by the heavy robe of the emperor and the obligation to the blindness of his subjects; they can thus see the unseeable and speak the unspeakable, "dissolving the shell of a god," as the author rightly concludes.

As Assy and Rolo tell us, Quilombismo transcends mere kinship or filiation, fostering intensive alliances that serve as both a point of dissolution of old paradigms and a foundation for constructing new narratives. It is an organization as much as it is a strategy, where the idea of justice is inherent to it and its workings. Chapter 5 uses the hidden people as a powerful agent to reach "the other," and "otherness," to let them become their own political and existential situation. Saavedra-Hernández describes in great detail the aims and challenges of the Zapatista struggle and how it was a form of coming together, a perfect example of hidden people in resistance creating novel spaces of truth.

After reading and sharing in the book, we hope to have answered the main question any interested reader may be asking: What sets the TEP apart? Well, many things, it's dealing of potentia/actuality, that means the effacing and overturning of the longest Western metaphysical tradition of *power as potestas*, alive since Plato and Aristotle (or at least the commodified reading of them since the dawn of modernity). The latter means the structuring of a novel relation of power and beingness built on immanence and becoming, not a naïve immanence nor a frictionless becoming, but as cores of a new form of penetrating the reality of power and resistance, of necessity and contingency, of the possible and the necessary. Even though this nucleus of the theory is complex and difficult to reduce to a formula, the results brought about by the entirety of the book are fundamental in clarifying and proving it. First, the nucleus of the theory offers an alternative logical reading of the problem of potential and actuality to prove, without a doubt, that being is power; hence, there is no justification (moral, epistemological, aesthetical) to condition being. Second, and consequently, it upends the relation of potestas/difference, which leads to an understanding of immanent difference that challenges any metaphysics of power anchored on transcendent and hidden models. This approach allows for a continuous and infinite exercise of difference (as resistance against potestas), which is crucial for any genuine political agency (genuine political agency that does not depend on the whim or encryption of power, but that is immanently grounded). Third, as a logical concatenation, it proves that the encryption of power of the people (in the terms pinned down by the theory) is not a minor or residual form of monopolizing and exercising power and of creating disenfranchised communalities and weak agencies, but that it is the central axiomatic trait of late coloniality.

As we have just grasped, from this cluster of theoretical underpinnings, the book advances the theory in many fields. We hope that the reader has seen a network of living ideas illuminate dark passages of power, evidencing strong links of political solidarity and communal practices where there seemed to be nothing, nothing at all according to the traditional disciplines of obedience such as constitutional law or traditional political science. Therefore, the book is a transforming force; it transforms not only the way in which we deem reality but also the tools with which said reality is apparently built.

NOTES

1. As we warned earlier, this is simply another singular reading and interpretation of the book, one that simply opens the way for what we hope will be multiple readings and reworkings of the book that turn it into many books, into an infinity. Our aim is to focus on its rhythm and harmony—a rhythm that each author, according to their unique needs and insights, contributes to, and a harmony born from a shared pursuit of decrypted justice.

2. Refer to https://criticallegalthinking.com/2021/11/22/many-worlds-interpretation-critical-theory-and-the-immanent-paradox-of-power/.

3. Among other things, decryption shows us how on one side there is a world of supposed order that is truly meager and dry, while on the other, the world manifests itself through abundant and multiple resources (spiritual, poetic, musical), frustrating the scientific pretense behind the drive of the first one to squeeze the life out of the latter one.

Index

About the Contributors

Bethania Assy (Brazil) is an associate professor of Philosophy of Law at the Pontifical Catholic University of Rio de Janeiro and the State University of Rio de Janeiro. She holds a PhD in Philosophy from the New School for Social Research, NY, United States, and is a co-coordinator of UNESCO Chair on Violence, Government and Governance at PUC-Rio. A former honorary fellow at Birkbeck Law School, London University (2012–2013), she has been a visiting researcher at Bremen University (2001), Frankfurt University (2003), Oldenburg University-Hannah Arendt Archive (2001, 2006, 2007), Max Planck Institute of History of Science-Berlin (2005), Free University of Berlin (2009), and a visiting professor at University of Nanterre, Paris X (2018, 2015, 2013).

Jaime Ortega (Mexico) is a political scientist and Latin American scholar. He participates in the "Interinstitutional Doctorate in Social Solidarity Economy" and is a professor in the Department of Politics and Culture at the Universidad Autónoma Metropolitana, Unidad Xochimilco-Mexico. He has written books and articles on various historical and theoretical topics.

Julián Trujillo-Guerrero (Colombia) is a lawyer, MA in philosophy, professor, and member of the Legal Clinic on Law and Territory of the Pontificia Universidad Javeriana. His research and political activism focus on the history of modernity and plebeian republicanism in Latin America, specifically, through the territorial conflicts faced by ethnic peoples in northern Cauca and the Colombian Amazon. He works as a legal advisor to black and Indigenous peoples in the defense of their rights, such as self-government and free, prior, and informed consent. Julián is also a bread baker, analog photographer, and a *vallenato* accordion apprentice.

Laura Edith Saavedra-Hernández (Argentina/Mexico) has a PhD in Anthropology from the Center for Research and Higher Studies in Social Anthropology (CIESAS-CDMX-Mexico). She is currently a researcher at the National Council of Humanities, Science and Technology in the master's degree program in human rights at the Autonomous University of San Luis Potosí. She is a member of the National System of Researchers in Mexico and an activist for Women's Human Rights. She is the winner of the 2019 Jan de Vos Prize for the best Doctoral Thesis. Her latest publication is the book: *Corazonar las justicias: Los saberes de las mujeres tseltales sobre violencias, justicias y derechos humanos*, publicado por CENEJUS-UASLP.

Luisa Gabriela Morales-Vega (Mexico) is a Law professor at the Autonomous University of the State of Mexico and a member of the National System of Researchers (Mexico). She holds a PhD in Law from the National University of Mexico. She has authored several publications on migration and asylum. Her primary area of research focuses on the legal framework of international migration and human rights at the national and international levels.

María Daniela Delgado-Álvarez (Colombia) is a consulting lawyer for Vivamos Humanos, an NGO seeking to humanize the internal armed conflict. She holds an LLB with an emphasis on human rights from Pontificia Universidad Javeriana, where she was awarded the Order of Academic Merit and has been a guest lecturer in History of Law II. Thanks to her work in Javeriana's Legal Clinic on Law and Territory. She is experienced in land restitution for campesino communities and in high-impact litigation on behalf of Indigenous peoples. She is an advocate for women, social justice, and all beings of nature.

María Elena Rojas (Mexico) is an economist. She founded and directed the "International Doctorate in Social and Solidarity Economy" at the Universidad Autónoma Chapingo (Mexico), where she has been teaching for more than three decades. She is the author of articles and book chapters that address the perspective of cooperative education as a way of teaching the principles and values of the social economy.

Marinella Machado-Araujo (Brazil) is a doctor in Administrative Law from UFMG, Brazil. She is a professor in the graduate and postgraduate programs at the Pontifical Catholic University of Minas Gerais—PUC Minas-Brazil—where she teaches General Theory of Public Law, Administrative Law, Urban, and Environmental Law. She is also the coordinator of the Legal Nucleus of Public Policies—NUJUP—at the Faculdade Mineira de Direito-PUC Minas. She has been a visiting researcher at Università di Firenze and the Max-Planck-Institut, Heidelberg, and a visiting professor at the University of Bologna. She is an editor of the book series *Decrypting Power and Coloniality: Philosophical Perspectives from and through the Global South.*

Michael Monclou-Chaparro (Colombia) holds an MA in History from the Universidad de los Andes in Colombia and an LLB from the Pontificia Universidad Javeriana in Bogotá. He is pursuing a PhD in Interdisciplinary Studies with a focus on Global Studies at the University of British Columbia, Okanagan. His research focuses on transitional justice, with a particular interest in power dynamics and land access for Indigenous and *campesino* communities. Michael has diverse experience in human rights research, public service, and consulting in Colombia and was a lecturer at the Pontificia Universidad Javeriana. He is a drummer, walker, and science fiction lover.

Oscar Guardiola-Rivera (Colombia/UK) is an award-winning author. Also, he is a professor of Political Philosophy and Human Rights at Birkbeck School of Law, Birkbeck College, University of London; founding director, Instituto de Estudios Sociales y Culturales—Pensar, Pontificia Universidad Javeriana (Bogotá); and visiting professor, PUC-Rio (Rio de Janeiro, Brazil). His poetic novel *Under the World, Night of the World* was launched in March 2024. His book *This Will Make You Hopeful* is forthcoming.

Rafael Rolo (Brazil) is a research fellow at the Humboldt-Universität zu Berlin (CAPES/DAAD Scholarship). He holds a PhD in Theory of State and Constitutional Law at Rio de Janeiro's Pontifícia Universidade Católica—PUC-RJ (2016–2020). He was a visiting student at the University of London, Birkbeck (2018), and holds a Masters in Procedural Law from Universidade do Estado do Rio de Janeiro, UERJ (2013–2015). A law graduate from Alma mater: Universidade Federal do Pará, UFPA (2004–2009), he has served as State Attorney for the Federal State of Pará, Brazil, since 2010. He is also a professor of law since 2019.

Ricardo Sanín-Restrepo (Colombia) is the author of *Decolonizing Democracy: Power in a Solid State* (2016) and *Being and Contingency: Decrypting Heidegger's Terminology* (2020) and editor of *Decrypting Power* (2018). He is also the author of *Ser y Contingencia* (2023) and *Teoría Crítica Constitucional* (2014) with *Tirant Lo Blanch* (Valencia-Spain) and editor of the book series *Decrypting Power and Coloniality: Philosophical Perspectives from and through the Global South.*

Sabelo J. Ndlovu-Gatsheni (Zimbabwe) is a full professor of History and Canada Research Chair Tier 1: Pluralistic Societies- Epistemic Pluralism and Ecologies of Knowledges, University of Calgary, Canada. Formerly a professor at the University of Bayreuth in Germany. Research professor and director of Scholarship in the Principal and Vice-Chancellor's Office at the University of South Africa (UNISA), South Africa. He is a leading decolonial theorist with over a hundred publications in the fields of African history, African politics, African development, and decolonial theory. His latest books are *Development and Knowledge in Africa: Turning over a New Leaf* (May 2020) and *Beyond the Coloniality of Internationalism: Reworlding the World from the Global* South (2024).

www.ingramcontent.com/pod-product-compliance
Ingram Content Group UK Ltd.
Pitfield, Milton Keynes, MK11 3LW, UK
UKHW041835031026
15587UKWH00002B/794

9 781666 961157